D0237135

WA 1043139 X

Industrial structure, capital markets and the origins of British economic decline

THE POLYTECHNIC OF WALES LIBRARY

Llantwit Road, Treforest, Pontypridd.

Telephone: Pontypridd 480480

Books are to be returned on or before
the last date below

2 7 MAR 1993

01. JUN 93

1 4 JAN 2005

Industrial structure, capital markets and the origins of British economic decline

William P. Kennedy

Department of Economic History
London School of Economics

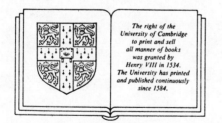

The right of the
University of Cambridge
to print and sell
all manner of books
was granted by
Henry VIII in 1534.
The University has printed
and published continuously
since 1584.

CAMBRIDGE UNIVERSITY PRESS

Cambridge
New York   Port Chester
Melbourne   Sydney

1043139 X   330.941
KEN

Published by the Press Syndicate of the University of Cambridge
The Pitt Building, Trumpington Street, Cambridge CB2 1RP
40 West 20th Street, New York, NY 10011, USA
10 Stamford Road, Oakleigh, Melbourne 3166, Australia

© Cambridge University Press 1987

First published 1987
Reprinted 1990

Printed in Great Britain at the University Press, Cambridge

British Library cataloguing in publication data

Kennedy, William P.
Industrial structure, capital markets, and
the origins of British economic decline.
1. Great Britain – Economic conditions –
19th Century   2. Great Britain – Economic
conditions – 20th century
I. Title
330.941′081   HC255

Library of Congress cataloguing in publication data

Kennedy, William P. (William Paca), 1944–
Industrial structure, capital markets, and
the origins of British economic decline.
Bibliography.
Includes index.
1. Great Britain – Economic conditions – 19th century.
2. Great Britain – Economic conditions – 20th century.
3. Great Britain – Industries – History.   4. Capital
market – Great Britain – History.   I. Title.
HC255.K45   1987   330.941   87–24411

ISBN 0 521 23018 7

TM

1.3.91

For Jean

Contents

Tables

Preface

This book is a product of my ongoing interest in long-term economic growth. It is concerned not with a success story of every-rising, confident growth, but with the perplexing case of a once indisputably successful economy that gradually lost the ability to sustain the innovation and development that had been the basis for its previous comparatively rapid expansion. The story of the virtuous spiral of rising real incomes generating higher levels of demand, thereby encouraging further innovations and productivity advances is a familiar one with an air of reassuring inevitability about it. The story of how such a spiral, after an existence that may be measured in decades, is stopped and then reversed is less familiar and devoid of reassurance for it almost suggests, in the manner of a Greek tragedy, that success contains the seeds of its own destruction. The story of a great economy's loss of dynamism, moreover, cannot be a simple one. People who have once experienced the benefits of rapid growth do not easily abandon them, so the story must be told in such a way as to show how experienced, rational economic decision makers could, collectively, produce such an undesired and unwelcome result. The details of Britain's troubled and controversial development in the late nineteenth century are of course unique, yet just as rapidly growing economies share certain fundamental characteristics, so those gradually losing their growth potential also exhibit fundamental similarities. Thus Victorian Britain's economic experience might interestingly be compared with that of the Dutch Netherlands in the eighteenth century or with the author's own native American Midwest in the mid-twentieth, although these comparisons must be deferred to other books.

The writing of this book has been a long process and in the course of it I have benefited from the help, encouragement, and suggestions of many whom it is my pleasure now to thank. Jonathan R.T. Hughes first indicated to me the significance of the puzzle of Victorian growth and offered encouragement and advice at crucial stages in the attempt to resolve it. Eric L. Jones and Michael J. Wagner extended encouragement and highly relevant practical advice. I am particularly indebted to Rachel E. Britton for programming assistance and for data processing, as well as for a sustained stream of shrewd and penetrating questions. Malcolm E. Falkus helped eliminate errors of fact and logic and also contributed greatly to making the book both shorter and more readable. Derek H. Aldcroft, Alfred D. Chandler, Stanley L. Engerman, Charles H. Feinstein, and Leslie Hannah each read drafts of the manuscript and responded with penetrating insights and questions. Conversations with Christopher J. Napier deepened my understanding of both the evolution and significance of accounting conventions. Conversations and correspondence with William C. Brainard, F. Trenery Dolbear, Michael Edelstein, and William H. Phillips helped sharpen and clarify the arguments of the book, as did seminars at Harvard University, Birkbeck College London, the University of Essex, the University of Warwick, the London School of Economics, the University of Newcastle-upon-Tyne, the University of South Carolina, and Washington University in St Louis. While I am grateful to all of them, none of these people can in any way be held responsible for my inability or unwillingness to benefit fully from their views.

I am also grateful to those who turned mountains of near illegible and heavily scratched-over foolscap pages into a neat typescript, Sheila Ogden, Penelope Ewles, Barbara Mistry, and Tess Truman, and for the patience and encouragement of my publishers. ESRC Grant HR4963 helped defray some of the costs of the computations reported in Chapter 3. The Macmillan Press and the editors of *Explorations in Economic History*, *The Journal of Economic History*, and *Research in Economic History* have kindly granted me permission to reprint selected passages from papers that they originally published.

Finally I wish to acknowledge my greatest debt of all, to my wife Jean, who sacrificed many hours to finding out what I was really trying to say and to enabling my prose to say it more effectively and who saw, with patience and forbearance, the project through from its beginning to the very end.

W.P.K.
London and Wivenhoe

1

Introduction

The British economy in the period of its dominance and relative decline performed as one would expect a competitive and prosperous economy to perform. Failures there were, but... there are isolated failures in any economy, the American and German no less than the British... British entrepreneurs [were competently] responsive to the opportunities available.
Donald N. McCloskey, *Essays on a Mature Economy: Britain after 1840* (1971)

Famous names still kept our station in a world which had no naturalist to equal Darwin, and no physicist to surpass Clerk Maxwell, but the springs of invention are failing, and, for the successors of the Arkwrights and Stephensons we must look to America, to France, even to Italy... and there across the North Sea, not in the armies only, but in the factories, schools, and universities of Germany, Late Victorian England instinctively apprehended its rival or its successor. Germany was abreast of the time, England was falling behind.
G.M. Young, *Victorian England: Portrait of an Age* (1936)

The puzzle of the Victorian economy: two perspectives

For most of the nineteenth century, the example of England – or more accurately, of Britain – served to define for the world the meaning of industrialization. More subtly, but even more fundamentally, Britain's example pressed home irresistibly, irrefutably, the significance of sustained economic growth in raising standards of living even while populations were reaching unprecedented sizes. In the last third of the nineteenth century the quickened pace of the economic and technological change which Britain had set in motion for the world more than a century earlier began to accelerate further (Schumpeter, 1939: 351–448; Landes, 1969: 235, 249–323). By 1914, however, many contemporary observers, both in Britain and abroad, had begun to question whether that acceleration, with its accompanying stimulus to real per capita incomes, was felt in Britain to the same extent as elsewhere.[1] Subsequent observers, too, have come to ponder the quality of

Victorian and Edwardian economic performance and in so doing have articulated an enduring and perplexing puzzle.[2]

On the one hand, no historical observer could fail to note that the British economy of the half century before 1914, as the direct historical product of the classical Industrial Revolution, was customarily considered foremost among the modern and advanced economies of the time. No other country before 1914 had experienced sustained economic growth more completely than Britain and no country had been more thoroughly transformed by that experience. Historians can measure the economic achievements of the Victorians and their predecessors by observing the eager and determined efforts with which the rest of the developed world sought to emulate British accomplishments, which included maintaining, up to 1914, the highest per capita incomes in Europe (Bairoch, 1976: 286, Table 6).[3] Historians can be justifiably impressed by the significant improvements – such as the development of central banking practice and the widespread introduction of limited liability for business owners – that the Victorians made to the revolutionary economic mechanism they had inherited. They can be equally impressed by the rich, cherished legacy of enterprise, skill, and endeavour which Victorian managers, workers, and entrepreneurs sought to maintain.

In contrast both to the period that had preceded theirs and to the period that was to follow, the apparent obstacles that individual Victorians faced in the self-interested disposition of their energies and assets were minimal. Government expenditures were low and, consequently, so were taxes – Lloyd George's controversial Budget of 1909 raised the standard rate of tax from 5% to less than 6% of taxable income (Mitchell and Deane, 1962: 128–9). The long, albeit increasingly tense, European peace, that lasted with only minor lapses for nearly a full century after Waterloo, spared Victorians the necessity or making vast, distortional provisions for wars. Although of potentially massive scale, the actual provisions for social expenditure, the full effects of which often elude conventional measurement, were in fact limited and made cautiously. Markets were amazingly free. If completely universal atomistic competition did not exist, contemporary industrial organization much more nearly approximated it than the monopolistic or oligopolistic alternative extremes (Hannah, 1976b: Chapter 2). While collusive agreements among domestic firms were not legally prohibited, such agreements were difficult to sustain and subject to foreign competition, inhibited only by distance and ignorance, and conspicuously *not* by meaningful tariff or other administered trade restrictions. Although British exports were hindered by trade barriers in some markets – most notably in the United States – nonetheless never had the international movement of commodities, capital, and people been freer or had the international economy flourished more vigorously. At home, British unions were weak and jurisdictionally British governments were unobtrusive in economic affairs and anxious to remain so.

Victorian Britain came perhaps as close as any society has ever done to approaching the ideal of economic *laissez-faire*. Naturally, therefore, the presumption deeply embedded in economic thought since Adam Smith's day, that the competitive forces inherent in *laissez-faire* will yield allocational efficiency, has led a distinguished succession of writers, from Victorian times to the present, to believe that whatever opportunities actually then existed were duly seized and that what was not done was either impossible or undesirable.

The presumed connection between competition and efficiency has exerted considerable influence in recent historical treatments of the Victorian economic experience. This influence is readily comprehended for it is difficult to over-estimate the logical force and intellectual grandeur of the competitive paradigm of economic behaviour. That paradigm has underlain virtually all rigorous economic thought since the eighteenth century and upon its insights has rested most of the justification for considering economics a science. Recently the competitive paradigm has been given a precise and reasonably comprehensive formulation that permits highly detailed analysis, a development that has served to magnify its impact even further. This formulation, commonly named after the men most closely associated with its final accomplishment, Kenneth Arrow and Gerard Debreu, provides rigorously both a definition of efficiency and a specification of the circumstances in which efficiency, even in the presence of uncertainty, will be obtained. Arrow and Debreu, building on a long analytical tradition, show formally that under carefully specified conditions, not excluding uncertainty, economic agents, each striving individually to maximize his own welfare, will attain collectively through competitive trade and production, as if guided by an 'invisible hand', a level of output such that no agent can be made better off without making some other agent worse off, a condition known as Pareto optimality (or Pareto efficiency).

Yet significant though this result is, it is only one aspect of the significance of Arrow and Debreu's work. Within the carefully drawn conditions by which Arrow and Debreu specify the competitive paradigm, the regulation of economic activity through competitive markets is extraordinarily sparing in terms of the burden of information that must be collected and analyzed in order to achieve Pareto optimality. Each agent must know only his own resource endowments, his own consumption preferences, the production technologies available to him, and the prices at which he can deal in marketed items. The factor and output prices generated by the competitive trading process provide concisely and plainly all the information individual agents need to co-ordinate their actions so as to achieve together the highly desirable Pareto optimal outcome. Thus not only is the classical competitive process efficient in a well defined, highly relevant sense, it is also 'automatic' in that the process itself both generates, in the most compact form possible, the information necessary to achieve efficiency and ensures the deployment of that information to guide individual agents. The competitive process systematically concentrates resources in those activities where their value in ultimately satisfying basic consumer wants is greatest and accomplishes this remarkable result entirely by an appropriate set of relative prices for both inputs and outputs. The availability of competitively determined prices permits a vitally important decentralization of economic decision-making to take place. No individual agent or institution determines the set of relative prices that regulates a competitive economy; the actions of all agents together determine those prices. In these circumstances, to obtain Pareto optimality it is only necessary that economic agents individually respond rationally to the competitive prices they face but cannot individually alter. There is no need to become concerned about the consequences of the complex and subtle interplay of the decisions of individual economic agents. The powerful Arrow-Debreu results ensure that this interplay is constructive, harmonious, and totally incapable of leading intelligent and rational men, engaged in voluntary trading, to outcomes palpably inferior to any potentially available to them.

It is precisely this singular property of efficient decentralized decision-making that has moulded and informed much of the recent historiography of the Victorian economy. As long as it could be shown on the one hand that individual decision-makers were price takers and on the other that they responded, for the most part, rationally and effectively to the prices they faced, it must follow that collectively they were also essentially efficient. A number of individual industry studies – in textiles (Sandberg, 1974), in machine tools (Floud, 1976), in iron and steel (McCloskey, 1968, 1973), and in financial services (Edelstein, 1971, 1974, 1976) – have shown that in the circumstances British entrepreneurs and managers conducted their businesses intelligently, competitively, and profitably. These studies have stressed that if the critics of late Victorian economic performance were suddenly somehow to find themselves transported back to nineteenth-century Britain, and asked to improve the situation, they would be able to find very few unexploited opportunities (McCloskey and Sandberg, 1971; Harley, 1974). And if it is admitted that, occasionally, British economic decision-makers suffered lapses of judgement and energy in pursuing opportunities – as in the chemical industry (Lindert and Trace, 1971) – similar lapses can be found in all other economies at all times. Furthermore, the corrective powers of competition were believed to have acted sufficiently quickly to render only temporary those lapses that did occur and, relative to the economy as a whole, to ensure that they were of only limited significance. The combined weight of such studies, therefore, serves to establish an impressive basis for the conclusion that the Victorian economic environment was robustly competitive and, therefore, efficient and consequently performing as well as could reasonably have been expected.

By adopting this theoretical stance which stresses both the feasibility and desirability of efficient decentralized competitive resource allocation, the task of historical research can also be decentralized and restricted to an industry-by-industry or firm-by-firm investigation, confident in the belief that competitive pressures will ensure that the ultimate outcome of many separate decisions will in aggregate be beneficial. The historiography this school of thought has produced, an historiography where both the conduct of research and the interpretation of results are guided by powerful analytical insights, is both persuasive and comforting – persuasive because of the inherent power and elegance of the competitive paradigm and comforting because of the implication that the virtuous Victorians had succeeded in achieving all that was reasonably possible.

This favourable perception of the Victorian economy arose out of an appreciation of the force of compelling logic and a recognition of the significance of economic growth long sustained in competitive conditions; however, this perception has rested uneasily with other, less comforting, if less sharply drawn, observations that escaped neither the Victorians nor subsequent writers. By the last quarter of the nineteenth century it had become unmistakably clear that other large and important economies were growing significantly more rapidly than Britain's and behaved, especially in the areas of technological advance and industrial practice, more dynamically (Landes, 1969: 231–358). It was seen by some as symptomatic of the age that German steel output, for example, after reaching parity with Britain's around 1890, should have surged to a level twice that achieved by Britain in 1913 (Webb, 1980: 327). Perhaps even more symbolically, where the transport possibilities of the steam engine had been decisively and dramatically demonstrated in England at Rainhill in 1829, the comparable establishment of the potential of alternating electrical current transmission was in Germany at Frankfurt in 1891. This symbolism can be given more concrete expression by noting that by 1913 three of the four largest electrical engineering firms in Britain were wholly owned subsidiaries of foreign enterprises, that the largest automobile producer in Britain was Henry Ford, and that the most dynamic British chemical firm, Brunner, Mond, depended crucially upon Belgian technical support. While it could reasonably be expected that other countries would benefit from Britain's example, and would, therefore, be able to industrialize more rapidly than Britain had done, it was more difficult to explain why, increasingly towards the end of the nineteenth century, foreign economic advances should have rested so heavily on industries which had never been important in Britain and which in some cases – such as electrical engineering, telephone communications, and dyestuffs – Britain appeared almost incapable of sustaining.

Moreover, this faltering technological ability can be only too easily seen to have highly damaging consequences. For example, the slow development of electrical engineering and the retarded extension of electrical applications in Britain not only deprived British producers of an important share of the rapid growth of world trade in electrical equipment, but also delayed the adoption and widespread application in Britain of production methods which depended heavily on electricity, most notably mass production assembly lines which required the uncluttered plant layout and the instant and accurate control possible only with electricity (Passer, 1953:344; Byatt, 1979:83–7; Hannah, 1979:18).[4] Furthermore, the successful utilization of mass production methods for the assembly of such products as typewriters, telephones, cash registers, electrical equipment (Passer, 1953:344), automobiles, and adding machines rested upon a flow of dependably made, accurately machined components of exacting tolerances, the inexpensive provision of which was feasible on the scale required only with the flexible but precisely controlled machining techniques that electrification made possible (Rosenberg, 1963; DuBoff, 1967).[5] Thus the slow exploitation of electricity was compounded by an inability to produce domestically and competitively a broad array of the instruments and devices necessary to meet the increased requirements for co-ordination, mobility, and control that have characterized so markedly economic development in the twentieth century. While the application of electricity is a particularly revealing example of the technological limitations of the late Victorian economy, it is far from being the only example, as the following chapters will show.

Such examples of technological weaknesses cannot be dismissed as too insignificant to yield a quantitative impact on the entire Victorian economy. Not only was the rate of per capita income growth less than that recorded for the more dynamic foreign economies of the period, but Britain's rate appeared to be slowing down sharply as that of other countries either accelerated or sustained previously strong performances (Matthews, *et al.*, 1982:30–3, 209, 497–507; Maddison, 1964:194–203). Thus as American per capita incomes in the years 1899–1913 continued to rise sharply, despite the inhibiting influence of enormous immigration flows, and as German per capita incomes rose similarly, despite a virtual cessation of the emigration that had earlier lessened the economic strain of industrial transformation, the British per capita income growth rate fell by more than 50%, *despite* the unprecedented levels of emigration that eased downward pressure on wage rates (Deane and Cole, 1962:50, Table 19B).

The apprehension properly aroused by this deceleration is reinforced when the pre-1914 growth rate is compared to that of the inter-war years. No one has seriously claimed that British growth in the inter-war years was as rapid as resources permitted; the enormous unemployment of men and machines is testimony of waste too great to support any view other than that of economic maladjustment on a vast scale. Yet per capita income growth in the inter-war period was at least as rapid as that achieved in the half century before 1914 and significantly greater than that of the decade and a half immediately preceding the war; the rate of growth of per capita income in the years 1899 to 1913 was only *one-third* of the rate of growth achieved in the years 1924–38. (See Tables 1.1 and 1.2.)

Table 1.1. *Growth rate of GNP*[1]

Period	Growth rate	Standard deviation of estimate	Durbin–Watson statistic	R^2	95% confidence interval
1871–1913[2]	0.0184	0.00063	1.93	99.10	0.0171–0.0197
1871–1899[2]	0.0187	0.00110	1.70	97.75	0.0164–0.0210
1899–1913[2,3]	0.0127	0.00126	1.47	89.66	0.0100–0.0154
1919–1938[3,4]	0.0199	0.00242	1.46	91.07	0.0148–0.0250
1924–1938[3,5]	0.0181	0.00541	1.72	84.73	0.0064–0.0298

Growth rate of GDP[1]

Period	Growth rate	Standard deviation of estimate	Durbin–Watson statistic	R^2	95% confidence interval
1871–1913[2]	0.0173	0.00075	1.96	98.87	0.0158–0.0188
1871–1899[2]	0.0176	0.00130	1.74	97.07	0.0149–0.0203
1899–1913[2,3]	0.0110	0.00126	1.49	86.11	0.0083–0.0137
1919–1938[3,4]	0.0196	0.00268	1.63	90.02	0.0140–0.0252
1924–1938[3,5]	0.0184	0.00550	1.80	84.12	0.0065–0.0303

Notes and sources:

[1] All results are obtained from equations of the type $\ln Y_t = \ln Y_o + rt + \varepsilon_t$, where r is the growth rate which is to be estimated and $\ln Y_t$ is the natural logarithm of output in year t. In all cases the data were transformed by the Cochrane – Orcutt iterative procedure before estimation in order to eliminate the first order autoregressive process which was highly evident in all data. Inspection of the residuals arising from the regressions run on the transformed data indicates that autoregression was in fact removed.

[2] Data for 1870 were used to calculate the extent of autoregression and the results were subsequently employed in the Cochrane – Orcutt iterative procedure. This meant, however, that estimates of output growth were available only from 1871 onwards. The data used were taken from C.H. Feinstein (1972), Table 5, column 8 (GDP at 1900 market prices), and column 10 (GNP at 1900 market prices). Data were not available before 1870.

[3] In order to measure the growth rate over the indicated years it was necessary to estimate the extent of autoregression by using data for the years preceding the beginning of the period. (See note 2.)

[4] Data for these years were taken from Feinstein (1972) Table 5, columns 8 and 10 for GDP and GNP respectively, both measured in 1938 market prices. The 1919 data were altered to exclude Southern Ireland by multiplying the 1919 figures by the ratio obtained by dividing Feinstein's 1920 estimate of U.K. GDP and GNP excluding Southern Ireland, by the estimate including Southern Ireland thus making the 1919 observation comparable to those from 1920 onwards where Southern Ireland is excluded.

[5] Data for 1924–38 are taken from the same source as data for 1919–38. Results from the shorter period are reported to indicate that although the variance of the growth estimates for 1924–38 are much greater than for 1919–38, the growth estimates for the longer period is itself much less severely affected. The greater variance of the growth estimate for the shorter period appears to be the natural consequence of reducing an already small number of observations by more than 25%. Thus the growth rate estimates are reasonably robust with respect to choice of dates over which to measure the growth, although elimination of the sharp slump of 1920–1 and the subsequent recovery does have the

Of course, the impact of the war and its aftermath is not entirely absent from the economic statistics. The variance of inter-war growth about its trend is much greater than the variance about trend which accompanied pre-1914 growth. Thus inter-war growth performance, comprising both the mean and the variance of the growth rate, may be judged inferior to the overall performance recorded in the half century before 1914, although not necessarily inferior to that recorded between 1899 and 1913 when the growth rate was much below the long-term pre-war average.[6] However, the very difficulties so obviously posed by post-1918 economic conditions, difficulties arising from the unprecedented violence of world economic fluctuations and from the inadequacy of international trade and payments arrangements, make by comparison the overall growth rate of the inter-war economy even more remarkable than at first sight. In fact, when account is taken of unutilized resources and of the weaknesses and disarray of the international economy upon which Britain relied so heavily, the driving forces of the inter-war economy emerge as possessing impressive power, especially when contrasted with the sluggish forces of the pre-1914 period that operated in markedly more favourable conditions (Matthews, *et al.*, 1982:469, 475–7). It must surely appear that if the greatly troubled inter-war economy could maintain a growth rate at least equal to (and probably greater than) the long-term rate of the pre-war years, then the pre-war economy must have been operating below its potential, especially in the early twentieth century. Since economic theory has identified technological advance as the primary means of achieving sustained growth in output per head (Solow, 1970:33–8; Kuznets, 1966:8–16), Britain's faltering economic growth performance offers powerful evidence of the cumulative significance of manifest technological shortcomings. Moreover, because the important technological changes of the late nineteenth and early twentieth centuries did not begin to alter markedly the structure of British industry until the 1920s, Britain's growth performance during the inter-

Notes to Table 1.1. (*cont.*)

effect of reducing the estimated growth in 1919–38 by approximately 10%. If the estimates of growth in 1919–38 were reduced to those of 1924–38, namely 1.81% per year for GNP and 1.84% per year for GDP, but the variance of the estimates for the longer period were retained, the 95% confidence interval for GNP would be 1.30% per year to 2.40% per year. Interpolating from a table of *t*-statistics indicates that there is less than a 20% probability that either GDP or GNP would be less than 1.54% per year even *if* the maximum growth rate of either of the two measures were estimated as only 1.81% per year with a standard deviation of 0.268%. Since there is only a 50% chance that growth rates for the years 1899–1913 were greater than 1.27% per year, there is less than a 10% chance that even for the reduced estimate of growth from 1919–38 would the growth in the period 1899–1913 have been as great as that for the later period. Furthermore, this 10% estimate is extremely generous for it makes no allowance for the fact that the probabilities of true growth rates being more than one standard deviation from their estimated values fall off very quickly as the distance from the estimated value increases further.

Table 1.2. *Population growth and per capita income growth*

Panel A
U.K. population

1870	31,257
1899	40,773
1913	45,649
1920[1]	43,718
1924[1]	44,915
1938[1]	47,494

Source: Feinstein (1972: Table 55, column 1).
Note:[1] Excluding Southern Ireland

Panel B
U.K. population growth rates

1870–1899	0.0092
1899–1913	0.0081
1870–1913	0.0086
1920–1938	0.0046
1924–1938	0.0044

Source: Rates were calculated from population data above according to the formula:

$$r = (1/t)(\ln P_{i+t} - \ln P_i) \text{ where}$$
P_{i+t} = population at end of span of t years
P_i = population at beginning of period,
t = time span
r = growth rate

Panel C
U.K. real per capita income (GNP) growth

1870–1899	0.0095
1899–1913	0.0046
1870–1913	0.0098
1920–1938	0.0153
1924–1938	0.0137

Source: Real per capita income was found by subtracting rate of population growth in Panel B above from the corresponding rate of real income growth shown in Table 1.1. The estimate of per capita income 1920–38 is biased downwards by using real income for 1919–38.

war years is most plausibly viewed as the consequence of tapping a backlog of unexploited technical advances that had accumulated during the preceding decades.[7]

These two facets of Victorian economic performance, on the one hand, the competitive and thus presumably efficient nature of the first industrial nation and, on the other hand, the increasingly rigid and obsolescent character of the economy's technological base, have produced sharply divided historical judgements of the period. Those who stress the benefits of competition generally are unable to find important examples of unusual missed opportunities – recognizing of course that no economy has ever been completely free of the errors of mistaken judgement and incompetence – and can support their findings by noting the undeniably low profitability in Britain of activities, such as electrical engineering and electricity supply, that were highly profitable elsewhere.[8] Moreover, such writers have often invoked the logic of optimization in free markets to show that their findings are what the rational observer must expect to find. Indeed, they have often used to tellingly good effect the logic of competitive optimization to expose the analytical haziness that underlies the writings of many of those who have sensed significant Victorian failure in grasping the opportunities of the period. For their part, those who stress the signs of technological rigidity and obsolescence have been substantially more at ease and more persuasive in recording those signs than in explaining how they came to be so painfully evident and why so little was done to improve the situation by free and competent decision-makers sustained by venerable traditions, great experience and high standards. How can these so differing interpretations be reconciled?

A first step towards resolution of the puzzle

The argument proposed in this book to achieve a reconciliation of the contrasting interpretations of Victorian economic experience holds that the Victorian manifestations of competitive behaviour were not even a crude approximation to the conditions necessary to secure the efficiency shown to be theoretically possible.[9] The argument offered here fully accepts the analytical power of the Arrow-Debreu paradigm of a competitive economy. But rather than quickly and unreflectively accepting that ostensible competitive behaviour can produce the potentially feasible efficiency, the argument emphasizes the inherent obstacles to the realization of that efficiency and the possibility that the cost of the failure to surmount the obstacles could be high. The fundamental insight taken from the precise formulation of the competitive paradigm is a sense of how difficult it is to achieve allocative efficiency. The Arrow-Debreu paradigm was not conceived as a description of the world as it actually is, much less as it actually was, but as a means of identifying what conditions must be met in order to bring about a world as we should like it to be. Thus Arrow (1974: 268), has written:

In my own thinking, the model of general equilibrium under uncertainty is as much a normative ideal as an empirical description. It is the way the world differs from the criteria of the model which suggests social policy to improve the efficiency with which [resources are] allocated.

When judged against the demands of the normative ideal, the tasks that confront the economic institutions through which individuals trade goods and exchange information are undeniably formidable. The conditions needed to ensure efficiency diverge, and have always diverged, greatly from what exists in reality. The shortfall between what is achieved by imperfectly competitive economies and what is possible is likely to be large. F.H. Hahn (1973: 14–15) has been provoked to declare:

This negative role of Arrow-Debreu equilibrium [in illustrating obstacles to efficient economic behaviour] I consider almost to be sufficient justification for it, since practical men and ill-trained theorists everywhere in the world do not understand what they are claiming to be the case when they claim a beneficent and coherent role for the invisible hand.

It is thus unacceptable to assume that ostensibly competitive conditions will yield a reasonable approximation to the possibilities inherent in an economy's resource endowments, the consumption preferences of its members, and the technologies available to it. The pervasive obstacles to the attainment of Pareto optimality virtually ensure that all economies at all times are inefficient to some degree. But there is no reason to believe that the degree of inefficiency has been uniform over time or among countries. The welter of price-setting conventions, investment behaviour, educational standards, research commitments, commercial laws, business conduct, taxation and subsidy policies, and so forth that have operated in different economies at different times cannot have had even an approximately similar impact on the efficiency of the economies in which they have been deployed. The procedures for evaluating the consequences of such a diverse body of practices will necessarily be complex, mirroring the complexity of the task of behaving rationally in a flawed, imperfectly competitive economy. In order, therefore, to evaluate Victorian economic performance it is necessary first to establish as a standard some measure of what was possible. That is the task of the next two chapters.

However, before taking up that task it will be useful, as preparation for subsequent analysis, to be as precise as possible in identifying the intrinsic obstacles to economic efficiency. The obstacles can be divided into two broad groups. The first group exists because efficiency in the Arrow-Debreu paradigm requires not only the familiar and demanding conditions that each agent by his own actions has no perceptible control over prices (thus constituting a restriction on the set of endowments consistent with Pareto efficiency) but also, more restrictively, that in both production and consumption there exist no externalities, indivisibilities, or increasing returns to scale. These latter conditions, however, are routinely and pervasively violated in modern economies. For example, scientific and technical research, upon which economic growth ultimately depends, creates extensive and critically important externalities. The operating efficiency of all producers is potentially enhanced by the knowledge discovered by any one of them. New advances, by widening comprehension, are likely to increase, not diminish, the value of the existing stock of knowledge. In an ideal world technical advances would be encouraged and rewarded by appropriate lump sum payments ('prizes') given to those whose efforts yielded the advance. Subsequently all producers, whether they contributed to the advance or not, would then be free to exploit the new knowledge in any way they saw fit. In such a system, full use of the new knowledge would be made, unhindered by payments that varied with the degree of use.

It is easy to see that the viability of such a system depends on how the lump sum payments – the research 'prizes' – are chosen and awarded. The valuation of new scientific and technical knowledge that potentially improves the welfare of all can thus be seen to be a complex and difficult problem where the pricing rules suitable for goods like bread, whose benefits in consumption can be allocated to specific individuals, are obviously inadequate. Knowledge gains in value from widespread use; a loaf of bread diminishes with each consumer's intake. The same system of pricing will not work for both. Most market economies have attempted to resolve the problem by the award of patents which create a temporary monopoly in the use of an idea. While such a system may create rewards for research and innovation, it is obviously inefficient because the social benefits of an advance in knowledge are artificially restricted. The rewards for more effectively resolving the problem created by externalities – especially those related to technical knowledge – are obviously great and differences in the efficacy of different national solutions to this problem must surely account in important measure for differences among countries in economic performance.

Indivisibilities and increasing returns to scale are closely related to each other and are both familiar features of modern economic growth. Indivisibilities arise when economic agents, in either production or consumption, cannot make adjustments to their plans in the amounts they would ideally wish, but must deal in large discrete units. Similar problems arise with factory based economies of scale. Such economies of scale permit unit production costs to fall as output levels increase. If the output range over which economies of scale occur is sufficiently restricted relative to the total size of the market, the problem is not serious. However, when the output range over which economies of scale occur is relatively large or, worse yet, completely saturates the available market, price formation will deviate from the conditions necessary for Pareto efficiency. This occurs for one of two reasons. First, the market may support only a few producers, or perhaps only one, who will then have the power to set prices. In such a case, optimization by the only (or few) producer(s) will not yield the social optimization, the Pareto efficiency, that is generated in the classical competitive case. Monopoly or oligopoly causes the invisible hand to fumble and grope. Alternatively, the market may not even support one producer if the rule, necessary to secure Pareto efficiency, that price must equal marginal cost, is adhered to. In such a case, marginal cost pricing alone would not cover total costs. As in the case of externalities some form of lump sum payment is necessary to support the activity efficiently. But once again, the critical, complex decisions governing who should pay and how much must be taken without unambiguous guidance by market prices. The varying success with which these problems are resolved in different countries and at different times also offers ample scope for differences in economic performance.

Externalities, indivisibilities and economies of scale – each one technically a condition that violates the convexity and continuity properties upon which the classical competitive mechanism depends in order to secure Pareto efficiency – destroy the informational compactness that lies at the heart of the competitive process (Reiter, 1977: 226–32). In the presence of these conditions some form of centralized intervention, that takes explicit account of the behaviour of individual agents and their interactions and sets bounds or limits to permitted actions, becomes necessary. It is not possible in these circumstances merely to ascertain the degree of competition within an economy in order to make assertions about overall efficiency. Instead it is necessary to evaluate in detail the institutional environment in which decisions are made and to consider how appropriate are the bounds and limitations institutions place on the permitted behaviour of individuals.

The second broad group of reasons for the persistent obstacles to economic efficiency arises from the problems that an uncertain future creates in co-ordinating economic activity among many people. If the problems of the first group arise because, in the presence of externalities, indivisibilities, and economies of scale, the informational requirements of decentralized decision-making are unmanageably great, the problems of the second group arise because much of the information required is intrinsically difficult, if not impossible, to acquire. Even without the complications of the first group, the minimal information necessary to secure efficiency is disconcertingly vast. There must be enough information to generate in a comprehensive array of spot and future markets a competitively determined price for every output and every input at every moment in time and under every conceivable circumstance or contingency. Such a set of markets would, for example, allow agents to insure themselves against *all* possibilities by making the appropriate forward contingent contracts to buy and sell goods and services. Yet the array of spot and future markets known to be required, even in well-behaved economies where the convexity and continuity properties necessary to secure Pareto optimality hold, have never existed. At best only a bare handful of future markets exist, and these for the comparatively simple limited contingency trading of highly homogeneous commodities for only short periods into the future.

A variety of reasons might plausibly be advanced to explain the non-existence of crucial contingency markets for future goods and services. Obviously the transactions costs involved in disseminating uniformly the required information would be huge, even if the data were readily available. Thus at best only the most essential contingency markets could reasonably be expected to exist, but even these are significantly incomplete. Arrow (1974:9–10) has suggested that the fundamental reason for the non-existence of the vital contingency markets lies in the fact that the minimal necessary co-operation among market users cannot generally be secured. Much crucial information is inherently asymmetrically distributed, particularly the information required for technological innovation and capital formation, activities which typically involve long planning horizons, demand much specialized and inaccessible knowledge of scientific, engineering and marketing factors, and are genuinely laden with intrinsic risk quite independent of attendant human shortcomings (Arrow, 1974:2–3, 9–10). Where the execution or completion of contracts are contingent on the occurrence of some event, all parties to the contract must ascertain without disagreement whether the particular event in question has occurred. Some parties, however, will gain by concealing information – a purchaser of fire insurance, for example, may not wish to reveal what he knows about the cause of a fire. Such behaviour creates a durable Prisoner's Dilemma that cannot be readily resolved in a large, complex economy. If all members of an economy faithfully agree to disclose fully, freely, and accurately certain specified information, even if this disclosure should occasionally be disadvantageous to them, in the long run they will be better off than if they fail to agree, for disagreement will preclude beneficial co-operation and will, therefore, be costly. However, if agreement is reached, the temptation for a few to violate the terms will often be so strong, and the disadvantages of full disclosure when some are concealing information so great, that most agreements are incapable of withstanding the subsequent pressure for concealment and non-co-operation by all. Such widespread concealment and non-co-operation often makes it impossible for important markets to function (Akerlof, 1970). The non-existence of these markets will prevent large groups of economic agents from reaching feasible efficient equilibria by means of desirable trades. Without the necessary markets the critical trades generally cannot take place. In addition, when the set of crucial markets is seriously incomplete, it is also discouragingly easy to show that the opening of a new market may actually make all agents worse off rather than, as one might reasonably have supposed, better off (Hart, 1975). Economic performance thus depends critically on the institutional and cultural arrangements devised to resolve – with the full knowledge that any proposed resolution will almost inevitably be incomplete – the fundamental problems created by the inherently asymmetrical distribution of vital information among people who can only too easily find co-operation difficult.[10]

Used in this broad, qualitative manner, the Arrow-Debreu paradigm can be extremely useful in identifying those aspects of economic activity most difficult to conduct efficiently and where the cost of flawed arrangements are likely to be greatest. These insights will be used in later chapters to assess the shortfall between what the Victorian economy actually achieved and what was reasonably possible.

2

Economic growth and structural change

Since an industry is a complex that reflects determining factors on the production-supply and output-demand sides, an adequate account of causes and consequences of trends in industrial structure will also constitute an account of much of the economic growth process... [We] should note first that technological change is clearly a major source of.... shifts [in industrial structure].
Simon Kuznets, *Modern Economic Growth: Rate, Structure, and Spread* (1966)

These industrial revolutions periodically reshape the existing structure of industry by introducing new methods of production – the mechanized factory, the electrified factory, chemical synthesis and the like; new commodities, such as railroad service, motor cars, electrical appliances; new forms of organization – the merger movement; new sources of supply... these results each time consist in an avalanche of consumers' goods that permanently deepens and widens the stream of real income.
Joseph Schumpeter, *Capitalism Socialism, and Democracy* (1962)

A procedure for evaluating structural shifts

The first step in the resolution of the issues raised by Victorian Britain's perplexing economic performance is to provide some quantitative estimate of what was possible – to determine in what sense, and to what degree, the economy of the period failed or succeeded. Without such an estimate there can be no clear grasp of the historical phenomenon that deserves investigation and explanation and, therefore, no clear analysis and, ultimately, no understanding either. The procedure adopted here to obtain such an estimate focuses directly on output growth.[1]

The aggregate average rate of growth of an economy may be defined as a weighted sum of the average rates of growth of the component sectors of the economy:

$$g = \sum_i g_i s_i, \tag{2.1}$$

where

g = economy's aggregate average growth rate,

g_i = average growth rate of the ith sector,

s_i = average value added in the ith sector as a proportion of GNP; hence $\sum_i s_i = 1$.

Equation (2.1) is an accounting identity which forms the basis for the necessary detailed examination of the economy. This is most easily done, however, by transforming the equation in order to focus on the consequences of particular rates of growth and their changes in the various sectors of the economy. This transformation is set out in equation (2.2):

$$\Delta g = \sum_i \Delta g_i s_i + \sum_i g_i \Delta s_i + \sum_i \Delta g_i \Delta s_i, \tag{2.2}$$

where Δg = change in aggregate average growth rate,

Δg_i = change in average growth rate of the ith sector,

Δs_i = change in the average size of the ith sector; since the relative share of total output gained by one sector must be lost by some combination of other sectors within the economy, then $\sum_i \Delta s_i = 0$.

Together, equations (2.1) and (2.2) provide the framework within which the performance of the individual sectors which comprise the economy can be examined to evaluate the contribution each makes to overall growth. In particular, it is possible to evaluate the contribution made by sectors that can be identified as 'strategic' in the process of economic growth.

In the long run, per capita income can only be increased by an augmentation in the stock of technical and organizational knowledge governing the transformation of production inputs into final consumption outputs. Sectors may, therefore, be defined as strategic to the extent that they can be identified either as an ultimate source of technological advance or as centrally instrumental in facilitating and supporting technological advance. The most obvious strategic sectors are those of engineering (broadly construed), chemicals, energy, and communications. These sectors provide collectively the largest portion of the means by which modern economic activity is conducted and controlled and by which productivity advances throughout modern economies are sustained. Extensive utilization of the output of these four sectors throughout the economy has required rapid growth of inputs into them; in the nineteenth and early twentieth century this meant most notably coal, steel, other construction materials, and construction effort.

The strategic nature throughout the past century of this complex of industries arises not from their role in the direct satisfaction of wants in modern society, although these sectors have provided directly important consumer goods and services, but, more importantly, from the fact that these sectors provide the intermediate inputs which are collectively indispensable in maintaining high levels of per capita output in modern economies. There is surprisingly little variation among societies in the broad objectives of economic activity, although there is considerable variation in the relative importance attached to each. The provision in varying proportions of food, clothing, shelter, warmth, light, sanitation, health care, security, mobility, and culture – the last objective interpreted widely to include art, science, philosophy, religion, and all aspects of entertainment – is a universal goal. The most important differences among societies reflect not differences in the objectives of consumption but the extent to which the ultimate objectives are satisfied indirectly rather than directly. In advanced, highly specialized economies most economic activity centres not on the direct provision of final goods and services but on the production of a vast array of intermediate goods and services which provides the machines, structures, transport, communications, and co-ordination that ultimately enables modern economies to achieve high levels of consumption. In less advanced societies, more effort is devoted directly to the production of final output and less to the production of facilitating intermediate goods and services. In the most primitive societies, characterized by relatively low levels of total factor productivity and, therefore, low levels of per capita consumption, almost all the final consumption that the society enjoys is produced directly, often by the final consumers themselves, with the aid of few intermediate inputs.

These general structural features of economic organization that permit identification of 'strategic' sectors also permit construction of a yardstick to measure overall economic performance. An indication of the relative sizes of the sectors most compatible with the historical process of rapid growth can be obtained by comparison of the structure of the British economy in the years 1870–1913 with the structures of those advanced economies – notably the U.S., Germany, Sweden and Switzerland – growing faster than Britain during that time. Such comparisons indicate two things. First, they indicate how large, relative to the rest of the economy, the rapidly growing strategic sectors of engineering, chemicals, energy and communications could become in an advanced, technologically progressive economy. Secondly, they indicate which sectors were most likely to experience relative decline as the strategic sectors expanded. Such a comparison would not, however, reveal the theoretical limits to nineteenth-century growth for, as argued in Chapter 1, all economies have suffered in varying degrees from defects in the mechanisms and procedures they employ to determine resources allocation. The comparison of Britain's economic structure with the structures of her most advanced nineteenth-century industrial rivals would reveal the extent to which the defects of the British economy were debilitating relative to the burdens of the defects sustained by other economies, not relative to a theoretically feasible ideal.

While such comparisons are extremely useful, since there can be no doubt that the output of the strategic sectors identified above were directly or indirectly the essential elements of late nineteenth-century productivity advance, their use cannot resolve all questions. Without measures of total factor inputs to accompany measures of net output, it is not possible to obtain a sectoral analysis of the gains, in total factor productivity, that constitute the fundamental sources of economic growth. Because the strategic sectors themselves do not necessarily exhibit unusually rapid rates of total factor productivity growth, the lack of a sectoral analysis of the incidence of total factor productivity growth means that an understanding of the precise means by which growth of the strategic sectors promotes rapid growth in the economy at large remains incomplete. Examples of both the coincidence and the divergence of relative sectoral output and productivity growth rates have been found by John W. Kendrick (1961: Tables 34, 58), who noted that while communications and public utilities achieved in the U.S. relatively rapid growth of both output and total factor productivity over the period 1899–1953, value added in electric and non-electric machinery output over the same period gained in relative importance despite a persistent tendency for measured productivity gains in the sector to be less than for manufacturing as a whole. Conversely, value added in textile manufacture rose less rapidly than did value added in all manufacturing, despite the fact that productivity gains there were greater than those achieved in all manufacturing.

The explanation for such divergence is not hard to find. The machinery sector played a vital role in boosting productivity in all sectors of the economy. Hence, whether its own productivity growth was unusually rapid or not, the relative importance of the machinery sector inexorably rose as the productivity gains made possible by its output were sought in all sectors of the economy (Kendrick, 1961: 179–181). Productivity gains in textile manufacture, on the other hand, had a much more limited impact, one insufficient to compensate for the fall in the relative price of textiles. In the case of textiles, above average productivity gains facilitated the transfer of resources from that sector to the rest of the economy rather than a relative increase in the sector's importance.[2]

It is cross-country comparison, then, that gives empirical and historical content to the identity defined in equation (2.2). In particular, equation (2.2) can be used to give quantitative expression to the long-held belief (Richardson, 1965) that too large a proportion of Victorian resources were committed to the slowly growing staples of mid nineteenth-century prosperity while far too small a proportion was committed to the sectors that constituted what David Landes (1969: 235) has called the 'Second Industrial Revolution'. From the historical data, g_i and s_i are known; they are respectively the average growth rate and the average size of the ith sector for the period 1870–1913. The Δs_i are derived by cross-country comparison. If, for example, an important strategic sector such as engineering were found in Britain to comprise only 2.48% of GNP on average over the period while in, say, the U.S. value added in engineering constituted on

average 3.34% of GNP for the same period, Δs_i would be set at 0.0086 (0.0334–
0.0248 = 0.0086). If, however, the U.K. engineering sector were to have grown so
rapidly as to increase its average share of GNP to 3.34% from the average 2.48%
of GNP that it actually achieved in the period, the growth rate of the sector would
also necessarily have been increased. In fact, since the proposed increase, the Δs_i,
amounted to approximately 34.7% of the industry's actual average size
(= 0.0086/0.0248), the growth rate of output would have had to have been
correspondingly more rapid in order to have produced this higher level of output.
Hence, for every change in s_i, there must be a corresponding change in g_i. When
the calculations indicated in equation (2.2) are performed, the impact on
aggregate growth of the hypothesized structural shifts is measured by Δg. To
perform the calculations only once, however, involves an obvious and significant
under-estimate of the magnitude of the ultimate impact of the hypothesized
structural changes. If, after one iteration of equation (2.2), Δg is not zero, all of the
g_i – but of course none of the Δs_i – must be recalculated. If Δg is greater than zero,
then the hypothesized structural changes are shown to have raised the average
aggregate growth rate.

Suppose after one iteration of equation (2.2) it were found that, because rapidly
growing sectors of the economy had been given a greater weighting while slowly
growing ones had been given a lesser weighting, the resultant Δg implied a level of
aggregate real output 10% higher than that which was actually achieved. The
implications of this increase might best be seen by considering the engineering
sector which had in fact grown at an average rate of 2.84% per year, its output
rising from 30 on the Lewis-Feinstein index in 1870 to 100 in 1913. By setting Δs_i
at 0.0086, implying an index number for engineering output in 1913 of 134.7
rather than 100, the counterfactual growth rate becomes 3.55% per year rather
than the actual 2.84%. But a growth rate of 3.55% is reached by assuming that the
expansion of the engineering sector occurs in isolation and had no impact on the
aggregate economy. But inspection of Δg, which is greater than zero (set at 10%
for illustration), shows that assumption to be false. For the entire hypothesized
structural change to occur, the 34.7% increase in engineering output would have
to relate to an economy whose index of *aggregate* output stood at 110 rather than
100; otherwise, the ultimate structural shift would be less than the 34.7% initially
assumed. The correction would require the engineering output index to rise from
30 to 148.1 (= 110 × 1.347), a level consistent with a 34.7% increase in relative
sector size in the now larger economy. It is obvious that the Δg_i calculated when
the index rose from 30 to 134.7 is inconsistent with the implied growth of the
index from 30 to 148.1. This inconsistency is removed by calculating the Δg_i
implied by movement of the index from 30 to 148.1 (or 0.94% [= 3.78% – 2.84%]
per year) and substituting this revised value into equation (2.2) in place of 0.71%
(= 3.55% – 2.84%). Recalculations are repeated until all the Δg_is (and thus Δg)
from repeated iterations converge to a limiting value, which was implicit in the

original values of g_i, s_i and Δs_i, all of which remained unchanged for each counterfactual possibility.

In general, then, this procedure yields an explicit estimate of the importance to an economy's growth of industrial sectors capable of sustaining unusually rapid growth over long periods. However, it is important to remember that the procedure will not in general measure potential 'optimal' growth but only the growth that would arise from marginal structural shifts within a given economic structure. To the extent that the actual development of the British economy in the period 1870–1913 was suboptimal, not only would rapidly growing sectors have had a smaller weight than was feasible while slowly growing sectors would have had relatively more importance, but also some sectors normally stimulated in rapid growth, such as construction, would exhibit unusually low growth rates while other sectors destined to long-term decline, such as manufactured gas, would exhibit inordinately rapid growth. To reverse these abnormal trends by counterfactually assuming that a rapidly growing sector, such as manufactured gas, would have grown more slowly and (consequently) would have a smaller average size and that a slowly growing sector, such as construction, would grow more rapidly and have a larger average size reduces substantially the gain in aggregate growth rates indicated by equation (2.2). Only if the relative rates of growth of the different sectors – regardless of their relative sizes – had been compatible with good overall performance, indicating that the economy was moving, albeit belatedly, towards a more progressive structure of output, would the counterfactual gain in output growth recorded by equation (2.2) even approximate the benefits of 'optimal' growth toward any given structural configuration. Additionally, it is important to recall that there are strong reasons to believe that no actual economy could achieve the optimal structural configurations implied by a given technology, a given pattern of resource endowments, and a given set of consumer preferences. Thus equation (2.2) measures the change in growth rates caused by a move from one suboptimal structure to another, less suboptimal structure, not the change in growth rates that would occur in moving from the historically given suboptimal structure to a theoretically optimal structure. Therefore, both because the actual relative rates of growth across sectors were suboptimal and because there exists no ideal 'model' economy to indicate the optimal size of desired structural shifts (the Δs_i), the use of equation (2.2) is best interpretated as measuring the lower bounds of the gains to be realized in moving toward an economic structure consistent with the technological opportunities of the period.

Despite the inherent limitations of this procedure for evaluating the possibilities and consequences of structural change, it nevertheless permits extensive clarification of the quantitative dimensions of Victorian economic performance. If it could be shown with this procedure that even if Britain in the half century before 1914 had had a structure of output as heavily weighted towards the strategic sectors as were the structures of the most dynamic contemporary economies, that nevertheless aggregate growth would have been little different, then it would be possible to argue that the British economy of the period was operating close to the historical limits to growth. In such a case, there would be little justification for concern over technological shortcomings and slowing growth rates. If, alternatively, it is possible to argue that a counterfactual shift of Victorian output in favour of the strategic sectors would have been expected to have raised sharply the aggregate rate of growth, then the approximate dimensions of any economic failure can be clearly drawn.

But more is at stake than an estimate of the limits to Victorian growth, although such an estimate is absolutely necessary to define intelligibly the historical problem to be resolved. If the limits to growth as indicated by structural comparisons were not approached, it is possible to see which sectors of the economy were most responsible for this failure and to ask detailed questions regarding both the extent of the allocation of resources to those sectors and the quality of the management of those resources actually committed. The structure of an economy by itself does not provide an explanation of performance but is rather only a manifestation of an underlying allocative process; it is, however, an extremely revealing manifestation and one worthy of the closest examination.[3]

The structure of output in the United States and the United Kingdom, 1870–1913

Although it would have been useful to have compared Britain with European countries such as Sweden, Switzerland, and Germany, all of which were well advanced and growing rapidly in the early twentieth century, the comparison used in this book is limited to that between the United States and the United Kingdom. The main justification for this choice is two-fold: first, American growth was perhaps the fastest in the world in the years 1870–1913 and thus offers the clearest comparison with Britain. Second, the structural changes that accompanied America's rapid growth were founded not so much on rich endowments of natural resources – although such endowments were undeniably an asset – as on an expanding technological capability. The pattern of rapid industrial expansion in the U.S., despite returns in extractive activities (predominantly agriculture and mining) considerably greater than those obtainable in the U.K., reveals most clearly the sectors offering the highest marginal yield to factors of production. The rapidly growing American industrial sectors were ones which might in fact have been expected to grow especially rapidly in Britain where a poorer natural resource base exercised an inherently weaker hold on factors of production.[4] Furthermore, the salient features of the American economy were also found prominently in the most progressive European countries, although with some differences in detail.

For example, one of the most distinguishing features of the contemporary German economy, one of the largest and the most dynamic of the European economies, was the extensive – the largest in Europe – technologically advanced, and rapidly growing engineering sector (Milward and Saul, 1977: 35–41). In both the U.S. and Germany, developments in the newest and most advanced branch of engineering, electrical engineering, were particularly striking, although this similarity was not repeated in all branches of engineering. If Germany was, compared with the U.S., slow to develop production of automobiles, office machines, typewriters, and cash registers, this backwardness was compensated by incomparable performance in the related strategic sector of chemicals and by a general technological and scientific capability that promised to limit to modest proportions any gaps in engineering which did occur while creating opportunities of industrial advances quite independent of American progress.

A highly capable, progressive engineering sector also lay at the heart of Swiss economic development throughout the nineteenth century, first in the production of watches, steam engines and textile machinery; later along broader lines, notably in electrical engineering where the Swiss firms of Brown, Boveri and Escher Wyss were among the world leaders in power station design and construction. For a nation whose citizens numbered only 3.9 million in 1914, those two Swiss firms alone, disregarding the numerous small firms in ancillary and allied trades, represented a massive commitment of talent and resources to the modern electrical engineering industry. Sweden's economic development in the half century before 1914 was perhaps the most spectacular in Europe, (Jörberg, 1973: 376; Milward and Saul, 1977: 65) transforming a relatively poor land into one of the wealthiest in Europe. In this transformation, the rapid growth and development of engineering, often based upon Swedish inventions, were particularly noticeable (Jörberg, 1973: 447; Sandberg, 1979: 232). Thus, if American expansion in the late nineteenth century was unique in its details it nevertheless shared enough important features with other advanced and rapidly growing economies of the period to support the belief that it offers a useful and illuminating basis for comparison with the U.K. A final consideration, not without its own substantial attractions, is that comparison is greatly aided by the similarity of American and British census techniques and classifications.

Tables 2.1 and 2.2 respectively set out the structure of domestic output for the U.K. in 1907 and for the U.S. in 1909. Table 2.3 presents a summary of the differences which existed in the early twentieth century between the two countries in the relative sizes of the major sectors. In the analysis that follows, except where explicitly noted otherwise, attention is focused on relative size (measured as in Table 2.3 as a proportion of the GNP of the respective countries) rather than on absolute size. Because of the marked differences in the absolute sizes of the two economies, output in the U.S. in almost every sector, measured at prevailing exchange rates, was greater than its U.K. counterpart, even when the *relative*

Table 2.1. *U.K. gross national product, 1907 (at modified market prices excluding duties on beer, sugar, and glucose)*

Sector	Value added	Percent of reference estimate
Agriculture and fishing	£148.0m	6.66
Construction, mining and manufacturing (CMM):	711.2	32.01
construction	£62.3m	2.80
mining	119.5	5.38
iron, steel trades	30.0	1.35
miscellaneous metal working trades	17.6	0.79
engineering	58.2	2.62
of which: electricity supply	(5.6)	(.25)
shipbuilding	21.0	0.94
cycle and motor trades	5.9	0.26
cutlery, tools and implements	3.2	0.14
small arms	2.1	0.09
railway carriage and wagon trade	21.1	0.95
road carriage	3.0	0.14
metal working (other than iron and steel)	7.5	0.34
textiles	94.3	4.24
clothing	49.8	2.24
food processing	44.6	2.01
alcoholic beverages	29.6	1.33
precious metals, jewels, watches	7.5	0.34
chemicals: class (a)	20.1	0.90
chemicals: class (b) – mainly agricultural by-products	4.4	0.20
paper, printing and allied trades	32.6	1.47
leather and canvas	5.6	0.25
timber trades	19.4	0.87
brick, cement, pottery	17.1	0.77
gas undertakings	17.3	0.78
telephones, telegraph systems	4.8	0.22
scientific instruments	1.5	0.07
musical instruments	1.1	0.05
miscellaneous industries	1.0	0.04
waterworks	9.1	0.41
Correction for CMM	50.0	2.25

Table 2.1. (*cont.*)

Sector	Value added	Percent of reference estimate
Domestic transportation	166.7	7.50
International shipping	37.5	1.69
Imputed income from dwellings	132.2	5.95
Wholesale-retail trade	407.8	18.35
Professional services	67.1	3.02
Personal services	42.0	1.89
Government sector services	92.0	4.14
Domestic service	74.3	3.34
International financial and commercial services	69.8	3.14
Net property income from abroad	144.0	6.48
Total	£2141.7m	96.39
Reference estimate	£2222.0m	100.00

Sources: Data Appendices A and C.

Table 2.2. *U.S. gross national product, 1909 (at modified market prices excluding excise taxes on alcohol and cigarettes)*

Sector	Value added	Percent of reference output
Agriculture and fishing	$5,240m	16.37
Construction, mining and manufacturing (CMM):	11,238	35.11
construction	$1,748m	5.46
mining	966	3.02
iron, steel trades	409	1.28
miscellaneous metal working trades	163	0.51
engineering	1,102	3.44
of which: electricity supply	(128)	(.40)
shipbuilding	42	0.13
cycle and motor trade	123	0.38
cutlery, tools and implements	46	0.14

Table 2.2. (*cont.*)

Sector	Value added	Percent of reference output
small arms	17	0.05
railway carriage and wagon trade	288	0.90
road carriage	84	0.26
metal working (other than iron and steel)	155	0.48
textiles	727	2.27
clothing	830	2.59
food processing	1016	3.17
alcoholic beverages	352	1.10
precious metals, jewels watches	115	0.36
chemicals: class (a)	287	0.90
chemicals: class (b) – mainly agricultural by-products	93	0.29
paper, printing and allied trades	753	2.35
leather and canvas	158	0.49
timber trades	867	2.71
brick, cement, glass	379	1.18
gas undertakings	114	0.36
telephone, telegraph systems	158	0.49
scientific instruments	49	0.15
musical instruments	48	0.15
miscellaneous industries	47	0.15
waterworks	102	0.32
Correction for CMM	793m	2.48
Domestic transportation	2585	8.08
International shipping	21	0.06
Imputed income from dwellings	1991	6.22
Domestic wholesale-retail trade	5475	17.11
Professional services	809	2.53
Personal services	736	2.30
Government sector services	889	2.78
Domestic service	525	1.64
International financial and commercial services	38	0.12
Net property income from abroad	− 39	− 0.12
Total	$30,301	94.68
Reference estimate	$32,005m	100.00

Sources: Data Appendices B and C.

sector size in the U.K. was larger, thereby rendering absolute size comparisons of limited interest.

The important feature that emerges from this general comparison is that *none* of the sectors that can readily be identified with late nineteenth-century technological change was larger in relative size in the U.K. than in the U.S. Furthermore, because of the crucial role the strategic sectors played in generating the means by which productivity was enhanced in the rest of the economy and in promoting rapid growth and development in general, the continued prosperity of the rest of the U.K. economy can be shown to have been unduly jeopardized by the stunted development of the strategic sectors. Such jeopardy, it will be argued below, affected particularly construction, shipbuilding, coalmining, international shipping, and international financial services, all sectors that were of great importance to the British economy of the nineteenth and early twentieth centuries.

Table 2.3. *Summary of differences in U.K. and U.S. distribution of output (measured as value added as proportion of total output)*

	U.K. (1907)	U.S. (1909)	*Difference*
Agriculture	6.66%	16.37%	−9.71%
Construction, mining, and manufacture (CMM):	32.01	35.11	−3.10
construction	2.80%	5.46%	−2.66%
mining	5.38	3.02	2.36
iron, steel trades	1.35	1.28	0.07
miscellaneous metal working trades	0.79	0.51	0.28
engineering	2.62	3.44	−0.82
of which: electricity	(.25)	(.40)	(−.15)
shipbuilding	0.94	0.13	0.81
motor and cycle trades	0.26	0.38	−0.12
cutlery, tools and implements	0.14	0.14	0.00
small arms	0.09	0.05	0.04
railway carriage and wagon trade	0.95	0.90	0.05
road carriage	0.14	0.26	−0.12
metal working (other than iron and steel)	0.34	0.48	−0.14
textiles	4.24	2.27	1.97
clothing	2.24	2.59	−0.35
food processing	2.01	3.17	−1.16
alcoholic beverages	1.33	1.10	0.23
precious metals, jewels, watches	0.34	0.36	−0.02

Table 2.3. *(cont.)*

	U.K. (1907)	U.S. (1909)	Difference
chemicals: class (a)	0.90	0.90	0.00
chemicals: class (b) – mainly agricultural by-products	0.20	0.29	−0.09
paper, printing and allied trades	1.47	2.35	−0.88
leather and canvas	0.25	0.49	−0.24
timber trades	0.87	2.71	−1.84
brick, cement, glass	0.77	1.18	−0.41
gas undertakings	0.78	0.36	0.42
telephone, telegraph systems	0.22	0.49	−0.27
scientific instruments	0.07	0.15	−0.08
musical instruments	0.05	0.15	−0.10
miscellaneous industries	0.04	0.15	−0.11
waterworks	0.41	0.32	0.09
Correction to CMM sectors	2.25	2.48	−0.23
Domestic transportation	7.50	8.08	−0.58
International shipping	1.69	0.06	1.63
Imputed income from dwellings	5.95	6.22	−0.27
Domestic wholesale-retail trade	18.35	17.11	1.24
Professional services	3.02	2.53	0.49
Personal services	1.89	2.30	−0.41
Government sector services	4.14	2.78	1.36
Domestic service	3.34	1.64	1.70
International financial and commercial services	3.14	0.12	3.02
Net property income from abroad	6.48	−0.12	6.60
Residual around reference estimate	3.61	5.32	−1.71

Sources: Tables 2.1 and 2.2

Detailed comparison of the structures of the U.S. and U.K. economies might most usefully begin with consideration of engineering and the closely related sectors of telecommunications and scientific instruments. The relative size of the engineering sector, which is comprised of mechanical and electrical engineering (including electricity supply), the motor, cycle and road carriage trades, and the working of non-ferrous metals, was 35.7% $\left(\dfrac{0.0456}{0.0336} = 1.357\right)$ greater in the U.S. than in the U.K. while the relative value added in the provision of telephone-

telegraph service and scientific instruments was $120.7\% \left(\dfrac{0.0064}{0.0029} = 2.207 \right)$ greater
in the U.S. than in the U.K. The full significance of these differences can be better
appreciated by three direct comparisons of output. Such comparisons are
especially useful for the large engineering sector which included the manufacture
of traditional products such as railroad equipment (excluding rolling stock and
track maintenance), steam engines and parts, general machinery and iron
castings, as well as those items distinguished by their rapid growth of production
in the late nineteenth and early twentieth centuries.[5] The comparisons, which are
of automobile, electricity, and telecommunications usage, were all selected
because they focused on sectors which were of unusual importance, which grew
with unusual speed in both countries, and which embodied to an unusual extent
the considerable technological progress of the period. The comparisons also serve
to emphasize that if British commitment of resources to the expansion of these
sectors where the rewards for prompt response were so great was laggard, then
the allocative response in other areas where the advantages were not so
extraordinary was also generally unimpressive.

The first comparison concerns the application of electricity to industrial uses.
This application was of signal importance for it wrought an expansion of useful
production opportunities throughout the economy, including important uses in
the large service sectors of distribution and transport. Table 2.4 indicates the
differences in both the level of electricity usage and the composition of usage
among industrial, commercial, and residential consumers in the two countries. In
1907, the U.K. produced 141 kilowatt hours per worker; in the same year the U.S.
produced 362, an output 2.57 times greater. The greater usage in the U.S. would
have been even more obvious had the comparison been restricted to electricity
consumption per *industrial* worker.[6] Since only 8.0% of all dwelling units in the
U.S. in 1907 were supplied with electric service, and only 15.9% in 1912, when it
was noted that residential users consumed only 3.64% total electricity output
(U.S. Bureau of the Census, 1975: series S109, S108, S120, S121), the appropriate
comparison is clearly to be made excluding residential users. Assuming that 60%
of the electricity used in the U.S. in 1907 was for industrial and traction
purposes – the bulk of the rest assumed to be used for commercial and public
lighting – then manufacturing, mining, construction and transportation used 547
kilowatt-hours of electric power per worker. If it is generously assumed that 64%
of the total electricity generated in the U.K. was used for industrial and traction
purposes, each British worker in the relevant industries used only 169 kilowatt-
hours of electricity per year. Thus each American industrial worker used on
average at least 3.2 times the electricity that his British counterpart used.[7]

Although the amounts of electricity generated before World War I were not
large by later standards (note, however, that in absolute terms Britain did not
reach the 1907 U.S. level of electricity production until 1933 nor the 1912 level

Table 2.4. *Generation and use of electricity in the U.S. and U.K., 1907–1912*

(All figures in thousands of kilo-watt hours)

	U.K. (1907)		U.S. (1907)	U.S. (1912)	
Industrial use	1,386,602	(51%)[1]		17,921,000	(76%)[2]
Transportation use	354,819	(13%)			
Residential – commercial use; miscellaneous	987,101	(36%)		5,517,000	(24%)[3]
Total	2,728,522	(100%)[4]	13,371,000[5]	23,438,000	(100%)[5]

Sources: U.S. – *Historical Statistics of the United States* (1975: series S120–132).
U.K.–Cd. 6320, pp. 15–18.

Notes:
[1] This figure includes an estimate of the output of private industrial generators for which the capacity was reported to the Census authorities but for which no output figures were returned. The capacity of these generators was 195,640 kilo-watts. If these generators produced the same amount of output as those generators for which both output and capacity figures are available their output would have been 339,862,000 kilo-watt hours. This figure was added to the reported 1,046,740,000 kilo-watt hours of power consumed by industrial users. It almost certainly represents an over-estimate of power used because the largest firms, which also tended to be the largest electricity users, were usually accurate in their reports while most of the inaccurate or incomplete reports were made by small users. Since firms were required to list the amount of 'stand-by' capacity they had, a large portion of the 195,640 kilo-watts of capacity which returned no output figures may have been quite inefficient and used only infrequently.
[2] This figure includes 6.671 billion kilo-watts listed in the category 'miscellaneous light and power'. Some of this may have been used by the extensive network of electric trams and railways but it is not possible to know how much. Some was probably also used for public and commercial lighting.
[3] This figure represents a residual calculated by subtracting the amount of industrial power plus the category 'losses and use unaccounted for' from the total figure given in series S120.
[4] The figure was in part for power *purchased* from electricity supply undertakings and hence does not include losses in generation and transmission. No allowance was made for losses incurred by firms that produced their own electricity.
[5] From the total amount of power used, an allowance for losses, an allowance equal to the proportion of losses to total output recorded in 1912, was made. This loss was 6.2% of total output in 1912.

until 1938), nevertheless electricity usage is perhaps one of the best indications of successful application of technology in the early twentieth century. The advantages of electrification were two-fold. First, electrification made possible large cuts in operating costs in a wide range of industries. By eliminating the awkward energy-wasting belt transmission of power and by allowing machines to draw power only when being used, electrification allowed, according to contemporary estimates, savings of up to 83% of the fuel costs of the same power supplied from continuously running steam engines (DuBoff, 1967:510–13).

Electrification also eliminated the need for heavy multi-storied buildings with reinforced floors capable of supporting on-site steam engines. Elimination of the steam engines themselves, together with their unwieldy and temperamental mechanical power transmission apparatus, and the subsequent concentration of power generation in a central plant reaping greater economies of scale, meant additional savings on expensive equipment and maintenance charges.

More importantly, however, electrification allowed a new flexibility in plant layout and design. The ability of electrical devices to control a vast and complex array of machine tools and other equipment with an ease, economy, and accuracy previously unknown opened up entirely new ranges of industrial techniques. Richard DuBoff (1967:518), a close student of the early process of electrification in the U.S., summarized the possibilities thus:

Electrification ushered in a period of 'efficiency' soon to become a watchword for the reorganization in manufacturing techniques that began after the turn of the century. Cost cutting became possible over much larger ranges of output than under steam. Subdivision and mobility of power units offered a wider array of labour, material and capital equipment combinations, from workshop, domestic-type activities reacting to irregular patterns of demand and supply often found in local markets, to factories sometimes surpassing the 'monster mills' of the Victorian steam era. Subdivision in turn meant greater diffusion of power needed to support a decentralized, less capital-intensive structure of industry. Smaller plants earned a new lease of life, since most of them could now afford power equipment commensurate with their operations.

Another important, technologically sophisticated product of the engineering industry whose use had a pervasive impact on the entire economy was the automobile and, to a lesser extent, the motor cycle and related forms of road transport. Table 2.5 compares the numbers in use in the two countries. Because the U.S. data are based on registrations rather than usage, the American figures are clearly under-estimates of the actual number of vehicles in use at any one time. Yet, despite substantial imports and the large scale assembly of vehicles in Britain by foreign firms before 1914, the numbers in use there were very much fewer relative to the population than in the U.S. at that time. In terms of the number of vehicles of all types per 1,000 inhabitants, the vehicle density in the U.S. (registrations only) was 2.8 times greater than in the U.K. If automobiles only are considered, the U.S. density is 5.5 times greater than that in the U.K. This greater density in the U.S. yielded benefits of two types. First, internal combustion vehicles speeded up the flow of goods and generally made the transportation and distribution systems more flexible and efficient. Secondly, because automobile manufacture constituted an unparalleled technological challenge to the engineering industry, requiring precise engineering yet subject to rough use while demanding a high degree of reliability, the successful response to this challenge brought important spin-offs to the rest of the economy. Metallurgy and machine-

Table 2.5. *Vehicles in use in the U.K. and U.S., 1904–1938* (in thousands)

	U.K.		U.S.[1]		
	Private cars	Buses, coaches, trams, taxis	Goods Vehicles	Automobiles	Trucks
1904	8	12	4	54	1
1905	16	15	9	77	1
1906	23	19	12	106	2
1907	32	22	14	140	3
1908	41	25	18	194	4
1909	48	27	22	306	6
1910	53	35	30	458	10
1911	72	44	40	618	20
1912	88	47	53	902	42
1913	106	51	64	1,190	68
1914	132	64	82	1,664	99
1924	474	108	203	15,436	2,176
1938	1,944	94	495	25,250	4,563

Sources:
U.K. – Mitchell and Deane (1962: 230).
U.S. – U.S. Bureau of the Census (1975: Series.Q, 153–5).

Note:
[1] Registrations only. Since registration of vehicles was not required in all U.S. states before 1921, part of the growth in numbers used represents increased registration rather than increased usage. This is especially important for trucks. For example in 1912 alone, sales of 22,000 motor trucks and buses were recorded (U.S. Bureau of the Census, 1975: series Q 150,155). Thus the 1912 output alone was more than 50% of the recorded 1912 stock, suggesting very substantial under-registration of goods vehicles and buses.

tool design and usage in particular were transformed by the endeavour to mass produce automobiles.[8]

The final instructive comparison concerns the use of the telephone. Abramovitz and David (1973: 435), in a comprehensive examination of American economic growth, observe that modern economic growth generates '... heightened needs for reliable performance of communication, co-ordination and control functions in an urban society within which the organizational scale and degree of specialization have been steadily pushed upward to take advantage of technical innovations in commodity production'. Leslie Hannah has elaborated this theme in describing the rise in Britain of the large scale firms that have been responsible for an ever increasing proportion of investment and output, especially in the technically oriented industries that have dominated twentieth-century growth. He (Hannah, 1974a: 256) cites the telephone as 'perhaps the most important new instrument of communication to become widely available to managers' and claims it 'provided a means of rapid communication between departments or between geographically dispersed branches and facilitated managerial control'. As with electricity, adoption of the telephone appears to have been a necessary prerequisite for utilization of many of the forms of technical advance which were becoming available in the late nineteenth century.[9] Tables 2.6, 2.7 and 2.8 show that Britain adopted the use of

Table 2.6. *Annual number of telephone calls made, U.S. and U.K., 1895–1914* (in millions)

	U.K.		U.S.	
	Trunk	Local	Trunk	Local
1895			18.5[1]	858.1[1]
1896			23.0[1]	960.0[1]
1897			27.4[1]	1131.1[1]
1898	5.9		34.7[1]	1395.4[1]
1899	7.1		48.5[1]	1888.5[1]
1900	8.1		70.4	2806.5
1901	9.0		93.1	3945.6
1902	10.1		122.6	5108.5
1903	11.6		132.5	5554.9
1904	13.5		153.7	6304.3
1905	15.5		188.3	7723.4
1906	18.1		232.1	9236.3
1907	19.9		257.0	10614.2
1908	22.1		256.2	11421.9
1909	23.6		278.9	12041.4
1910	26.7		314.6	12884.1
1911	30.7		332.5	13592.2
1912	33.7		369.7	14452.5
1913	36.0	797	393.5	14561.7
1914	38.2	934	387.3	14586.9

Not until 1960 did trunk calls in the U.K. equal in number those made in the U.S. in 1914. Local calls in the U.S. in 1905 were greater than the number of local calls made in the U.K. in 1966.

Sources:
U.K. – Mitchell and Jones (1971: 112–13).
U.S. – Calculated from U.S. Bureau of the Census (1975: Series R9–12).

Note:
[1] Bell system only.

Table 2.7. *Telephones in use, U.K. and U.S.,*
1914–1940

	U.K.	U.S.
1898	–	681,000
1902	–	2,371,000
1906	–	4,933,000
1910	–	7,635,000
1914	803,543	10,046,000
1920	914,923	13,329,000
1925	968,433	16,936,000
1930	1,323,314	20,202,000
1935	1,579,062	17,424,000
1940	1,976,605	21,928,000

Sources:
U.K. – Hannah (1974a: 257).
U.S. – U.S. bureau of the Census (1975: Series R1).

Table 2.8. *Indicators of telephone usage*

	U.K. Telephones/ worker	U.S. Telephones/ worker
1914	0.04	0.25
1955	0.25	0.82

Sources:
U.K. Telephones –
   1914 – Hannah (1974: 257).
   1955 – G.P.O communication to Mr L. Hannah, January 1969.
U.K. Labour force – Feinstein (1972: Table 126,
   column 3).
U.S. Telephones – U.S. Bureau of the Census
   (1975: Series R1).
U.S. Labour force – U.S. Bureau of the Census
   (1975: Series D1, 1914, Series D12, 1955).

telephones even more slowly than the use of electricity. While the contrast with
the U.S. is particularly stark, Britain also lagged behind many Western European
countries in telephone usage, despite higher per capita real incomes that tended
to stimulate the demand for better communications (Milward and Saul,
1977: 544, Table 96).

The relatively small size of strategic industries in Britain cannot be attributed to a lack of demand. That impressive demand for these goods did, in fact, face British producers is revealed clearly by international trade and capital flows, although satisfaction of this manifest demand depended upon a price response which only technological advance could sustain. While Britain's share of world trade was bound to fall eventually as other nations industrialized, it was certainly not inevitable that the decline should have been so pronounced in the trade of those goods whose production required the highest levels of industrial skills and technological capability. The changing structure of British exports in fact reversed the pattern experienced by other developed nations of the period. The normal pattern was for advanced nations to sustain a decline in the rate of growth of output in those industries whose technology and skills were most accessible to poorer countries, while expanding the relative rate of output in the more technologically demanding spheres of production (Maizels, 1970: 162–73). While Britain actually increased its share of the slowly growing world trade in both the traditional industries of textiles and clothing in the early twentieth century, it was fast losing its share in the rapidly expanding trade in industrial equipment, electrical goods and motor vehicles (Tyszynski, 1951). When, between 1899 and 1913, the value of world manufactured exports more than doubled, while the share claimed by exports of textiles and clothing fell from 40.3% to 35.0%, Britain's share of total world exports of textiles rose marginally from 44.4% to 44.8% and its share of world exports of clothing rose even more, from 23.5% to 25.7%. This export achievement represented an increase of £87.8m in the value of exports between 1899 and 1913, although the increase in domestic value added was much smaller since the price of imported raw cotton doubled over the interval while the price of cotton sheeting rose by only 56% (Tyszynski, 1951: 277–8; U.S. Bureau of the Census, 1975: series E126 and E128).

On the other hand, Tyszynski's figures show that the categories of industrial equipment, electrical goods, and motor vehicles comprised 7.4% of the value of manufactured exports of the eleven major trading countries in 1899, rising to 13.6% in 1913. By 1913, Britain's share of trade in industrial equipment had fallen from the 40% registered in 1899 to 28%; for electrical goods, from 33% to 23%; and for motor vehicles, from 24% to 17% despite the very rapid growth of total British exports after 1904. Had Britain simply managed to maintain in 1913 the share of exports of industrial equipment, electrical goods, and motor vehicles that had been held in 1899, British exports of those goods, given the actual level of world trade in 1913, would have been £64.9m rather than £45.6m, an increase of £19.3m, equal to 42.3% of the actual 1913 level of British exports of those goods. Moreover, almost all this increase would have represented increased value added by British resources.

Britain contributed to the growth of international trade in manufactured goods as a major importer as well as an exporter. Indeed, a sizeable portion of the growth in world trade in sophisticated industrial goods was due to Britain's increasing prominence as an importer. To some extent, the rapid rise in British imports reflected the increased trade of manufactured goods among all industrial nations caused by the multiplicity of new competitive sources of supply, the increasingly international character of scientific advance and technological innovation, and the growing internal demands of complex, technically sophisticated economies. To a much larger extent, however, rising imports reflected a failure of British producers to adjust successfully to changing technical opportunities and domestic requirements. Examination of British import statistics documents these trends (see Table 2.9). In technologically sophisticated areas of trade such as chemicals and automobiles, Britain's imports relative to her exports were large and quickly growing.

Even superficially successful performances in these areas must be qualified. The

Table 2.9. *Value of U.K. foreign trade in selected commodities, 1895–1913* *(£000,000)*

	Chemicals		Electrical goods		Automobiles	
	Imports	Exports	Imports	Exports	Imports	Exports
1895	5.6	11.4				
1896	6.3	11.7				
1897	6.5	12.0				
1898	6.3	11.6				
1899	6.6	12.2				
1900	7.1	13.1				
1901	9.9	12.1				
1902	10.5	12.8				
1903	11.1	13.5	1.3	2.9		
1904	11.2	13.6	1.3	2.1		
1905	11.9	14.5	1.4	3.1		
1906	13.2	15.5	1.6	2.7		
1907	14.5	17.1	1.7	3.0		
1908	13.9	16.3	1.6	3.3		
1909	14.3	16.8	1.6	3.7	4.3	1.6
1910	15.8	18.6	2.0	5.8	5.3	2.6
1911	16.9	20.1	2.2	4.6	6.0	3.2
1912	17.4	21.0	2.3	6.0	7.1	3.7
1913	18.3	22.0	2.6	7.6	7.4	4.4

Sources:
Chemicals: Data for exports from Mitchell and Deane (1962:304–5), data for imports from H.W. Richardson (1968:293).
Electrical goods: Byatt (1968:257).
Automobiles: British Parliamentary Papers, *Annual Statement of Trade* (1914:23).

appearance in Table 2.9 of a favourable balance of trade in electrical products is deceptive. I.C.R. Byatt (1968: 273) noted that: 'the main function of the British electrical goods industry before 1914 was to produce the less sophisticated types of equipment for the home market and for export to the underdeveloped world'. In general, had trade figures been included for machine tools and certain other kinds of advanced industrial equipment, the significance of imports would have been magnified.[10] Although Britain could have reduced the level of these imports had her governments rashly erected tariff barriers as other countries did, the trend, especially in the trading of newer types of goods, could have been reversed only by a more fundamental response.

Moreover, the trade figures, which were ominous enough, would have been worse had not foreign investment within Britain in the early twentieth century occurred on an important scale. In several new and important industries destined to be crucial to Britain's future, foreigners detected investment opportunities going unseized by domestic entrepreneurs at a time when Britain's own foreign investment flows were at an unprecedented and subsequently unequalled peak. By 1913, Henry Ford had become the largest automobile manufacturer in Britain, producing more cars than the next two largest British manufacturers combined (Saul, 1962b: 25, Table 3). In electrical engineering, British-based subsidiaries of German and American companies – Siemens, General Electric, and Westinghouse – dominated the British domestic market (Byatt, 1962: 369–70; Byatt, 1968: 255–8).[11] British subsidiaries of American companies producing printing presses, typesetting and line adjusting machines similarly dominated British markets in those products (Dunning, 1956: 246–7). It is significant that American investment, which probably accounted for the bulk of foreign direct investment in Britain, was concentrated almost entirely in the new fields of production; the older established industries attracted little foreign investment (Dunning, 1956: 257), a pattern implying that foreigners expected the rate of return in the 'new' industries to be substantially higher than in the old. Undoubtedly this belief stemmed largely from the absence of British domestic investment and competition in the new lines. Thus, the structure of foreign investment in Britain reinforces the conclusion reached by examination of the pattern of Britain's foreign trade – it was in the reaction to opportunities for new, technologically sophisticated products that British response was weakest and most laggard.

The limited commitment of resources to the most technologically advanced sectors of the British economy of the late nineteenth and early twentieth century had direct ramifications in the rest of the economy. An important example of these effects may be seen clearly in the small size and technological backwardness of the British construction industry. In size, relative to GNP, the U.S. industry was almost twice as large – 95.0% $\left(\dfrac{0.0546}{0.0280} = 1.950 \right)$ larger to be exact – as its

U.K. counterpart. In turn, the relatively small size of the construction industry naturally restricted the size of those supply industries most dependent on construction, notably brick, cement, and glass manufacture. Relative to GNP the U.S. sector of brick, cement, and glass manufacture was 53.2% $\left(\dfrac{0.0118}{0.0077} = 1.532 \right)$ larger than its U.K. counterpart.

Two powerful, reinforcing influences operating on demand for new construction contributed to this result. One operated directly, as failure to exploit more completely the possibilities offered by industrial electrification, the telephone, and the automobile restricted demand for new construction since older buildings and sites continued to be used unaltered and new ones were not required. The other influence operated indirectly through the periodic waves, intense and persistent by contemporary European standards, of emigration from the U.K. (Green and Urquhart, 1976: Tables 1 and 2). Failure to exploit technological innovations and to expand more rapidly the sectors most directly contributing to, or benefiting from, technological advance held domestic incomes below what they would otherwise have been and thereby may plausibly be believed to have encouraged emigration, although the precise determinants of the complex decision to emigrate are still unclear (B. Thomas, 1973: 94–5, 103–7). Clearly, however, heavy emigration served, *ceteris paribus*, to reduce the demand for new housing and the social infrastructure related to it.[12]

Weak demand impulses were further attenuated by a poor supply response by the British construction industry itself. British construction methods in the late nineteenth century lagged far behind both American and German practice in the use of new construction materials – most notably steel I-beam load bearing frames and steel reinforced concrete which permitted the construction to stronger, lighter, taller, and more fireproof buildings than had been possible with only masonry techniques (Bowley, 1966: 12–22). The slow adaptation and relatively high price of electricity, together with the equally slow improvement in the availability of electrical equipment (e.g. drills, saws, sanders) for use on building sites, further hobbled productivity growth in construction. The notable lack of architectural training and awareness among those most intimately involved in the construction either of industrial structures – rail stations and terminals were a clear exception that demonstrated the general rule – or of low cost housing made those buildings as a distinct group less attractive, functional, and comfortable than they might have been (Bowley, 1966: 354).

Weak demand for new construction and slow improvement in building materials and construction techniques interacted with slow advance in the engineering sector to compound inherent economic weaknesses. In Britain there was no stimulus such as that which occurred in the U.S. with the rapid adoption of tall steel frame skeleton buildings in response to sharply increasing site costs, a development which created, virtually alone, a vast market for elevators, complex internal plumbing systems, and related equipment. In this manner, innovations in related industries reinforced each other. The initial stimulus to construction techniques and possibilities created by the steel frame skeleton and by steel reinforced concrete resulted in a flow of novel demands on the engineering industries. The successful response to those demands further increased the design options open to engineer-architects and thereby sustained a fruitful interaction of challenge and response between construction and engineering far beyond the initial possibilities created by the simple steel frame skeleton and steel reinforced concrete.

Another important industry becoming increasingly dependent on the most technologically progressive sectors of the economy was shipbuilding. Shipbuilding was a vital part of the British economy and one where Britain's performance down to the opening decade of the twentieth century was undeniably impressive. In 1913, Britain was still by far the world's largest shipbuilder, a position which had been held since the mid nineteenth century (Hughes and Reiter, 1958: 468–9). In the decade before World War I, Britain alone produced approximately twice as much tonnage of new shipping as the rest of the world combined (Pollard, 1957: 426–7). The relative size (in terms of a proportion of GNP) of the U.S. industry in 1909 was only 13.8% $\left(\dfrac{0.0013}{0.0094} = 0.138\right)$ of that of its British counterpart in 1907. In absolute terms, value added in the American shipbuilding industry in 1909 was only 41.2% of the value added in the British industry in 1907. Yet the circumstances that had created and sustained this dominating position of the British shipbuilding industry were, even before 1914, rapidly changing and the new conditions, magnified by the turbulent aftermath of the First World War and an unsettled international economy, were to reduce savagely the sector's importance in the British economy.

There were three main reasons for this. First, shipbuilding, in the last half of the nineteenth century, increasingly became an industry assembling components made in other sectors of the economy. Where once builders in shipyards would have flanged, turned, centre-bored, slotted, and otherwise prepared the iron and steel they used, by the end of the nineteenth century steel works increasingly supplied the finished goods to them ready for assembly. Auxiliary equipment – such as winches, pumps, steering gear, electric generating plant, refrigeration equipment, ventilating systems, electrical equipment and navigation aids – which came to comprise an increasing proportion of the value of a completed ship, was also supplied by specialist builders (Pollard and Robertson, 1979: 90–91). As the machinery became more complex, supplier specialization increased. Thus the competitiveness of the shipbuilding industry increasingly came to depend on the competence of an ever-widening range of component suppliers in the engineering and metal fabricating industries. If these suppliers as a group faltered, the shipbuilding industry would be dangerously threatened. Of course, components could be imported, as American, French, and even German yards demonstrated before 1914 by depending upon British-made components to varying extents (Pollard and Robertson, 1979: 91–2). However, as American, French and German experience before 1914 also demonstrated, heavy reliance upon remote suppliers for critical components condemned the domestic industry to a subsidiary position relative to the country whose yards were in closest contact with the component suppliers.

Close contacts with supplying industries were especially important for British shipbuilders. A long tradition of adoration of 'practical' men with 'practical' experience – experience gained with dirty hands from long years' labour in yards and workshops without recourse to books – left the great bulk of British shipbuilders unable to apply systematically new scientific developments to their own work. Pollard and Robertson (1979: 74) cite only Wigham Richardson and C.A. Parsons, of all Victorian shipbuilders and designers, as examples of men whose positions of pre-eminence were based on technical knowledge and study rather than practical training. As in the past, the practical, empirical tradition of British shipbuilding continued to generate a respectable flow of innovations, but by the closing decade of the nineteenth century more and more innovations in shipbuilding – perhaps the majority of them – were coming from outside industries, in steelmaking, electrical and mechanical engineering, where contact with formal science was pursued more enthusiastically and comprehensively (Pollard and Robertson, 1979: 148–50). Moreover, the lack of technical and scientific training among shipbuilders left them in a poor position to give supplier industries useful guidance in the solution of technical problems specific to shipbuilding or to understand how new developments appearing elsewhere could best be applied to shipbuilding. For example, the slow development in Britain of the diesel motorship, destined to be the fastest growing segment of the world's shipbuilding industry during the inter-war period, owes much to the fact that diesel engineering sprang, unlike steam propulsion, from a technological tradition not well represented in Britain (Saul, 1968a: 219, 221). In contrast, innovations in steam were rapidly taken up although steam propulsion represented the past, not the future. In this manner weaknesses in the most technologically advanced areas of engineering and metallurgy were transmitted to the large, traditionally important sector of shipbuilding.

The second, closely related reason for the increasing weakness and vulnerability of the pre-1914 British shipbuilding industry, a weakness incompletely veiled by the apparent prosperity of the period, arose from changes in construction techniques. British predominance in ship construction was solidly based on the traditional engineering skills required for steam and iron work. As long as new techniques could be readily comprehended, mastered, and applied by workers steeped, by education and experience, in traditional methods, British shipbuilding could adopt and assimilate the new techniques (Pollard and

Robertson, 1979: 129). But when the pace of change exceeded these comparatively narrow limits, British yards increasingly operated at a disadvantage, both because there existed in them no reliable body of experience and knowledge in the use of techniques more capital and technology intensive than the traditional ones and because British industry was badly prepared to supply them with modern, sophisticated equipment useful in shipbuilding. For example, not only were British shipyards unusually slow to provide electricity for powering tools, (Pollard and Robertson, 1979: 129), but the backward state of the British electrical engineering industry, a backwardness temporarily left undisturbed by foreign firms too busy coping with their own burgeoning domestic markets to look elsewhere, obliged British shipbuilders in the 1890s to construct, if they could, their own electrical machinery (Pollard and Robertson, 1979: 121). In a related manner, the relatively high cost of electricity in Britain, combined with the retarded development of the electrical engineering industry, helps to explain why in Britain so little interest was shown in electric welding, which ultimately was to replace altogether, not merely to complement, the traditional alternative technique of riveting (Pollard and Robertson, 1979: 123).[13]

The third source of pressure on Britain's shipbuilding industry was the deceleration in the growth of the volume of international trade, from a rate of increase Kuznets estimated at roughly 50% per decade between 1820 and 1880 to a decadal rate of 37% between 1881–5 and 1911–3 (Kuznets, 1966: 304–305, Table 6.3). The implications for British shipbuilding of the deceleration in the growth of world trade were magnified because Britain's share of world trade, the share which generated the greatest proportionate demand for British ships, was declining rapidly from 19.1% in 1881–83 to 12.2% in 1913 (Kuznets, 1966: Table 6.3, row 3, panel B, Hilgerdt's data). This situation was made worse by the subsidies which foreign governments insisted on lavishing on their own shipbuilding industries just as the global demand for ships was slackening.

Not surprisingly, these cumulative pressures on British shipbuilding increasingly squeezed both profits and wages in the industry, although not as violently as was to occur after 1920. Wages were under particular pressure. Pollard and Robertson (1979: Table 9.7) show, for a representative shipyard for which good records exist, that pre-1914 real earnings for all workers peaked in 1902 and even in 1913, which was a comparatively good year, real earnings for all workers were below the level reached as early as 1894. Moreover, this pressure on the real wages of all workers was not uniform across all skill groups but was concentrated most heavily on the most highly skilled workers, precisely those groups whose abilities were most crucial to Britain's traditional competitive strength (Pollard and Robertson, 1979: Table 9.8), clearly indicating the extent to which Britain's established advantages in shipbuilding were being eroded.

In the circumstances of the late nineteenth century, the only way that shipbuilding could contribute to the more rapid expansion of the British economy was by transferring the skills, resources and experience of shipbuilders to other, more rapidly growing industries while maintaining shipbuilding output through improved productivity. The prospects for this beneficial outcome were not good, however. It is important to note that no major British shipbuilder before 1914 was able to diversify successfully into other flourishing engineering industries, such as electrical engineering or automobile manufacture. Beardmore, Armstrong-Whitworth, and Vickers all made expensive if ultimately futile efforts to manufacture automobiles (Checkland, 1977: 10–12; Irving, 1975), but were never able to obtain even a faint semblance of the success achieved by former bicycle manufacturers and others whose background was in light engineering. The determination of many shipbuilders to diversify successfully was weakened by the lucrative attractions of naval construction. By 1914 perhaps as much as 20% of British shipbuilding activity was sustained by perceived military requirements (Pollard and Robertson, 1979: Table 2.1, columns 4 and 5), rather than by commercial orders, thereby temporarily obscuring the ominous failure to achieve viable diversification in comparatively favourable conditions.

An industry that shared important characteristics with shipbuilding was that of chemicals. But where the competitive pressures that were ultimately to destroy Britain's shipbuilding industry were not felt until the 1920s, they emerged in chemicals half a century earlier, in the 1870s. The fundamental nature of the competitive pressures operating on the two industries was similar – the replacement of an older, empirical, labour-intensive production tradition by one firmly based on scientific principles, a condition which tended to increase capital intensity of operations and which certainly increased the dependence of operations, both in terms of processes and products, on a programme of systematic research and development.

The core of the late nineteenth-century chemical industry may be usefully considered to have consisted of three parts – explosives; heavy inorganic chemicals, of which acids, alkali, and fertilizers were the most important products; and organic and fine chemicals, of which dyestuffs were the single most important product (although other products, notably pharmaceuticals and photographic materials, which promised prodigious expansion in the future, began to appear with increasing frequency in this branch of the chemical industry after the turn of the century). The explosives branch was well and truly established in Britain with the founding in 1871 in Scotland, of the British Dynamite Company by Alfred Nobel, a Swede (Reader, 1970: 16–36). Nobel set up operations in a number of countries to exploit his inventions, and he took care to see that Britain, because of its wealth and extensive use of explosives in mining, civil engineering, and armaments, was included among them. Because of Nobel's actions and the ready reception granted to his product in Britain, the performance of the British explosives industry matched, but no more than matched, the performances of the explosives industry in the U.S. and in Germany. In heavy inorganic chemicals, where the size of the industry before 1870 completely dwarfed that of explosives and where, accordingly, the British stake in the industry was much greater, performance was seriously flawed. And in the third and most rapidly growing branch, that of organic and fine chemicals, where the industry had never been of great size in Britain despite the first synthetic dye having been produced there in 1856, British producers quickly fell away to insignificance before German firms and the rest of British industry just as quickly came to depend upon imports, particularly from Germany, for their growing organic and fine chemical needs.

By virtue of its size and contribution to industrial expansion, inorganic chemistry constituted, in 1870, the most secure basis for the Victorian chemical industry's future. It was precisely in that sector of the industry, however, that a major technological and commercial weakness developed – the continued dependence on the Leblanc process of making alkali, the most important inorganic chemical product of the period. American and Continental producers switched to the Solvay process, which offered, despite significant further improvements in the Leblanc process, a much richer basis for future developments (Lindert and Trace, 1971; Reader, 1970: 90–124). The British inorganic chemical industry, however, did not simply collapse before superior foreign technology, Rather, that technology, firmly in the grip of Ernest Solvay and his Belgian company (which had important commercial links all over the world, not least in the U.S. and Germany), was impregnably established in Britain by the firm Brunner, Mond, which had secured the British rights to Solvay's process and subsequent improvements. Unfortunately for the pre-war growth of the British chemical industry as a whole, however, Brunner, Mond, relying on their increasingly valuable rights to the Solvay technology, used their complete technological superiority over the rest of the British heavy inorganic chemical industry to sustain a stolid, measured, but unremitting expansion, earning all the while supernormal profits, which, at nearly 15% per year (Reader, 1970: 478, 513) were from at least 25% to 50% greater than the average rate of profitability elsewhere in British industry.

Thus, while Brunner, Mond expanded at a carefully controlled pace, the United Alkali Company, a huge merger of all the obsolete alkali producers in Britain and, for a very brief moment at the time of its creation in 1891, perhaps, the largest industrial company in the world, stagnated or contracted. Consequently, the aggregate size of the British heavy inorganic chemical industry expanded only slowly, as commercial strength flowed from United Alkali to Brunner, Mond and as other companies found growing markets for products such as fertilizers and paints.[14] The measured, focused expansion of Brunner, Mond created a secure basis for a firm that, as one of the core firms that merged in 1926 to form I.C.I., was to play a decisive role in ensuring that in the twentieth century Britain possessed a world-class chemical company. But Brunner, Mond's success was by itself no substitute for vigorous performance elsewhere in the

British chemical industry. Indeed, the lack of competitive pressure from any source other than United Alkali, a firm hamstrung by its utter commitment to an obsolete technology, was the most important factor in making possible Brunner, Mond's supernormal profits. Furthermore, the market overhang of United Alkali's vast high-cost output capacity and Brunner, Mond's strong hold on Solvay technology effectively blocked any further entry in the domestic British heavy chemical industry. Brunner, Mond's growing profits, however, were used only to preserve and strengthen Brunner, Mond's cost advantages in the manufacture of alkali and related products, not to seek out actively, as did the German chemical giants, other possible areas of expansion. Had the enormous demands of the First World War not forcibly widened the technical and commercial horizons of the whole British chemical industry, the British heavy inorganic chemical industry might in time, on the basis of its pre-war performance, have been reduced to a few highly specialized, possibly profitable, firms operating in an economy almost totally dependent on foreign sources for the bulk of its chemical technology and the bulk of its chemicals.

Thus the competitive erosion only just gathering force in shipbuilding in 1913 had been plainly operating for more than forty years in the chemical industry and the extent of the erosion is seen in the relative sizes of the American and British chemical industries. Whereas in 1870 the American chemical industry was barely established, by 1909 the American industry was equal in relative terms, and vastly larger absolutely. The equality in the early twentieth of the relative importance of this strategic industry in the two countries was entirely a legacy of the early and mid nineteenth century when the British industry flourished without serious competition. The principal uses of chemicals then, in cleaning and dyeing textiles, in manufacturing the artificial fertilizers used by progressive farmers, and in producing iron and steel, ensured this result, for in all of these activities Britain was the most prominent pioneer until late in the century. Britain's dominant position faded as its chemical industry became uncompetitive or only marginally competitive in the manufacture of one traditional product after another, without the capability of generating significant new products or processes to stem the erosion of both export and import markets. This condition was well advanced by 1913, as indicated by the virtual disappearance of an export surplus in chemicals; yet this erosion was slow enough, and Britain's mid century dominance had been great enough, to leave still a comparatively large industry in 1913. The U.S., on the other hand, had neither British mid century dominance nor overall German technical capability to aid in establishing a large industry. The growth of the American industry, which took place behind substantial tariff barriers, was based on a steady diffusion of the techniques, pioneered in Europe, needed to produce the chemicals so prodigiously required in modern industrial growth. The diffusion was accelerated and facilitated by an increasing American ability to achieve important technological breakthroughs, as occurred in electro-chemical techniques and products and in the thermal cracking of petroleum (Freeman, 1974: 53–69). These American innovations, while certainly not seriously challenging the overall German technological superiority, nevertheless constituted evidence of a greater ability to sustain an important chemical industry than was apparent in Britain before 1914 and at least facilitated more rapid and successful emulation of the German example (Svennilson, 1954: 164).

Unlike differences in the sizes of the strategic sectors, some of the structural differences noted in Tables 2.1 and 2.2 can easily be explained by differences in natural resource endowments in the two countries. The most obvious example of this is agriculture. Britain, as befitted the first industrial nation, had begun shifting resources out of agriculture much earlier than had the U.S. and hence, although the sector's share in output in both countries was falling throughout most of the nineteenth century, Britain by 1907 had a much smaller agricultural sector than did the U.S. Relative to GNP, the sector in the U.S. in 1909, was 245.8% of the size of its U.K. counterpart in 1907. A small part of this difference reflects the comparative advantage which size and geography conferred upon U.S. agricultural production,[15] but the bulk of the difference arose from the greater British success in transferring resources out of this slowly growing sector. The sector's large size in the U.S. economy clearly reduced U.S. aggregate growth below what it would have been had agriculture shed resources more rapidly, as the repeated 'crises' of American agriculture in the nineteenth and twentieth centuries made abundantly clear.[16] The relatively large size of the timber, food processing, and, to a lesser extent, leather-making industries in the U.S. was due, like agriculture, to inherent differences in resource endowment. This observation, however, does not prepare one for the finding that mining, by 1900 predominantly coal, was nearly twice as important to the U.K.'s economy as it was to the U.S.'s. This was in part due to the large export trade, amounting to one-third of national coal production by 1913, which Britain acquired by virtue of the location of her major coal fields near ports, thereby offering easy sea access to major foreign markets (Taylor, 1968: 41).[17] The large size of the U.K. mining industry, however, may also have been due in part to the failure of other sectors of the economy effectively to bid resources away from it.[18] Had British wages been higher, some markets would have been irretrievably lost and the rent acquired by location would have been correspondingly reduced. Furthermore, had coal costs been higher, even greater incentives than actually existed would have operated to accelerate the pace of electrification, since electricity rather than steam or manufactured gas was (and still is) a much more efficient means of providing power for ultimate industrial and commercial uses. The failure of other sectors to exert more wage pressure on British mine owners, in addition to causing the British mining sector to be relatively large, had unfortunate consequences for the future, since relative labour abundance appears to have deterred ambitious programmes of capital investment and modernization (Taylor, 1968: 59). For example, only when demand was buoyant and labour markets tight did mine owners begin, although reluctantly at first, to introduce electric equipment (Byatt, 1962: 290–94). The legacy of using labour so prodigiously for so long as a cheap substitute for equipment and scientific organization of mine operations was bitterly reflected in the mining industry's tortured labour relations of the inter-war years.

Only slightly less surprising than the large share of mining in Britain's national income was the large share still claimed by textile manufacture. Although the U.S. was the world's largest producer of raw cotton while Britain had no domestic supplies at all, nevertheless the relative size of the U.K. textile industry, predominantly centred on cotton, was more than twice as large as its U.S. counterpart. The U.S. clothing industry, however, was marginally larger than its U.K. counterpart. This difference is explained by the vast export market for textiles which Britain had acquired and maintained during the late eighteenth and early nineteenth centuries. However, the preservation and expansion of textile export markets in the period 1870–1914 was progressively becoming more difficult, offering a faint hint of the great troubles that were to emerge after 1920 (Lazonick, 1981a; 1981b). By the beginning of the twentieth century, and perhaps earlier, the growth of world trade in both textiles and clothing was falling as industrialization spread to countries which previously had been important textile and clothing importers. There is nothing mysterious about the prominence of the mechanization of textile and clothing manufacture in the early stages of industrialization (Maizels, 1970: 180–183). All pre-industrial societies produce textiles and clothing, albeit typically in small establishments, often cottages, without extensive equipment. Thus a large, reliable market for textiles and clothing exists everywhere. Compared with other capital goods, textile machinery has been, since the eighteenth century, relatively inexpensive and the low minimum optimal scale of operations has invited easy entry into the industry. Even more than textiles, clothing manufacture has been small scale and labour intensive and has, therefore, tended to be less important in world trade.

The combination of large, universal markets and relatively low-cost, easy entry into the industry has acted to make textile and clothing manufacture not only in Britain but almost everywhere invariably the first sector to undergo modernization (Maizels, 1970: 52–5). The process was further aided in the last half of the nineteenth century when textile machinery, after more than a century of dramatic development, experienced only slow if steady further improvement; it thus became progressively easier as the nineteenth century came to a close for a late-comer to adopt the latest vintage equipment and, with the aid of very cheap labour by English standards, mount a real competitive challenge to the textile industries of the wealthiest nations.[19] International trade in textiles was further hindered as most industrialized countries in the late nineteenth century erected tariff barriers to protect domestic producers from (and to deprive consumers of) the consequences of the growing low wage competition.

The same dynamic of development characterized the clothing industry. The main innovation of the nineteenth century in the clothing industry was the sewing machine, the deployment of which fitted easily into the smallscale, cottage organization of the industry. The low initial costs and the reliance on skills well known in pre-industrial societies acted, as with textiles, to give low-wage, industrializing economies an important competitive advantage which could only be partially countered by sophisticated physical plant, elaborate organization and superior product design.

It is, therefore, ironic that as the world-wide trend towards national self-sufficiency in both textile and clothing manufacture gathered momentum in an environment of only moderate technological advance, British cotton textile and clothing producers achieved one of the undeniable entrepreneurial triumphs of the half century before 1914 by succeeding in holding so much of their huge share of a diminishing, increasingly competitive global market.[20] When the value of world manufactured exports more than doubled between 1899 and 1913 while the share claimed by exports of textiles and clothing fell from 40.3% to 35.0%, nevertheless Britain's share of total world exports of textiles rose marginally from 44.4% to 44.8%, and her share of world exports of clothing rose even more, from 23.5% to 25.7%.[21] What could not be achieved in the areas where the rewards were great and increasing was accomplished in an area where the ultimate rewards were not only comparatively small but shrinking (Sandberg, 1974: 172–4, 221–45).

Textiles, and to a somewhat lesser extent clothing, were not the only British industries to develop large export markets on the basis of an early start. Iron and steel, railroad rolling stock and liquor were all industries in which a comparatively large size in the U.K. can be linked generally to the early development of the industry in the U.K. and the subsequent growth of exports as industrialization took hold in other countries; in the case of iron, steel and rolling stock export demand was a function of the capital requirements of new developing economies (often colonial economies). In the case of liquor, export demand was related to rising incomes and consumption levels abroad, particularly among British emigrants.

The only significant manufacturing industry that remains to be considered is paper, printing and publishing. The American industry was, relative to GNP, $59.9\% \left(\dfrac{0.0235}{0.0147} = 1.599 \right)$ larger than its equivalent in the U.K. This difference in relative sector size is more closely related to levels of economic development than to natural resource endowments. The sector has grown faster than GNP in Britain since the mid nineteenth century.[22] Growth has accelerated in the twentieth century and by 1938 the relative importance of the industry in Britain was almost exactly equal to the U.S. sector's relative size in 1909.[23] Nor are Britain and the U.S. unique in having the industry increase its relative importance steadily over time; the same trend has been noted in all OECD countries since 1945 (Hill, 1971: Table 12). The universally rapid growth of paper, printing and publishing is most easily linked to the consumption demands of increasingly literate and educated populations, to the advertising and packaging requirements arising from the mass distribution of goods, and to the heightened requirements of communications and co-ordination in increasingly complex economies. Kendrick's data (1961) suggest that the latter two considerations were dominant in the industry's unusually rapid growth in the U.S. in the period 1870–1913. Kendrick notes that paper, printing and publishing output grew much more rapidly than did public consumption of books, magazines and newspapers in the period for which comparable data are available, 1899–1909.[24]

The most obvious explanation of the divergence between the U.S. and the U.K. in the growth experience within the paper, printing and publishing sector, during the nineteenth century, centres perhaps most convincingly on the emergence in the U.S., during this period, of giant enterprises engaged in mass production and mass distribution, while similar developments within the U.K. were much less widespread. In a number of diverse industries, ranging from complex capital goods such as electrical products to common items of everyday consumption such as biscuits and canned meat, production and distribution in the U.S., in the late nineteenth century, was increasingly dominated by a small number of increasingly large firms. These firms usually marketed output on a national or international scale, required a large volume of diverse inputs from many different suppliers and depended upon high volume production runs to achieve the low costs per unit made necessary by large overheads. To make such enterprises viable at all – many failed outright and others were severe disappointments to their creators and owners – required manufacturing firms to devote unprecedented attention to advertising, marketing and internal co-ordination. Before the 1870s only the communication and co-ordination problems facing governments and railroads even remotely resembled those facing the large firms created in the late nineteenth century (Hannah, 1976b: 12, 81). Thus the communications and internal control problems that had earlier belonged only to a few organizations now became the lot of a much larger number. Moreover, as the number of distinct processing stages of manufacture increased, and as services, including those provided by governments, became more complex and heterogeneous, the demands placed on information flows upwards and command flows downwards also became more numerous and complicated (Chandler, 1962: 7–17). The result was an explosion of paperwork and documentation which paralleled the massive increase in telecommunication usage in developed countries. Just as in the case of telephone usage, the greater importance in the U.S. of paper manufacture, printing and, to some extent, publishing reflected the greater needs for co-ordination, control and communication in the U.S. economy.[25] The satisfaction of the needs that generated the explosion of paper flows within U.S. organizations also generated a vast demand for typewriters, calculating machines and office equipment in America which simply was not matched in the pre-war British economy.[26]

Growth of demand for, and mechanization of, clerical work was also related to explosive growth and radical changes in the U.S. clerical labour force (Rotella, 1977: 106, Table 4.1, 112). In 1870 the Bureau of the Census identified 74,200 American clerical workers, of which 1,800 were women. By 1910, American clerical workers numbered 1,523,900 and their share of the non-agricultural labour force had risen five-fold to 5.91%. But the really remarkable change had been in the sex composition of the clerical labour force; by 1910 women made up nearly 40% of the total. Where male clerical employment had risen 12-fold between 1870 and 1910, female employment had increased over 300-fold. Thus the factors that generated the huge demand for paperwork and documentation not only supported an entirely new branch of the engineering industry, that of office equipment, it was also responsible for a revolutionary change in the nature of female labour force participation (Rotella, 1981: 51–2). The much smaller British demand for paperwork and documentation, that the relatively small British sector of paper, printing and publishing reveals, is also reflected in the miniscule size of the British office equipment industry and the small proportion of the non-agricultural labour force – 3.64%, or 61.6% of the American proportion for 1910 (Kennedy, 1975: 200–4, 206–7, 216–17) – engaged in specifically clerical occupations in 1911. In that year women comprised only 26.7% of the British clerical labour force.

Internal demands for paperwork and documentation were not the only means by which large American firms, in the late nineteenth century, contributed to the relatively large size of the American paper, printing, and publishing sector. Marketing and distribution also generated large demands for paper and for printing services. Mass produced items had to be distributed, and that required newspaper advertising on an unprecedented scale and also the widespread use of catalogues and printed circulars. The items themselves had to be wrapped and packaged as they left factories and processing centres for destinations often hundreds of miles distant. All of this consumed prodigious amounts of paper and print and further helped to account for the relatively large size of the American sector.

It is not only within the broad sectors of agriculture, construction, manufacturing and mining that the differences in the growth experiences of the U.K. and the U.S. over the years 1870–1914 are mirrored. The same findings emerge from examination of the rest of the economy, of the service sectors which are so often held to be of signal importance in modern economies.[27] Table 2.10 presents a summary of differences in the relative importance of five major categories of services provided to the respective domestic economies of the two countries. Of the five categories, only that of professional services can be said definitively to

Table 2.10 *Summary of U.K. and U.S. differences in distribution of output (measured as value added) among selected
service sectors within the domestic economy*

		U.K. (1907)	U.S. (1909)	Difference
1	Domestic transportation	7.50	8.08	− 0.58
2	Domestic wholesale-retail trade	18.35	17.11	1.24
3	Professional services	3.02	2.53	0.49
4	Personal services	1.89	2.30	− 0.41
5	Government services (including military)	4.14	2.78	1.36
5a	Government services (excluding military)	(3.20)	(2.57)	(0.63)
		34.90%	32.80 %	2.10 %

Source: Table 2.3 and Data Appendices.

have an income elasticity greater than unity. Although the category of
professional services was clearly larger in the U.K. than in the U.S., the
interpretation of this difference is not straightforward for it is highly probable
that differences in industrial organization between the two countries influenced
the relative sizes of this service sector to a greater extent than for any other sector.
Professional services as defined in Table 2.10 refer only to those services provided
to the public by independent individuals or firms. Thus the value of the services of
a lawyer employed by, for example, a manufacturing corporation would be
included in the value added by the manufacturing sector, not the professional
sector. On the other hand, if the lawyer were a partner in a law firm retained by a
manufacturing corporation but not working directly as an employee of the
corporation, the value of his services would be included in the professional sector
and counted as an input into manufacturing. There is no doubt that U.S. firms by
the beginning of the twentieth century were both larger and more likely to employ
directly professional staff than their British counterparts[28] and, therefore, the
smaller size of the U.S. sector recorded in Table 2.10 may not mean that
professional services were less important in the U.S. economy. This possibility is
strongly supported by the finding that when the distributions of the labour forces
of the two countries across occupations (rather than across industries) are
compared, the proportion of professional workers in law, science, accounting and
engineering in the two countries are much more equal than is indicated in
Table 2.10.[29]

Of the other categories in Table 2.10, provision of government services is more
clearly subject to the special requirements of national security and other

collective social needs than it is, as a whole, to increasing income as such. Before the First World War, the manpower strength in absolute numbers of the U.K. armed forces stationed in the British Isles was nearly three times that of U.S. forces in continental America, although the U.S. labour force was 80% again as large as that of the U.K. Pay in cash and kind of H.M. forces amounted to 22.8% of total British government outlays on wages and salaries whereas U.S. forces pay comprised only 11.1% of U.S. government payments for labour services; these payments comprised 0.945% of U.K. GNP but only 0.210% of U.S. GNP. The relative importance of value added in the provision of non-military government services in the U.K. is only 24.5 % $\left(\dfrac{0.0320}{0.0257} = 1.245\right)$ greater than that for the U.S. Most of this remaining difference can be explained by differences in the levels of urbanization in the two countries in the early twentieth century, since high urban densities require more of the government services of police and fire protection, sanitation and welfare (possibly because the urban poor, without access to even poor land, are less able to take care of themselves).

Transportation and personal services have shown no clear tendency to increase their share of total output in the twentieth century. Thus it is not possible to relate their relatively larger size in the U.S. to the inevitable demands of an economy in the process of rapid growth. Domestic transport's relatively larger size in the U.S. may be caused, on the one hand, by the much larger geographical expanse of a country comparatively well endowed with natural resources and by the increased demand for transport services which accompanies high levels of economic development, due to both a highly income elastic demand for leisure travel and to a tendency for firms to exploit ever larger plant requiring an increase in transport (and communications) inputs relative to other factors. On the other hand, the impact on economic structure of the tendency for demand for transport to increase at least as rapidly as incomes have risen has been tempered throughout the twentieth century by rapid technological progress in transport; in the early part of the century, the rapid spread of the truck and automobile must have sharply lowered the real cost of transport of both people and goods. Thus, even if demand were highly income elastic yet price inelastic, the revenue accruing to factors of production in transport, in relative terms, would have fallen *if* the supply of transport services had increased sufficiently, an increase which was certainly possible.[30] It is not possible at this point to weigh the relative merits of these conflicting tendencies and thereby ascertain the nature of transport's relative position within a modern economy. It is reasonably clear, however, that the net effect, whatever it is, is not great.

The size of the personal service sector in the period 1870–1914 was dependent, like transport, on a number of conflicting tendencies. As incomes rose and people had more leisure and indulged in more travel for pleasure, the demand for restaurant, hotel and other services increased. This tendency was heightened to the extent that many of these personal services had been previously provided in the home by the ultimate consumer and thus not recorded in the conventional national income accounts. Hence, the growth of the personal service sector may not necessarily have indicated, for example, that more laundry was being done, although that may have been true, but rather that fewer people were doing it at home and more were having it done by professional cleaning firms. The relatively large size of the sector in the U.S. may also be related to the much smaller importance of domestic servants in the U.S. economy. However, most of the workers in the sector were relatively unskilled and the huge waves of immigration into the U.S., in the early twentieth century, made such labour easily available. Thus expansion of sector supply could take place without incurring labour costs to the extent of increasing the sector's relative share of total output. Furthermore, although such domestic household appliances as washing machines, vacuum cleaners, refrigerators and electric steam irons were only just appearing for the first time before 1914, their use may have even then acted to a small degree to hold down demand for publicly provided personal services.

A more telling indication of the extent of British resources committed to relatively slowly growing sectors is found in examination of wholesale-retail distribution, an important activity in which the U.S. sector in 1909 was only $93.24\% \left(\dfrac{0.1711}{0.1835} = 0.9324 \right)$ of the relative size of its U.K. counterpart in 1907. In the U.S. since 1909, growth in this sector has failed, barely, to keep pace with the growth of GNP.[31] In the U.K. since 1907 the sector's relative importance has declined sharply.[32] That the sector has declined at all in either country must be attributed to the extensive, systematic use of labour-saving equipment (including transport improvements) for the volume, diversity and complexity of the goods and services entering the distribution network has steadily and manifestly increased apace with economic growth. As William Baumol (1967) has shown in a simple but convincing demonstration, unless a labour intensive service such as distribution,[33] which faces a high income but low price elasticity of demand, can somehow utilize technological advance to increase productivity, the service will tend to absorb an ever increasing share of the economy's resources.

The key to the more rapid American rate of technological progress in distribution was clearly the substitution of new kinds of capital equipment for labour. The use of calculating machines, punch-filing systems, cash registers, typewriters and telephones was a prominent feature of American growth in the early twentieth century. In fact, the demand for such office and business equipment, demand which arose in large part from the distribution sector (Barger, 1955: 51), helped to create a new and prominent engineering industry in the U.S. whereas the industry was not mentioned in the U.K. 1907 Census of Manufactures. The faster development of the business machinery industry in the U.S. can be further gauged by the fact that U.S. companies have consistently accounted for about half of all *London* (let alone Washington) patents for calculating machinery since the early decades of the twentieth century (Freeman, 1974: 130). Therefore, the relatively high proportion of GNP originating in distribution in Britain, combined on the one hand with a comparative absence there of all of the mechanical and electrical aids of telephones, cash registers, typewriters, adding machines, and semi-automatic filing systems and on the other with a comparatively less flexible transportation system, suggests that Baumol's arguments may be invoked directly to explain the difference in distribution's relative share of GNP in the two countries in the early twentieth century.

Distribution, for all practical purposes, is an intermediate good in the process of consumption. It is the goods and services provided by the distribution network rather than the circumstances of their provision which is of paramount importance. Demand for distribution services may, therefore, be assumed to possess an income elasticity of demand little greater than that registered for the goods and services which the distribution system dispenses. This instrumental rather than direct character of the demand for distribution services easily permits the inference that the price elasticity of demand is low. It is well known that the opening of new distribution outlets does not increase total sector sales (OECD, 1973: 12). Lower distribution charges at a given establishment increase sales there at the expense of other outlets; at the aggregate sector level, except through income effects, demand for distribution services is highly insensitive to distribution charges. Accordingly, if technological progress permits a rapid downward shift of the aggregate supply curve, the revenue earned by the industry as a whole will fall absolutely. Taking adequate account of the increased demand caused by rising incomes explains why value added in distribution has in fact fallen over time in both countries only relatively and not absolutely.

American advances in communications, information handling, transportation, and storage facilities (such as refrigerators) encouraged larger stores handling more diverse goods and services. Larger stores generated inventory savings and more intensive utilization of space, personnel, and equipment and also facilitated increased specialization of personnel and equipment, especially in purchasing merchandise and keeping accounts (Hall, *et al.*, 1961: 62–5), thereby permitting a sharp increase in the capacity and efficiency of the U.S. distribution system. Moreover, technological progress favourably altered the characteristics of demand as well by reducing the monopolistic competition that previously pervaded the provision of distribution services (Hall, *et al.*, 1961: 77–80). Improved information flows and greater personal mobility acted to transform monopolistic competition into more effective competition, reducing the economic waste caused by too many outlets each operating at a suboptimally small scale. The technological advances of the period thus not only increased the optimal scale of distribution activity in each establishment but also simultaneously ensured that a more complete exploitation (via a more horizontal demand curve induced by greater awareness of alternative prices and a greater ability, through greater mobility, to act on this awareness) of the enhanced possibilities took place.[34] By technologically induced alterations of both supply and demand functions it was possible to achieve an important reduction in the relative level of resources allocated to the provision of distribution services. These shifts took place earlier and with greater impact in the United States and account for the lessened importance (relative to GNP) there of distribution services. The shifts depended utterly on equipment and service inputs from the strategic sectors.

Of all of the economic activity in the service sector, however, it was that of domestic service which delineated most clearly the failure of the British economy to shift resources out of sectors capable only of very slow growth and into sectors capable of profitably expanding output rapidly. For the purposes of measuring the ease with which structural change in modern economies can be accomplished, the size of the domestic service sector is perhaps the most reliable indicator available. Domestic service, even more than agricultural labour, has been the employment of last resort, and, unlike agricultural labour, has always required little complementary physical capital. Output in domestic services is almost exclusively produced by unaided human effort. As the 'servant problem' indicates, it appears universally true that as economic growth expands opportunity, employment in domestic service is sharply reduced. The obverse of this phenomenon holds historically as well. Charles Booth, observing the rapid increase in the proportion of domestic servants in Ireland after the potato famine wrote: 'The only explanation that suggests itself is that servants are more numerous where poverty makes service cheap.'[35]

When contrasted with the U.S., the relatively large number of people employed as domestic servants in Britain after 1870, may, therefore, be taken as a measure of the slow pace at which structural change occurred and as a measure of the lack of opportunity elsewhere in the economy. Although the majority of servants were women (see Table 2.11) and were prepared neither by training nor by experience for alternative work in other sectors of the economy, the ability of domestic servants as a group to perform successfully other tasks was clearly demonstrated during the First World War. That the redeployment of servants in general, and women in particular, which occurred during the war did not take place sooner owes more to lack of occasion than to anything else. For example, there was no pressure in the British female labour market to compare, even remotely, with the vast American demands for female clerical workers, demands that elicited an extremely vigorous supply response fuelled by the higher wages, better working conditions, and higher status available to women in clerical work compared with any other occupation then open to them (Rotella, 1977: 44–6, 245).

The four sectors of Tables 2.1 and 2.2 remaining to be considered – imputed income from dwellings, international shipping, international commercial and

Table 2.11 *Distribution of servants*

	U.S. (1909)		U.K. (1911)	
Males	182,744	(8.3%)	415,370	(19.8%)
Females	2,022,231	(91.7%)	1,682,905	(80.2%)
Total	2,204,975	(100.0%)	2,098,275	(100.0%)

Sources:
U.K. – Data Appendix A.
U.S. – U.S. Bureau of the Census (1914a: 428–432).

financial services, and net property income from abroad – were, with the exception of imputed income from dwellings, each larger in Britain than in the U.S. The size of income attributed to the ownership of private dwellings may be due in part to errors of measurement since the value of output in both countries was estimated indirectly and, therefore, subject to greater error than measurement in most other sectors. It should be noted, however, that the difference in relative sizes was not large; the American sector was only 4.54% larger than its British counterpart $\left(\dfrac{0.0622}{0.0595} = 1.0454\right)$.

Geography, the advantages conferred by early industrialization, and the buoyant state of world trade help explain the enormous importance to the U.K. economy of international shipping and financial services, services which were of negligible importance in the U.S. economy. This advantage of position was reinforced by both Britain's role as largest trader in the world and as centre of the world's largest empire. What was not formally controlled was often dominated, or at least strongly influenced, by British contact and British law and commercial customs. Not only did merchants and industrialists find it useful to transport their imports and exports in British ships, but they also tended to find it easier in London than anywhere else to raise money on good collateral and to insure themselves against any contingency. The provision of these services was generally profitable and their relative importance to Britain was, in certain respects, a sign of entrepreneurial skill and commercial vitality in the pre-war economy. In another sense, Britain's position also depended upon fortunate circumstances, the rapid growth of an international economy whose overall fate was determined only remotely by British actions. British provision of international finance and shipping also depended upon the performance of the rest of the domestic economy to maintain its dominant position. Slow growth in the British economy restricted British imports and exports, trade flows which generated an important demand for the services of the merchant navy. Although the British merchant navy was also active in that part of the world's carrying trade which was not related to British trade directly, the largest source of demand arose from the ports of the British Empire and sluggish activity in those ports was quickly translated into sluggish demand for the British merchant fleet (Aldcroft, 1968: 329). Poor domestic performance thus directly depressed demand for the services of the merchant marine. In addition, an unprogressive engineering industry acted to make the capital costs (including costs of repairs) and eventually the operating costs of the British merchant fleet higher than they otherwise would have been, thereby further curtailing the prospects for the continued expansion of British shipping services.

Similar arguments apply, somewhat more subtly, to the provision of international financial services. The decline in Britain's role in the world economy, which followed upon long decades of relatively slow growth, would have inevitably eroded, but not necessarily destroyed, London's position as the world's premier capital market. Sooner or later, countries growing more rapidly would have had, in absolute terms, more resources available for investment abroad. However, the main engine of decline was more indirect. It will be argued below that the operations of British capital markets played a central role in first creating, and then maintaining an industrial structure capable of only limited growth. If this argument is accepted, two implications immediately follow. First, inherent capital market failings limited the services which British financial intermediaries could offer. Because possibilities for diversifying risks across financial assets representing both industrial and social overhead capital were so limited in London, risk-taking was inhibited and this was reflected in low rates of return on the majority of widely traded British financial assets (Kennedy, 1974: 425–34). By not accurately registering the potential demands of ultimate borrowers, particularly industrial borrowers, pre-1914 British capital markets failed in their primary function to link most effectively ultimate lenders with ultimate borrowers. Because of obstacles in concentrating resources in risky, technologically progressive activities, especially in engineering and related industries, the rates of return which British intermediaries could offer were fundamentally restricted and, therefore, so also were the portfolios which could be constructed from British assets. This limitation in the world-wide competition for funds ultimately guaranteed a decline of the London markets' relative importance. Secondly, and of more fundamental importance, the enormous activity of the London market, with its foreign orientation, served to distort the sectoral pattern (and perhaps the level) of domestic capital formation. Given the institutional arrangements as they actually existed in Victorian Britain, the vast flow of net property income from abroad was not compatible with efficient, dynamic domestic investment and growth.[36] Thus the enormous proportion of GNP earned on British assets located abroad, while offering great strength to the U.K. balance of payments before 1914, may be more usefully viewed as an indication of institutional distortion of relative prices than as an unqualified benefit to the economy.

In summary, then, the structural reasons for the slow and hesitant growth of Victorian Britain are clear. Not only did Britain have a relatively smaller proportion of total value added generated by the most technologically advanced activities of the period – activities where net outputs were growing substantially more rapidly than the economy as a whole – but weaknesses in these advanced areas were transmitted through supply and demand linkages to the rest of the economy, not least to large, long-established activities such as shipbuilding, textiles and financial services. More is being claimed here than the tautological fact that if Britain had a smaller proportion of its assets in rapidly growing sectors than did the U.S. then it must have had a larger proportion in more slowly growing sectors. Because the rapidly growing, technologically advanced sectors provided productivity enhancing inputs for the rest of the economy (and also often provided markets for the output of more traditional sectors as in the case of the steel chassis and textile seats used in automobile manufacture), the vitality as well as the aggregate growth of the entire economy depended crucially upon the advanced sectors as a group. While international trade could make good isolated deficiencies in these sectors, trade could not, in the long-run, make good wholesale failure, for in such a case British tradeable output would be concentrated in precisely those sectors experiencing the greatest competitive pressures and facing the least promising future. It now remains to provide a quantitative assessment of the consequences of Victorian Britain's increasingly outmoded structure of production.

3

The consequences of structural change
in the Victorian economy:
a counterfactual estimate

In the calculations which follow, an answer is offered to the question: How fast could the Victorian economy have grown had there been a greater commitment of resources to those sectors capable of sustaining rapid expansion and technological progress? The calculations are made in two phases. First, the sectors most capable of sustaining a relative increase in importance are selected and a counterfactual gain in relative size for them posited in conjunction with a corresponding counterfactual reduction in the relative size of sectors elsewhere in the economy. Equation (2.2) of Chapter 2 is then used to determine the consequences of the suggested counterfactual structural change. In order for this procedure to be creditable, the sectors chosen both to expand and to contract must conform to the historical experience of growth.[1] The sectors for one such counterfactual shift are set out in Table 3.1. Column 2 is the historical relative average size of the sectors listed in Column 1 over the period 1870–1913. The construction of the estimates of relative average size is described in Appendix D (Calculation procedures). Column 3 is the change in relative sector size implied by the new counterfactual structure; negative numbers denote counterfactual loss in relative sector size; positive numbers denote gain. Column 4 is the historical growth rate of the sector in the period 1870–1913. Column 5 is the estimated index number of output in each industry in 1870 (1913 = 100). Tables 3.2 and 3.3 set out the average index numbers of output and the average growth rates of output for each of the listed sectors in the two countries over the decades before 1914.

The criteria which governed the selection of sectors both for counterfactual expansion and contraction can be summarized under four main considerations. First, the counterfactually expanding sectors can all be closely associated causally or instrumentally with the rapid technological change of the period whereas no such close association is possible with the counterfactually contracting sectors. Second, the expanding sectors (with the exception of construction and related industries) were those already growing comparatively rapidly in the U.K.

Table 3.1. *Low growth variant*

(1)	(2)	(3)	(4)	(5)
Industry	S(I)	ΔS(I)	G(I)	O(I)
1 Textiles	0.0445	− 0.0026	0.0111	56.9
2 Domestic service	0.0464	− 0.0227	0.0050	85.9
3 Agriculture	0.0972	− 0.0057	− 0.0005	101.5
4 Domestic wholesale-retail trade	0.1764	− 0.0039	0.0198	43.4
5 Gas undertakings	0.0046	− 0.0023	0.0458	15.5
6 Net property income from abroad	0.0457	− 0.0083	0.0370	22.2
7 Construction	0.0382	0.0168	0.0057	83.2
8 Iron, steel trades	0.0120	0.0000	0.0254	35.5
9 Engineering	0.0248	0.0074	0.0275	30.6
10 Paper, printing and publishing	0.0101	0.0146	0.0335	23.4
11 Electricity, telecommunications, scientific instruments	0.0024	0.0035	0.0610	8.5
12 Bricks, cement, glass	0.0105	0.0014	0.0057	83.2
13 Chemicals: class (a)	0.0061	0.0018	0.0405	20.0
14 Rest of economy	0.4811	0.0000	0.0218	39.2
	1.0000	0.0000		

$$\sum |\Delta S(I)| = 0.0910$$

Sources:
Column (2) – Column (3), Table D1, Appendix D and text Appendix D (for 'rest of economy').
Column (3) – see main text.
Column (4) – see text, Appendix D.
Column (5) – see text, Appendix D.

whereas the contracting sectors (with the exceptions in the U.K. of gas, net property income from abroad, and, more marginally, of distribution) were those growing slowly. All of the sectors designated as expanding were growing comparatively rapidly in the U.S. while those designated as contracting were growing there less rapidly than the economy as a whole with the single exception of gas undertakings. The counterfactual analysis thus examines the consequences of the expanding sectors achieving greater preponderance in the economy earlier than they did in fact achieve. Third, the expanding sectors had all – with the single marginal exception of the iron and steel trades – become larger, relative to the economy, in the U.S. during the course of rapid growth before 1914 than they had become in the U.K. by that time, whereas the contracting sectors – with the

Table 3.2. *U.K. sectoral data, 1870–1913*

(1) Industry	(2) Average sector size (1913 = 100)	(3) Growth rate (per annum)	(4) 95% Confidence interval for growth rate	(5) Estimation procedure
1 Textiles	72.2	0.0111	0.0091–0.0131	CORC 2
2 Domestic service	95.6	0.0050[1]	0.0025–0.0075	OLS
3 Agriculture	100.4	−0.0005	−0.0019–0.0009	CORC 1
4 Domestic wholesale- retail trade	66.1	0.0198	0.0186–0.0210	CORC 2
5 Gas undertakings[2]	40.5	0.0458	0.0427–0.0489	CORC 1
6 Net property income from abroad	48.5	0.0370	0.0288–0.0452	CORC 1
7 Construction	94.0	0.0057	−0.0114–0.0228	CORC 1
8 Iron, steel trades	60.8	0.0254	0.0224–0.0284	CORC 2
9 Engineering	54.8	0.0275	0.0247–0.0303	CORC 2
10 Paper, printing and publishing[3]	47.5	0.0335	0.0172–0.0498	CORC 2
11. Electricity, telecommunications, scientific instruments[4]	30.4	0.0610	0.0512–0.0708	CORC 2
12 Bricks, cement, glass	94.0	0.0057	−0.0114–0.0228	CORC 1
13 Chemicals: class (a)	47.0	0.0405	0.0378–0.0432	CORC 2
GNP	68.6	0.0184	0.0171–0.0197	CORC 1

The relationship between average sector size and growth rate is affected by the pattern of the variance of annual data around the trend rate; hence there is not a unique relationship between average sector size and sectoral growth rate.

Sources:
Column (2) – see calculation Appendix D.
Column (3) – growth rate calculated from annual index of sector's output; see text Appendix D.
Column (4) – confidence interval implied by regression estimate of growth.
Column (5) – CORC 1 = Cochrane – Orcutt iterative procedure for first order autocorrelation.
   CORC 2 = Cochrane – Orcutt iterative procedure for second order autocorrelation.
   OLS = ordinary least squares (employed due to lack of observations).

Notes:
[1] Calculated over the years 1861–1911.
[2] Calculated over the years 1870–1902.
[3] Calculated over the years 1886–1913.
[4] CORC 1 estimate 0.0282; F- statistic for CORC 1 better than for CORC 2 but Durbin–Watson statistic less satisfactory.

Table 3.3. *U.S. sectoral data, 1869–1913*

(1) Industry	(2) Average sector size (1913 = 100)	(3) Growth rate[1] (per annum)	(4) 95% Confidence interval for growth rate	(5) Estimation procedure
1 Textiles	51.0	0.0403[2]	0.0376–0.0430	CORC 2
2 Domestic service	69.1	0.0213	0.0169–0.0257	OLS
3 Agriculture	76.5	0.0163[3]	0.0095–0.0231	CORC 1
4 Domestic wholesale-retail trade	48.3	0.0383[4]	0.0284–0.0482	OLS
5 Gas undertakings	30.9	0.0708[4]	0.0663–0.0753	OLS
6 Construction	48.3	0.0458[4]	0.0392–0.0524	OLS
7 Iron, steel trades	40.8	0.0678[5]	0.0591–0.0765	CORC 1
8 Engineering[6]	37.1	0.0535[7]	0.0420–0.0644	CORC 1
9 Paper, printing and publishing	50.4[8]	0.0338[8]	0.0279–0.0397	CORC 1
10 Electricity telecommunications, scientific instruments	27.4	0.1169[4]	0.1086–0.1252	OLS
11 Bricks, cement, glass	48.3	0.0458[9]	0.0392–0.0524	OLS
12 Chemicals: class (a)	42.2	0.0467[10]	0.0390–0.0544	CORC 1
GNP	47.9	0.0401[3]	0.0365–0.0437	CORC 1

The relationship between average sector size and growth rate is affected by the pattern of the variance of annual data around the trend rate; hence there is not a unique relationship between average sector size and sectoral growth rate.

Sources:
Column (2) – see calculation Appendix D.
Column (3) – growth rate calculated from annual index of sector's output; see Appendix D.
Column (4) – confidence interval implied by regression estimate of growth.
Column (5) – see Table 3.2 for list of abbreviation.

Notes:
[1] Except where otherwise indicated, the growth rate for each series was calculated over the years 1889–1913.
[2] 1870–1913.
[3] Calculated over the years 1869, 1879, 1889–1913.
[4] Census years only, 1869–1909.
[5] 1880–1913.
[6] Excluding electricity supply.
[7] Calculated over the years 1869, 1879, 1889–1913. Inclusion of 1869, 1879 significantly lowered rate.
[8] There is serious disagreement for the years 1899 to 1909 between Kendrick's measures of output

notable exception of agriculture – were all smaller in the U.S. than in the U.K. Fourth, in the course of economic growth in both countries after 1918 all of the pre-war expanding sectors (except construction in the U.S., see note 9) became even larger relative to the economy while the contracting sectors became smaller, indicating that the pattern of growth in the late nineteenth and early twentieth centuries was no temporary aberration but a stable characteristic of modern economic growth. These criteria are further justified by recognition that British production in the expanding sectors was less than the level warranted by market conditions as indicated by British loss of market share in export markets, by the rising level of imports into Britain of goods produced by the expanding sectors, and by the volume of foreign investment into Britain directed towards the expanding sectors. Those British industries, like construction and construction materials, including iron and steel,[2] designated for counterfactual expansion but not attracting foreign investment and/or not entering into foreign trade,[3] derived stimulus for their growth from other expanding industries which were both absorbing foreign funds and growing in international demand.

Concerning specific sectors, the textile industry was included as a sector losing relative size for two main reasons: (1) as the industry became more competitive on a global basis the possibilities for continued expansion became increasingly remote (Sandberg, 1974: 207–220); (2) the industry's smaller relative size in the U.S. in 1909 was a more accurate indicator of the sector's viable size in the long-run than was the sector's relative size in the U.K. in 1907. The argument for domestic service is similar. In both countries, domestic service was a very slow growing industry but very much larger in the U.K. than in the U.S.; had more rapid growth occurred in the U.K., the sector's relative size certainly would have contracted (Hunt, 1973: 140). The same argument is true of agriculture, although the sector's relative size was much smaller in the U.K. than in the U.S.; nevertheless, the pressure on rents, wages and land prices in the U.K. after 1873 indicated that the decline had not gone far enough fast enough.[4] Had more rapid growth of other sectors occurred, offering more inviting alternative uses of men and money than existed historically, the flow of resources out of agriculture would have been even larger than it was historically (Matthews, *et al.*, 1982: 275). Agriculture in Britain not only failed by a vast margin to grow as rapidly as the

Notes to Table 3.3. (*cont.*)
(Kendrick, 1961: 471) for paper, printing and publishing and those used here, which indicate a much lower growth rate and, therefore, a much higher average index number of outputs than is shown by Kendrick's data. The lower estimate was deliberately used without alteration in order to bias the comparisons of U.S. and U.K. performance against the counterfactual argument, although in this case the comparison is misleading for it implies that the paper, printing and publishing sector grew less rapidly than GNP when in fact it almost certainly grew faster.
[9] Growth rate estimated by same series used for construction.
[10] Growth conservatively proxied by U.S. manufacturing growth over the years 1869, 1879, 1889–1913. Inclusion of 1869, 1879 significantly lowered growth rate.

economy as a whole, but between 1870 and 1913 actually recorded a negative growth rate. While this negative rate was not, at the 95% confidence interval, significantly different from zero, it was very much less than the growth rate of the American sector, which was certainly positive even if only 40% of the growth rate of the U.S. economy as a whole. Thus, even without the emergence in the U.K. in the early twentieth century of highly visible growth sectors comparable to automobile manufacture and electrical engineering in the U.S., British agriculture contracted rapidly and might, therefore, have been expected to have contracted yet more rapidly in a more dynamic environment.

The sector of wholesale and retail trade was also assumed to contract (in relative terms) more rapidly in a situation of faster growth than was true historically. Although the sector grew marginally more rapidly than aggregate output in the U.K., it grew less rapidly than output in the U.S.[5] Furthermore, the twentieth century has not been conducive to the relative expansion of the sector in either country. Had more rapid growth taken place in the British economy before 1914, distribution services would very likely have been less important to the pre-war economy than they in fact were. Such an outcome is especially plausible when recalling that the technological changes of the period, in which advances in communications and transportation were particularly prominent, permitted substantial productivity gains in the inherently labour intensive, price inelastic activity of the distribution of goods and services.

Manufactured gas output was growing comparatively rapidly in both countries yet its relative size was vastly larger in the U.K. in 1907 than it was in the U.S. in 1909. The reason for this difference is clearly bound up with the greater use of electricity in the U.S. for lighting and power. Since eventually the U.S. practice of electricity replacing manufactured gas for most uses was adopted in the U.K., it is reasonable to assume that faster growth in the U.K. would have favoured expansion of electricity output at the expense of gas manufacture.[6]

The last sector selected for counterfactual contraction was that of net property income from abroad. This sector was already large in Britain by historical standards by the mid nineteenth century, the stock of foreign assets amounting in 1860 to perhaps 28% of the domestic capital stock in industry and commerce (Feinstein, 1978:81, Table 23). Between 1860 and 1914 the stock of foreign assets grew until by 1913 net property income from abroad accounted for more than 7% of GNP at market prices (it had been only 3% in 1870) (Feinstein, 1972: Table 3, columns 6 and 7). The assets which generated this vast income from abroad were valued in 1913 at 64% of the gross value of the domestic capital stock excluding dwellings.[7] Never before or since, has a major industrial nation made a commitment of resources abroad on such a scale.[8] Furthermore, British foreign investment was, in aggregate, highly conservative, weighted towards well known government and transport issues. Neither at home nor abroad was British investment heavily directed towards those activities most closely associated with the rapid technological progress of the period. Given this feature of British foreign investment, the large flow of income from abroad was inconsistent with rapid growth. Rapidly growing economies generate demands for domestic capital formation on such a scale that only relatively small amounts of resources are available for foreign investment, especially foreign portfolio investment; Germany is a particularly good illustration of this proposition (Feis, 1930: 60–2). Furthermore, as the twentieth century was to reveal, the maintenance of comparatively high levels of income from abroad depended ultimately upon the capabilities of the domestic economy. Assets abroad could not compensate in the long run for economic inefficiencies at home. Consequently more rapid growth in Britain would inevitably have reduced in relative terms the massive accumulation of foreign assets which in fact occurred.

Of the sectors chosen to expand, iron and steel, chemicals, engineering, instrument production, paper and printing, electricity, and telecommunications were already growing comparatively rapidly in both the U.S. and the U.K. The sectors of construction and construction materials (brick, glass, cement) while expanding much more slowly than the overall economy in the U.K., were, in the U.S., both relatively large (compared with the U.K.) and growing faster than the American economy as a whole. It is difficult to imagine a process of rapid growth which would not place heavy demands on the construction sector and on those industries which produce construction materials. The relatively small size of construction and related sectors in the U.K., in the early twentieth century, is obviously linked with the slow development of the economy at that time rather than with any unique British ability to achieve rapid growth without extensive construction activity. Hence it is reasonable to assume that more rapid British growth would have both required and supported a larger construction sector.

The fact that the expanding sectors were not only those growing comparatively rapidly before 1914 but also those which tended to become even larger in both countries in the years after 1918[9] indicates that no inherent barrier to expansion existed in Britain before 1914 but rather that the relatively small size of the rapidly expanding sectors before the war was due to a failure to transfer to them resources swiftly and effectively from the staple sectors of mid nineteenth-century development. Indeed, the relatively good growth performance of the British economy in the inter-war period, when external conditions were so unfavourable to growth, may be explained in part by a structural shift which could have been begun on a large scale long before 1919. As a result of the delayed shift, very substantial opportunities for technological and commercial arbitrage of factor yields among sectors emerged which were not effectively exploited until after 1914.

The criteria by which the sectors capable of more rapid growth can be identified are more objective than those which govern the extent of the counterfactual changes. Although the degree of counterfactual expansion and contraction is, in part, arbitrary, the consequences of various choices can be examined to assess the sensitivity of the conclusions to a particular choice. The choices made here in the first, low growth variant, were determined by setting the hypothetical sizes of the expanding sectors in the U.K. equal to their American counterparts. The iron and steel trades, already marginally larger than their American counterparts, were allowed no counterfactual expansion. The result was a gain of 4.55% of average GNP by the expanding sectors as a group. This loss was distributed among the six contracting sectors as follows: domestic service, manufactured gas production and distribution were reduced to the sizes of their American counterparts, accounting for 63.5% of the hypothesized sectoral shifts. The remaining 36.5% of the shift was allocated to textiles, agriculture and net property income from abroad by assuming half – or 0.83% – of the required shift of 1.62% of GNP would be taken from foreign incomes' share and the other half from textiles and agriculture in proportion to their relative sizes. This resulted in textiles' losing 0.26% and agriculture 0.57% of their share of average GNP over the period 1870–1913. The procedure used here to determine the extent of the counterfactual sectoral shift requires that the size of the gains made by the expanding sectors be calculated first.

The losses calculated for the sectors of domestic service, manufactured gas and distribution are thus based on comparison with the U.S., while textiles, agriculture and net property income from abroad are residual contracting sectors, the extent of their contraction depending upon the size of the counterfactual shift. The details of the impact of this shift upon growth are reported in Tables 3.4 and 3.5. From Table 3.5, it is found that the aggregate growth rate would have been increased by 0.56% per year. Had aggregate growth been 0.56% per year more rapid, at 2.40% per year rather than the 1.84% actually achieved, output by 1913 would have been 126.8% of the actual 1913 level. This is, in fact, a large increase. To appreciate just how large an increase in per capita terms this counterfactual level of output implies, it may be noted that a peacetime level of per capita GNP equal to 126.8% of the 1913 figure was not reached until 1946.[10]

The procedure just described is nevertheless very conservative in evaluating the possibilities for growth arising from structural change despite its estimation of an income level not reached in Britain until 1946. No allowance is made for the fact that in 1870 a much larger proportion of British than American resources were committed to sectors that were to be the key to subsequent growth. Had British performance in those strategic sectors only been comparable, rather than markedly inferior, to the performances of the other advanced economies of the period, the relative sizes of the British strategic sectors would still have been substantially larger than their American counterparts in 1907. The best way to recognize the considerable structural advantages of Britain's early industrialization is by first setting appropriate relative sector sizes for the contracting sectors

Table 3.4.[1] *Effects of structural change: details – low growth variant. End of first iteration*

(1)	(2)	(3)	(4)	(5)	(6)	(7)
	Change in growth rate $\Delta G(I)$	Change in sectoral share $\Delta S(I)$	Acceleration effect $\Delta G(I)S(I)$	Shift effect $G(I)\Delta S(I)$	Interaction effect $\Delta G(I)\Delta S(I)$	Total contribution to change of growth $\sum(\Delta G(I)S(I) + G(I)\Delta S(I) + \Delta G(I)\Delta S(I))$
Industry						
1 Textiles	0.0006822[2]	−0.0026	0.000030	−0.000029	−0.000002	−0.000000
2 Domestic service	−0.017016	−0.0227	−0.000790	−0.000114	0.000386	−0.000517
3 Agriculture	−0.001250	−0.0057	−0.000122	0.000003	0.000007	−0.000112
4 Domestic wholesale-retail trade	−0.000728	−0.0039	−0.000129	−0.000077	0.000003	−0.000203
5 Gas undertakings	−0.018189	−0.0023	−0.000084	−0.000105	0.000042	−0.000147
6 Net property income from abroad	−0.006194	−0.0083	−0.000283	−0.000307	0.000051	−0.000539
(subtotals)		−0.0455	−0.001376	−0.000629	0.000488	−0.001517
7 Construction	0.007136	0.0168	0.000273	0.000096	0.000120	0.000488
8 Iron, steel trades	−0.001023[2]	0.0000	−0.000012	0.000000	0.000000	−0.000012
9 Engineering	0.006683	0.0074	0.000166	0.000204	0.000049	0.000419
10 Paper, printing and publishing	0.022591	0.0146	0.000228	0.000489	0.000330	0.001047
11 Electricity, telecommunications, scientific instruments	0.020389	0.0035	0.000049	0.000213	0.000071	0.000334
12 Bricks, cement, glass	0.001514	0.0014	0.000016	0.000008	0.000002	0.000026
13 Chemicals: class (a)	0.003900	0.0018	0.000024	0.000073	0.000007	0.000104
(subtotals)		0.0455	0.000743	0.001083	0.000579	0.002405

14 Rest of economy	0.000888	0.0000	0.000427	0.000000	0.000000	0.000427
15 Total net increase in growth rate			−0.000206	0.000454	0.001067	0.001315

Sources:

Column (3) – Table 3.1, column (3).

Entries in columns (2), (4), (5), and (6) by calculation. See algorithm, Appendix D.

Column (7) – Sum of columns (4), (5), and (6).

Notes:

[1] Totals may not equal column sums due to rounding error of ± 0.000001.

[2] Because the actual growth rate is estimated by regression while the altered growth rate at the beginning of the first iteration is calculated by comparing the output index for 1870 with the output index for 1913 (= 100) reduced by the proportionate change in the sector's share of total output, for small changes $\Delta G(I)$ may have the wrong sign. A comparison of row 1 with row 8, the two instances where this occurred in Table 3.4, indicates that the resulting bias acts to lower the final counterfactual growth rate. The algorithm was altered to replace any $\Delta G(I)$ of the wrong sign by zero. This had no impact on the final outcome although more iterations were required to reach convergence. Hence the results from the original algorithm are reported here.

Table 3.5.[1] *Effects of structural change: details – low growth variant.*
End of final iteration (34)

(1) Industry	(2) Change in growth rate $\Delta G(I)$	(3) Change in sectoral share $\Delta S(I)$	(4) Acceleration effect $\Delta G(I)S(I)$	(5) Shift effect $G(I)\Delta S(I)$	(6) Interaction effect $\Delta G(I)\Delta S(I)$	(7) Total contribution to change of growth $\sum(\Delta G(I)S(I) + G(I)\Delta S(I) + \Delta G(I)\Delta S(I))$
1 Textiles	0.006280	− 0.0026	0.000279	− 0.000029	− 0.000016	0.000234
2 Domestic service	− 0.011550	− 0.0227	− 0.000536	− 0.000114	0.000262	− 0.000387
3 Agriculture	0.004273	− 0.0057	0.000415	0.000003	− 0.000024	0.000394
4 Domestic wholesale-retail trade	0.004910	− 0.0039	0.000866	− 0.000077	− 0.000019	0.000770
5 Gas undertakings	− 0.012503	− 0.0023	− 0.000058	− 0.000105	0.000029	− 0.000134
6 Net property income from abroad	− 0.000491	− 0.0083	− 0.000022	− 0.000307	0.000004	− 0.000325
(subtotals)		− 0.0455	0.000945	− 0.000629	0.000236	0.000552
7 Construction	0.012739	0.0168	0.000487	0.000096	0.000214	0.000796
8 Iron, steel trades	0.004645	0.0000	0.000056	0.000000	0.000000	0.000056
9 Engineering	0.012405	0.0074	0.000308	0.000204	0.000092	0.000603
10 Paper, printing and publishing	0.028434	0.0146	0.000287	0.000489	0.000415	0.001191

11 Electricity, telecommunications, scientific instruments	0.026372	0.0035	0.000063	0.000213	0.000092	0.000369
12 Bricks, cement, glass	0.007087	0.0014	0.000074	0.000008	0.000010	0.000092
13 Chemicals: class (a)	0.009678	0.0018	0.000059	0.000073	0.000017	0.000149
(subtotals)		0.0455	0.001334	0.001083	0.000840	0.003257
14 Rest of economy	0.003808	0.0000	0.001832	0.000000	0.000000	0.001832
15 Total net increase in growth rate			0.004111	0.000454	0.001076	0.005640

Source: Same as sources for Table 3.4.

Note:
[1] Totals may not equal column sums due to rounding error of ± 0.000001.

Table 3.6. *Medium growth variant*

(1) Industry	(2) S(I)	(3) ΔS(I)	(4) G(I)	(5) O(I)
1 Textiles	0.0445	− 0.0142	0.0111	56.9
2 Domestic service	0.0464	− 0.0227	0.0050	85.9
3 Agriculture	0.0972	− 0.0122	− 0.0005	101.5
4 Domestic wholesale – retail trade	0.1764	− 0.0039	0.0198	43.4
5 Gas undertakings	0.0046	− 0.0023	0.0458	15.5
6 Net property income from abroad	0.0457	− 0.0205	0.0370	22.2
7 Construction	0.0382	0.0168	0.0057	83.2
8 Iron, steel trades	0.0120	0.0052	0.0254	35.5
9 Engineering	0.0248	0.0214	0.0275	30.6
10 Paper, printing and publishing	0.0101	0.0146	0.0335	23.4
11 Electricity, telecommunications, scientific instruments	0.0024	0.0061	0.0610	8.5
12 Bricks, cement, glass	0.0105	0.0065	0.0057	83.2
13 Chemicals: class (a)	0.0061	0.0052	0.0405	20.0
14 Rest of economy	0.4811	0.0000	0.0218	39.2

$$\sum |\Delta S(I)| = 0.1516$$

Sources:
Column (2) – column (3), Table D1, Appendix D and text of Appendix D (for 'Rest of economy' sector).
Column (3) – see main text.
Column (4) – see text of Appendix D.
Column (5) – see text of Appendix D.

and then distributing among the expanding sectors the differences between the counterfactually altered contracting-sector sizes and their actual historical average sizes. Had the textile sector declined to an average level equal to 125% of the relative size of its U.S. counterpart during the period 1870–1913[11] – a contraction equal to 1.42% of GNP – while assuming agriculture's loss over the same period to be 1.215% of GNP[12] and the loss in net property income from abroad to be 2.05% of GNP, the expanding sectors would have registered a further increase of 3.03% of GNP in addition to that assumed in the low growth variant, thus causing the sectors of iron and steel, chemicals, electricity generation, telephone-telegraph communication, bricks, cement, and glass, and engineering to be relatively (but not, of course, absolutely) larger than their American counterparts. The increase of 3.03% of GNP was apportioned among the five sectors according to their relative sizes, engineering being the most affected. The sector of electricity generation, telecommunications and scientific

Table 3.7.[1] *Effects of structural change: details – medium growth variant. End of first iteration*

(1) Industry	(2) Change in growth rate $\Delta G(I)$	(3) Change in sectoral share $\Delta S(I)$	(4) Acceleration effect $\Delta G(I)S(I)$	(5) Shift effect $G(I)\Delta S(I)$	(6) Interaction effect $\Delta G(I)\Delta S(I)$	(7) Total contribution to change of growth $\sum(\Delta G(I)S(I) + G(I)\Delta S(I) + \Delta G(I)\Delta S(I))$
1 Textiles	− 0.006916	− 0.0142	− 0.000308	− 0.000158	0.000098	− 0.000367
2 Domestic service	− 0.017016	− 0.0227	− 0.000790	− 0.000114	0.000386	− 0.000517
3 Agriculture	− 0.002959	− 0.0122	− 0.000288	0.000006	0.000036	− 0.000245
4 Domestic wholesale – retail trade	− 0.000728	− 0.0039	− 0.000129	− 0.000077	0.000003	− 0.000203
5 Gas undertakings	− 0.018189	− 0.0023	− 0.000084	− 0.000105	0.000042	− 0.000147
6 Net property income from abroad	− 0.015616	− 0.0205	− 0.000714	− 0.000759	0.000320	− 0.001152
(subtotals)		− 0.0758	− 0.002311	− 0.001206	0.000885	− 0.002631
7 Construction	0.007136	0.0168	0.000273	0.000096	0.000120	0.000488
8 Iron, steel trades	0.007589	0.0052	0.000091	0.000132	0.000039	0.000263
9 Engineering	0.015402	0.0214	0.000382	0.000588	0.000330	0.001300
10 Paper, printing and publishing	0.022591	0.0146	0.000228	0.000489	0.000330	0.001047
11 Electricity, telecommunications, scientific instruments	0.029610	0.0061	0.000071	0.000372	0.000181	0.000624
12 Bricks, cement, glass	0.009903	0.0065	0.000104	0.000037	0.000064	0.000205
13 Chemicals: class (a)	0.012630	0.0052	0.000077	0.000211	0.000066	0.000353
(subtotals)		0.0758	0.001226	0.001925	0.001130	0.004280
14 Rest of economy	0.001649	0.0000	0.000793	0.000000	0.000000	0.000793
15 Total net increase in growth rate			− 0.000292	0.000719	0.002015	0.002442

Sources:

Column (3) – Column (3), Table 3.6.

Entries in columns (2), (4), (5), and (6) by calculation. See algorithm Appendix D.

Column (7) – sum of columns (4), (5) and (6).

Note:

[1] Totals may not equal column sums due to rounding error of ± 0.000001.

instruments was given a double weighting in this procedure. The other sectors – construction and paper, printing and publishing – were left unchanged from the previous calculation.

Where the structural shifts in the low growth variant were constrained by the relative sizes of the rapidly growing American sectors and the sectoral changes within the contracting sectors were determined as a residual, the structural shifts in the medium growth variant were constrained by the relative sizes of the contracting sectors and the sectoral changes within the expanding sectors were determined as a residual. In this case, counterfactual 1913 output would have been 155.5% of the actual level of output, a level of per capita output not surpassed until 1955. (See Tables 3.7 and 3.8 for the details of this second counterfactual estimation. From Table 3.8, it is found that the aggregate growth rate is increased 1.05% per year, rising from 1.84% to 2.89% per year.)

This second calculation still cannot be considered to probe the limits to growth in pre-1914 Britain. To accomplish that, a Britain which had significantly larger engineering, chemical and telecommunications sectors must be imagined. Such a counterfactual situation is set out in Table 3.9. These values were chosen by setting all of the expanding sectors except that of electricity, telecommunications, and scientific instruments equal to the relative size they obtained in 1970 (CSO, 1976: 18–19). The remaining sector of electricity, telecommunications and scientific instruments was expanded by the same proportionate amount as that required to shift the engineering sector from its 1907 size to that of 1970.[13]

Such a shift meant a gain for the expanding sectors of 13.85% in all. This shift was off-set by reductions of equal magnitude in the contracting sectors. The reductions were chosen by first setting the relative size of distribution equal to 15.5% of GNP.[14] The remaining 12.79% was distributed among the other five contracting sectors in proportion to their relative sizes, with net property income from abroad given double weight in order to concentrate counterfactual reductions in that sector. Details of this high growth variant are shown in Tables 3.10 and 3.11. The counterfactual 1913 income, in the high growth variant, is 371.5% of the actual 1913 level, an implicit growth rate of 5.00% per year from 1870 to 1913 rather than the rate of 1.84% actually recorded. This counterfactual growth rate is almost 25% faster than that of the nineteenth-century American economy and approximately equal to that achieved by France over the period 1950 to 1969, a period which saw France, on a per capita basis, become one of the wealthiest countries in Western Europe while experiencing growth at a rate unprecedented in her history. In the counterfactual calculation the final result was the product of maintaining an historically rapid rate of growth for an unprecedentedly long period. It is of little surprise, therefore, that the subsequent per capita income levels generated by these very large counterfactual structural shifts are remarkably high. The level of 1913 income implied by the most extreme counterfactual structural shift considered here is greater than any which might

Table 3.8.[1] *Effects of structural change: details – medium growth variant. End of final iteration (37)*

(1) Industry	(2) Change in growth rate $\Delta G(I)$	(3) Change in sectoral share $\Delta S(I)$	(4) Acceleration effect $\Delta G(I)S(I)$	(5) Shift effect $G(I)\Delta S(I)$	(6) Interaction effect $\Delta G(I)\Delta S(I)$	(7) Total contribution to change of growth rate $\sum (\Delta G(I)S(I) + G(I)\Delta S(I) + \Delta G(I)\Delta S(I))$
1 Textiles	0.003453	− 0.0142	0.000154	− 0.000158	− 0.000049	− 0.000053
2 Domestic service	− 0.006814	− 0.0227	− 0.000316	− 0.000114	0.000155	− 0.000275
3 Agriculture	0.007331	− 0.0122	0.000713	0.000006	− 0.000089	0.000629
4 Domestic wholesale-retail trade	0.009795	− 0.0039	0.001728	− 0.000077	− 0.000038	0.001612
5 Gas undertakings	− 0.007577	− 0.0023	− 0.000035	− 0.000105	0.000017	− 0.000123
6 Net property income from abroad	− 0.005069	− 0.0205	− 0.000232	− 0.000759	0.000104	− 0.000886
(subtotals)		− 0.0758	0.002011	− 0.001206	0.000100	0.000905
7 Construction	0.017595	0.0168	0.000672	0.000096	0.000296	0.001063
8 Iron, steel trades	0.018256	0.0052	0.000219	0.000132	0.000095	0.000446
9 Engineering	0.026171	0.0214	0.000649	0.000588	0.000560	0.001798
10 Paper, printing and publishing	0.033497	0.0146	0.000338	0.000489	0.000489	0.001316
11 Electricity, telecommunications, scientific instruments	0.040872	0.0061	0.000098	0.000372	0.000249	0.000720
12 Bricks, cement, glass	0.020391	0.0065	0.000214	0.000037	0.000133	0.000384
13 Chemicals: class (a)	0.023505	0.0052	0.000143	0.000211	0.000122	0.000476
(subtotals)		0.0758	0.002333	0.001925	0.001944	0.006202
14 Rest of economy	0.007107	0.0000	0.003419	0.000000	0.000000	0.003419
15 Total net increase in growth rate			0.007765	0.000719	0.002043	0.010527

Source: Same as sources for Table 3.7.

Note:

[1] Totals may not equal column sums due to rounding error or ± 0.000001.

Table 3.9. *High growth variant*

(1) Industry	(2) S(I)	(3) ΔS(I)	(4) G(I)	(5) O(I)
1 Textiles	0.0445	− 0.0205	0.0111	56.9
2 Domestic service	0.0464	− 0.0212	0.0050	85.9
3 Agriculture	0.0972	− 0.0422	− 0.0005	101.5
4 Domestic wholesale– retail trade	0.1764	− 0.0106	0.0198	43.4
5 Gas undertakings	0.0046	− 0.0020	0.0458	15.5
6 Net property income from abroad	0.0457	− 0.0420	0.0370	22.2
7 Construction	0.0382	0.0258	0.0057	83.2
8 Iron, steel trades	0.0120	0.0131	0.0254	35.5
9 Engineering	0.0248	0.0552	0.0275	30.6
10 Paper, printing and publishing	0.0101	0.0178	0.0335	23.4
11 Electricity, telecommunications, scientific instruments	0.0024	0.0053	0.0610	8.5
12 Bricks, cement, glass	0.0105	0.0015	0.0057	83.2
13 Chemicals: class (a)	0.0061	0.0198	0.0405	20.0
14 Rest of economy	0.4811	0.0000	0.0218	39.2
		$\sum |\Delta S(I)| = 0.2770$		

Sources:
Column (2) – column (3), Table D1, Appendix D and text of Appendix D (for 'Rest of economy' sector).
Column (3) – see main text.
Column (4) – see text of Appendix D.
Column (5) – see text of Appendix D.

reasonably have been achieved in reality. Only the Japanese have maintained a growth rate of such size for a comparable period of time and they have had the opportunity to adopt a large backlog of technical progress in a manner not open to Britain in the mid nineteenth century.

What is important here, however, is that the upper bound is very large indeed, indicating that plausible structural shifts affecting more than 9% but less than 28% of the economy would lead to a very substantial increase in the rate of economic growth, yet one with numerous historical precedents.

Moreover, as a little experimentation with the algorithm described in Appendix D will quickly show, this general result can be achieved in a wide variety of ways and does not depend on the specific structural changes proposed in the illustrative counterfactual growth variants of Tables 3.1, 3.6, and 3.9. As these three variants indicate, within wide limits, changes in the allocation of output

Table 3.10.[1] *Effects of structural change: details – high growth variant.*
End of first iteration

(1)	(2)	(3)	(4)	(5)	(6)	(7)
	Change in growth rate $\Delta G(I)$	Change in sectoral share $\Delta S(I)$	Acceleration effect $\Delta G(I)S(I)$	Shift effect $G(I)\Delta S(I)$	Interaction effect $\Delta G(I)\Delta S(I)$	Total contribution to change of growth rate $\sum(\Delta G(I)S(I) + G(I)\Delta S(I) + \Delta G(I)\Delta S(I))$
Industry						
1 Textiles	-0.012345	-0.0205	-0.000549	-0.000228	0.000253	-0.000524
2 Domestic service	-0.015605	-0.0212	-0.000724	-0.000106	0.000331	-0.000499
3 Agriculture	-0.012997	-0.0422	-0.001263	0.000021	0.000548	-0.000694
4 Domestic wholesale–retail trade	-0.001667	-0.0106	-0.000294	-0.000210	0.000018	-0.000486
5 Gas undertakings	-0.015255	-0.0020	-0.000070	-0.000092	0.000031	-0.000131
6 Net property income from abroad	-0.060185	-0.0420	-0.002750	-0.001554	0.002528	-0.001777
(subtotals)		-0.1385	-0.005651	-0.002168	0.003709	-0.004111
7 Construction	0.010712	0.0258	0.000409	0.000147	0.000276	0.000833
8 Iron, steel trades	0.017609	0.0131	0.000211	0.000321	0.000231	0.000763
9 Engineering	0.028804	0.0552	0.000714	0.001518	0.001590	0.003822
10 Paper, printing and publishing	0.025675	0.0178	0.000259	0.000600	0.000460	0.001319
11 Electricity, telecommunications, scientific instruments	0.027106	0.0053	0.000065	0.000323	0.000144	0.000532
12 Bricks, cement, glass	0.001710	0.0015	0.000018	0.000009	0.000003	0.000029
13 Chemicals: class (a)	0.033141	0.0198	0.000202	0.000802	0.000656	0.001660
(subtotals)		0.1385	0.001878	0.003720	0.003360	0.008958
14 Rest of economy	0.004847	0.0000	0.002332	0.000000	0.000000	0.002332
15 Total net increase in growth rate			-0.001440	0.001551	0.007067	0.007178

Sources:
Column (3) – Table 3.9, column (3).
Entries in columns (2), (4), (5) and (6) by calculation. See algorithm, Appendix D.
Column (7) – sum of columns (4), (5), and (6).

Note:
[1] Totals may not equal column sums due to rounding error of ± 0.000001.

Table 3.11.[1] *Effects of structural change: details – high growth variant. End of final iteration (46)*

(1) Industry	(2) Change in growth rate ΔG(I)	(3) Change in sectoral share ΔS(I)	(4) Acceleration effect ΔG(I)S(I)	(5) Shift effect G(I)ΔS(I)	(6) Interaction effect ΔG(I)ΔS(I)	(7) Total contribution to change of growth rate Σ(ΔG(I)S(I) + G(I)ΔS(I) + ΔG(I)ΔS(I))
1 Textiles	0.018607	−0.0205	0.000828	−0.000228	−0.000381	0.000219
2 Domestic service	0.015056	−0.0212	0.000699	−0.000106	−0.000319	0.000273
3 Agriculture	0.017575	−0.0422	0.001708	0.000021	−0.000742	0.000988
4 Domestic wholesale– retail trade	0.029885	−0.0106	0.005272	−0.000210	−0.000317	0.004745
5 Gas undertakings	0.016682	−0.0020	0.000077	−0.000092	−0.000033	−0.000048
6 Net property income from abroad	−0.029913	−0.0420	−0.001367	−0.001554	0.001256	−0.001665
(subtotals)		−0.1385	0.007216	−0.002168	−0.000536	0.004512
7 Construction	0.042210	0.0258	0.001612	0.000147	0.001089	0.002849
8 Iron, steel trades	0.049904	0.0131	0.000599	0.000321	0.000654	0.001574
9 Engineering	0.061538	0.0552	0.001526	0.001518	0.003397	0.006441
10 Paper, printing and publishing	0.058499	0.0178	0.000591	0.000600	0.001047	0.002238
11 Electricity, telecommunications, scientific instruments	0.060826	0.0053	0.000146	0.000323	0.000322	0.000792
12 Bricks, cement glass	0.032930	0.0015	0.000346	0.000009	0.000049	0.000404
13 Chemicals: class (a)	0.066413	0.0198	0.000405	0.000802	0.001315	0.002522
(subtotals)		0.1385	0.005225	0.003720	0.007873	0.016819
14 Rest of economy	0.021324	0.0000	0.010262	0.000000	0.000000	0.010262
15 Total net increase in growth rate			0.022703	0.001551	0.007338	0.031592

Source: Same as sources for Table 3.10.

Note:
[1] Totals may not equal column sums due to rounding error of ± 0.000001.

shares among expanding and contracting sectors alters only the details of the calculations, not the broad results which depend most crucially on the total size and not the composition of the sectoral changes. Thus per capita incomes of between 150% and 200% of what they actually were in the U.K. in 1913 would appear to constitute an historically plausible upper bound to British economic performance in the years 1870–1913. To achieve the output levels implied by this upper bound would have required commitment of resources to technologically progressive sectors on a scale somewhat greater, in relative terms, than that made in the U.S. during the same period. But given Britain's industrial tradition and the weaker hold of natural resources on mobile factors of production, such a commitment does not, in retrospect, appear to have been unattainable.

4

Limits to British growth? The balance of payments and supply of labour

Although the structural changes proposed in the growth variants of the previous sections are to some extent arbitrary in size, they are not arbitrary in kind. It should be noted first that greatly improved performance did not require a radical restructuring of the economy. All that was necessary to have achieved more rapid growth was that Britain had sustained the processes of structural change and technological advance which she had pioneered.[1] If Britain, by the standards of the late nineteenth century, had been as aggressive and successful in exploiting the uses of electricity, the internal combustion engine, scientific chemistry, rapid communications and the other technical advances of the time as she had been in first exploiting, by the standards of the late eighteenth century, the steam engine, textile machinery and the metallurgical improvements of that period, a per capita British income in 1913 at least 50% greater than that actually achieved appears to have been eminently feasible.[2] The plausibility of these counterfactual re-structurings depends in fact only upon the belief that sufficient markets for the expanded outputs existed; that is, that the only constraints lay on the demand side, for the necessary technological capability was readily available as the performance before 1914 of the U.S., Germany, Sweden, and even France showed. Had the technology of the period been fully exploited, a task which would have entailed a substantial increase in rates of domestic human and fixed capital formation, any potential shortages of labour or materials may readily have been surmounted or by-passed.

The importance of markets in discussions of counterfactual levels of output has been demonstrated by Charles Kindleberger (1964: 264–71) in his forceful rejection of John Meyer's counterfactual model of British export-led growth in the period 1872–1907.[3] Meyer postulated that if Britain had maintained between 1872 and 1907 the rate of export growth achieved from 1854 to 1872, then the rate of growth of the British economy would have been over twice that actually recorded. He used an input–output table constructed from the 1907 Census of Production to reach this conclusion. Meyer assumed that the structure of exports and the economy would have remained unchanged had greater growth been achieved in the late nineteenth century. He calculated what exports in 1907 would have been, had the relative importance of the various exported goods retained their actual 1907 positions with total exports reaching a higher level than actually occurred. This procedure implied that in 1907 textile exports would have been worth £493m rather than £129m; iron, steel, engineering and ship exports would have been worth £205m instead of £95m and total visible exports would have been worth nearly three times their actual 1907 value of £477m. Doubtless had such an enlarged level of export demand in the pattern of 1907 existed in that year and had the input–output relationships in the economy remained unchanged as well, the total value of output would have been twice as large as it actually was. However, Kindleberger points out (1964: 269–70) that this particular version of export-led growth is untenable because of the structural pattern of both production and consumption which it implies:

The law of diminishing returns in consumption ensures that a given bill of goods cannot expand at a constant rate either indefinitely or over decades... The world demand for exports is not infinitely elastic at existing prices, any more than the supply of British exports may be. The input–output technique may provide a useful *reductio ad absurdam*: British growth could not have been achieved through expanding exports in an *unchanged* pattern. It would have produced a ridiculously large amount of textile exports, in terms both of production and of consumption abroad. (Emphasis added.)

The growth variants of the previous section avoid this difficulty of Meyer's work. The growth patterns suggested here are broadly consistent with both the actual trading patterns of the period and the broad trends of modern economic growth. By these criteria, the sector output levels in terms of value added implied by the medium growth variant are not wildly large in comparison with the actual value of output. Of course, implicit in these patterns and trends are assumptions concerning British price and quality competitiveness which is fundamentally determined by the realized technological advances and entrepreneurial skills that are the essence of productivity improvements. But nothing in this regard is assumed for Britain which was not actually shown to be possible elsewhere in the late nineteenth and early twentieth centuries. The counterfactual model, therefore, is simply a means of exploring the level and structure of output that would have been achieved had Britain exploited the technological and commercial opportunities of the period as effectively and as successfully as was done elsewhere in Europe and in America. Table 4.1 compares the actual level of value added in various sectors in 1907 with those yielded by the medium growth variant.

If an input–output table accurately reflecting the postulated structural changes were available, both the inputs required for the higher counterfactual levels of output and the output capacity of the economy resulting from the full

Table 4.1. *Total GNP: actual and medium growth variant*

(1)	(2) Actual value in 1907 (£m)	(3) Actual sector size (1907) (fraction of GNP)	(4) Counter-factual value added in 1907 (medium growth variant)	(5) Counter-factual sector size in 1907 (medium growth variant) (fraction of GNP)
1 Textiles	£94.3m	0.0424	£106.8m	0.0329
2 Domestic service	74.3	0.0334	57.8	0.0178
3 Agriculture	148.0	0.0666	193.7	0.0596
4 Domestic wholesale-retail trade	407.8	0.1835	580.9	0.1789
5 Gas undertakings	17.3	0.0078	13.2	0.0041
6 Net property income from abroad	144.0	0.0648	120.0	0.0370
(subtotal)	£885.7m	0.3985	£1072.4m	0.3303
7 Construction	£62.3m	0.0280	£118.4m	0.0365
8 Iron, steel trades	30.0	0.0135	57.7	0.0178
9 Engineering[1]	69.0	0.0311	175.2	0.0539
10 Paper, printing and publishing	32.6	0.0147	106.1	0.0327
11 Electricity, telecommunications, scientific instruments	11.9	0.0054	48.2	0.0148
12 Bricks, cement, glass	17.1	0.0077	36.0	0.0111
13 Chemicals: class (a)	20.1	0.0090	45.9	0.0141
(subtotal)	£243.0m	0.1094	£587.5m	0.1809
Rest of the economy:				
14 Mining	£119.5m	0.0538	£174.7m	0.0538
15 Shipbuilding	21.0	0.0094	30.5	0.0094
16 Food processing	44.6	0.0201	65.3	0.0201
17 International shipping	37.5	0.0169	54.9	0.0169
18 Clothing	49.8	0.0224	72.7	0.0224
19 Timber trades	19.4	0.0087	28.2	0.0087
20 Personal services	42.0	0.0189	61.4	0.0189
21 Professional and government services	159.1	0.0716	232.5	0.0716
22 Domestic transportation	166.7	0.0750	243.6	0.0750
23 International financial and commercial services	69.8	0.0314	102.0	0.0314
24 Miscellaneous[2]	363.9	0.1638	532.0	0.1638
(subtotal)	£1093.3m	0.4920	£1597.8m	0.4920
Error[3]			(−10.1)	(−0.0031)
25 TOTALS	£2222.0m	1.0000	£3247.6m	1.0000

exploitation of the technological changes of the period could be directly examined. At this time, however, the necessary input–output table is not available. The assessment used here, therefore, compares the output requirements for exports, investment and consumption in circumstances of more rapid growth with the historical pattern of output shown in the first two columns of Table 4.1.

Since by the early twentieth century even a slowly growing Britain had become highly dependent on world trade for food and industrial raw materials, and since

Notes to Table 4.1. (*cont.*)

Sources:

Column (2) – Table 2.1.

Column (3) – Table 2.1.

Column (4) – Entries in rows 1–13 inclusive were calculated by first finding the 1870 level of value added in each sector implied by the actual 1907 value (from Table 2.1) and by the sector's historical growth rate (from Table 3.6, column 4). The counterfactual 1907 value for each sector was then found by expanding the implied 1870 value added by the annually compounded counterfactual growth rate, which was taken to be the *sum* of the historical growth rate (as before, taken from Table 3.6, column 4) *and* the counterfactual change in growth rate (taken from Table 3.8, column 2). Note that if the counterfactual change in growth rate is positive, counterfactual 1907 sectoral value added will be greater than actual 1907 value added; if negative, counterfactual 1907 sectoral value added will be less than actual 1907 value added; if zero, the counterfactual and actual 1907 values will be equal. The entry in row 25 was calculated in a similar manner by finding first the 1870 level of GNP implied by the actual annual growth rate of 1.84% and the actual (adjusted) level of GNP, £2222.0m (taken from Table 2.1). The implied 1870 GNP was £1131.78m. This figure was then expanded by the annually compounded counterfactual growth rate (1.84% *plus* 1.05%) (taken from Table 3.8, column 7, row 15), to yield £3247.6m. Row entries 14–24 inclusive were then calculated assuming the relative size (as a fraction of GNP) of each sector was equal to its actual proportionate size in 1907 (thus mining value added is 0.0538 × £3247.6m = £174.7m); this assumption also yields column (5) for those rows. Column (5) – Calculated from column (4).

Notes:

1 Defined as engineering (excluding electricity supply), motor and cycle trades, road carriage, and non-ferrous metal working in Table 2.1.

2 The most important components of this category are imputed housing services, waterworks, railway equipment, preparation of alcoholic beverages, musical instruments, and other miscellaneous production, including the residual in Table 2.1.

3 The error term indicates the degree of inconsistency in the estimates. Since the counterfactual value added of the sectors designated for counterfactual expansion or contraction were calculated on a different basis from those sectors whose sizes were left unchanged, some inconsistency was inevitable. The inconsistency arises from the fact that average growth rates, calculated by regression, were used for calculating the altered size of the thirteen sectors whose share of GNP was counterfactually changed, and for calculating total GNP, yet the actual size of the thirteen sectors and of GNP in 1907 was not necessarily on the regression line. Judging from the sign of the error term more sectors were above the trend growth path in 1907 than were below it – since the sum of the separately distinguished sectors was £10.1m greater than the required total of £3247.6m. However, given the small size of the error, further investigation is not warranted. Such investigation would, however, indicate the contribution of each of the thirteen distinguished sectors to the total error.

Table 4.2. *British foreign trade – 1907: actual and implied level (medium growth variant)*

	(1) 1907 (actual)	(2) 1907 (implied)
Imports (CIF)		
1 Retained imports of food	£235.1m	£279.4m
2 Retained imports of material for textiles	96.2m	109.0m
3 Retained imports of manufactured and other goods (non-textiles)	97.3m	142.2m
4 Retained imports of raw materials (other than textile material)	92.8m	178.5m
5 Retained textile imports	33.2m	33.2m
Total retained imports of goods	£554.6m	£742.3m
5(a) of which: payment for shipping and commercial services	43.5m	58.2m
(A) Total foreign currency costs of goods exclusive of transport and handling charges (sum of rows 1 through 5 minus 5(a))	£511.1m	£684.1m
Exports (FOB)		
6 Food, drink, tobacco	£22.7m	22.7m
7 Textile exports (manufactured)	161.1m	161.1m
8 Raw materials	55.0m	36.7m
9 Non-textile manufactures	180.9m	249.9m
10 Miscellaneous exports	6.3m	6.3m
Total exports of goods	£426.0m	£476.7m
11 Net export of services	106.0m	154.9m
12 Net foreign income	144.0m	120.0m
(B) Total receipts of foreign exchange (sum of rows 6 through 12)	£676.0m	£751.6m

Sources and Notes:
Actual trade in 1907: Figures for the trade in goods, rows 1 through 10, were taken from British Parliamentary Papers, Annual Statement of Trade, 1907 (Cd. 4100). The estimate of the total payment for services included in the import of goods was derived by subtracting Feinstein's estimate (1972: Table 15, column 9) of total imports of goods, valued at £603.0m excluding insurance, freight and other handling charges, from the figure reported in the Annual Statement of Trade covering all imports (including re-exports in transit) valued on a CIF basis. This latter figure was £646.5m, yielding a figure of £43.5m for total service payments incurred in the importation of goods. Row 11 was obtained from Feinstein (1972: Table 15, column 2 minus column 10). Row 12 was also taken from Feinstein (1972: Table 15, columns 3 and 4 minus columns 11 and 12).

Derivation of import level implied by medium growth variant: ROW 1 – The actual retained import of foodstuffs, drink, and tobacco in 1907 was £235.1m. Domestic agriculture and fishing production was worth £148.0m (Table 2.1). Total agricultural consumption (excluding textile materials) was thus £383.1m in 1907. The income elasticity of demand for food was calculated by assuming that the entire

Notes to Table 4.2. (*cont.*)

per capita increase in imported food was explained by rising incomes alone. In this manner, the 75% increase in the nominal value of imported foodstuffs, drink, and tobacco between 1870 and 1913 was accounted for by a 46% increase in population (from 31.257m people to 45.649m) and a 57% increase in per capita income (at 1900 prices). These figures were taken from Feinstein (1972: Table 55, column 1 for population and Table 5, column 13 for GNP in constant 1900 prices). The portion of the 75% increase attributed to rising income was 29% (0.75–0.46), the per capita increase in consumption. This still over-estimates the income elasticity of demand for food for two reasons: (1) food prices fell sharply between 1870 and 1913 according to both the Rousseaux and Sauerbeck-*Statist* indices and some of the increased demand was certainly due to falling prices; (2) part of the increase in food imports was caused by declining domestic production. In this manner the income elasticity of demand was conservatively estimated at 0.51 (= 0.29/0.57). From Table 4.1, the hypothetical increase in the per capita income in the medium growth variant is 46.2% greater than the actual 1907 levels; hence food consumption is assumed to be 23.5% (= 0.462 × 0.51) greater, or £90.0m more, than that actually achieved in 1907. From Table 4.1 counterfactual domestic food production was calculated to be £193.7m, requiring £279.4m of food imports to achieve the hypothetical increase.

ROW 2 – From Table 4.1 it was calculated that the counterfactual increase in textile output was 13.2%. The value of retained textile materials was increased by the same proportion. Any upward bias induced by price increases caused by increased British demand would be more than offset by the presumption that the actual pattern of the industry's development, a progressive movement towards production of material of higher and higher counts, would have been accelerated in a condition of higher overall growth. Thus the resulting estimate of £109.0m of retained textile material imports may be considered an over-estimate of counterfactual requirements.

ROW 3 – Retained imports of manufactured and other goods (excluding textiles) were assumed to have an income elasticity of unity. Although highly industrialized, wealthy countries do generally have a high level of imports of manufactured goods, it was assumed that the greater competitiveness and technological capability secured by the counterfactual successful shift in resource allocation in favour of industries that produced or helped produce the manufactured goods Britain was importing so heavily would have limited the increase in imports. By this reasoning the estimate of imports in this category of £142.2 (= 1.462 × £97.3) is an over-estimate.

ROW 4 – Many of the imports of non-textile related raw materials consisted of ores or minerals not found in Britain at all or, like timber, found only in insufficient quantities and qualities. Therefore, more rapid growth would have forced imports of these materials up. It was assumed that imports in this category would have doubled when net output rose by 50%. Although much of the net increase in the value of output would have taken place in industries which were heavy users of imported ores and metals, the emphasis which growth places on the production of technically sophisticated goods tends to reduce, often dramatically, the relative importance in final output of raw materials. The increase of £85.7m in the level of non-textile raw materials is thus a compromise between the tendency of the engineering and construction industries to be particularly heavy users of raw materials and the tendency for raw material inputs to become less important relative to the value of final output. The compromise chosen here almost certainly overstates the raw material requirements of the counterfactual growth pattern set out in the medium growth variant.

ROW 5 – In 1907, domestic production of £33m of cotton textiles and £39m of woollen textiles were consumed in Britain. In addition, £33.2m of imported textiles were retained in the U.K., yielding total internal consumption of textiles of £105.2m. Assuming that the income elasticity of demand for textiles is 0.25, the subsequent increase in domestic consumption of £12.2m (= 0.462 × 0.25 × £105.2m) is assumed to come entirely from increased domestic production (see note to row 1 above and row 1 Table 4.1).

ROW 5a – Payments for shipping and commercial services were assumed to rise at precisely the same rate as total imports (CIF), thereby maintaining in the counterfactual variant the same proportionate expenditure on services as was realized in 1907.

Notes to Table 4.2. (*cont.*)

ROW 6 – There was assumed to be no change in the value of British exports of food, drink, and tobacco.

ROW 7 – Exports of manufactured textiles (including yarns) were left unchanged from the actual 1907 figures.

ROW 8 – The most important British export of raw materials was coal, with an FOB value in 1907 of £42.1m. The counterfactual level of total raw material exports was reduced by one-third on the assumption that diminishing returns in mining combined with increased needs in engineering, metallurgy, and households would have eroded Britain's competitive position. This erosion would have been limited by increased use of mechanized power equipment in mines – thereby acting to raise output per man – and by the increased use of centrally generated electricity, a much more efficient use of coal than direct steam power.

ROW 9 – The value of exports of non-textile manufactured goods was taken from Table 4.3, columns (3) and (4). Column (3) represented a purposely low estimate of the impact of improved British technological performance on world export markets while column (4) represented a more optimistic estimate, yet one well within the bounds of the largest plausible estimate that could be suggested. The procedure was to add to column (3) half of the difference between columns (3) and (4). This procedure was a conservative one for it makes only limited allowance for the impact of improved British export performance on the level of world trade. See source notes to Table 4.3 and text. The estimates taken from Table 4.3, columns (3) and (4), were adjusted to reflect the difference in actual trading between 1907 and 1913. The adjustment factor was 0.811, the ratio of British domestic exports in 1907 to the corresponding figure for 1913. This represented a more severe adjustment than either of the plausible alternatives – adjustment by the expansion of total trade (0.828) or by the counterfactual growth of the economy (0.843). The historical trade data were taken from Mitchell and Deane (1962: 284).

ROW 10 – The value of miscellaneous exports were left unchanged from actual values.

ROW 11 – The value of the net export of services was estimated by assuming that such exports would bear counterfactually the same relationship to GNP as actual net exports of services in 1907 bore to actual GNP (which was 4.77%). It should be noted that this implies a faster rate of growth of trade in services than in commodities. The counterfactual expansion of trade in commodities is 23.8% greater than the actual 1907 value of trade in commodities while the expansion of (net) trade in services is 46.2% greater than the actual 1907 trade in (net) services. This procedure is, interestingly enough, entirely consistent with the counterfactual output levels of international shipping, financial and commercial services shown in Table 4.1, rows 17 and 23. Although actual British trade in services grew less rapidly than British trade in commodities between 1870 and 1913 – expanding only 2.26 times the 1870 value compared with an expansion of 2.58 times for commodities (Feinstein, 1972: Table 15 columns 1 plus 9 for commodities and columns 2 plus 10 for services) – over the last century trade in services has grown substantially more rapidly than trade in commodities. Between 1870 and 1938, commodity trade (nominal values) grew by a factor of 2.68 whereas services grew by a factor of 3.29. Between 1870 and 1965 the nominal value expansion factors were 18.72 and 33.41 for commodities and services respectively. See text for further discussion.

ROW 12 – The counterfactual figure for net property income from abroad was taken from Table 4.1, column (4), row 6. This sum was £24m less than that actually earned in 1907. It should be noted that the level of foreign investment implied by Table 4.2 (row B minus row A, column 2) is £67.5m. The implicit yield in this counterfactual level of investment was estimated to be 5.0%, compared with an actual yield, calculated on the same basis, of 4.7%. The yield rates were calculated as follows. The counterfactual level of net investment abroad in 1907 was £67.5m, or 2.08% of counterfactual GNP. The counterfactual average aggregate growth rate for the entire period 1870–1913 is 2.89% per year, a rate that yields an implict 1870 GNP of £1132m in constant 1907 prices. Feinstein's estimate of 1870 GNP in 1900 prices is £1118. Adjusting this latter estimate for the change in the implicit GNP deflator (see Feinstein, 1972: Table 61, column 5), which rises from 93.2 in 1900 to 95.4 in 1907 (1913 more rapid growth would have required even greater imports, the balance of payments constituted the most obvious barrier to more rapid expansion. The best method of assessing the plausibility of changes of growth rates and structure on the scale suggested in Table 4.1, therefore, is to begin with an examination of the imports and exports which such changes would most probably have generated. Table 4.2, with the accompanying notes describing the table's construction, indicates that an increase of Britain's growth rate by approximately 50% would have required surprisingly few changes in world trade before 1914. In essence, the results of Table 4.2 imply that raw material imports would have increased more rapidly than income and that this increase would have been compensated by a relatively small increase in Britain's imports of highly manufactured goods, by an increase in sales of British trading services sufficient to maintain the proportionate relationship between net British service exports and GNP that actually existed in 1907, and by an increase in British exports of manufactured goods.

The comparatively slight increase in British imports of manufactured goods may be seen as the natural consequence of the hypothetical growth of British industrial capabilities, a growth that would have made import penetration into the British home market more difficult and less profitable than it actually was, despite the greater import potential implicit in the higher counterfactual income levels. The growth of service exports would in part be the natural accompaniment to higher levels of trade. Net exports of British services in 1907 amounted to 11.3% of the total value of British commodity trade, taken as the sum of commodity exports and imports. Maintaining the same proportion of total commodity trade in the counterfactual variant would yield an increase in net exports of services equal to £25.3m.

The remaining increase in service exports of £23.6m would most plausibly

Notes to Table 4.2. (*cont.*)

= 100) yields a reference estimate of £1144m. Using the lower of the two estimates, and applying to that estimate the counterfactual 1907 level of net investment abroad yields a figure of £23.5m for net investment abroad in 1870 (= £1132 × 0.0208). The average of £23.5m and £67.5m is £45.5m, which is taken to represent the average rate of net foreign investment for each year in the period 1870–1907. The actual yield of 1870 of foreign investment was £35m (Feinstein, 1972: Table 3, column 6).

If the pre-1870 stock of foreign investment is assumed to remain intact, and the income flow from that stock is also assumed to remain unchanged, then the incremental return on the annual net investment abroad between 1870 and 1907 is taken to be the actual 1907 value of £144m less the 1870 value of £35m, or £109m. The flow of £109m was obtained by investing a total of £2333m abroad between 1870 and 1913. The figure of £2333m was obtained by summing the net investment abroad for each year from 1870 to 1907 (Feinstein, 1972: Table 15, column 16). Note that £109m/£2333m = 0.047. Similarly the counterfactual income from abroad of £120m was assumed to be composed of the earnings flow on pre-1870 investment plus the average yield on the accumulated post-1870 investment. If the average counterfactual net investment abroad for the period 1870–1907 was £45.5m, the total accumulated stock would be £1683.9m (= £45.5 × 37). The incremental yield would be £120m less £35m, or £85. Note that £85m/£1683.9m = 0.050. See text for further discussion.

have come from increased sales of insurance and other services of financial intermediaries. Such increased sales would be the natural accompaniment of the improved financial intermediation needed to undertake and support the timely and aggressive exploitation of the technical changes of the period and the more rapid domestic structural change such exploitation would have required. By holding more diversified portfolios while investing more intensively and directly in the industrial and commercial activities most closely linked to the important technological advances of the period, intermediaries would have been able to offer foreigners (as well as domestic clients) services and asset yields more attractive than those actually offered. Had the investment portfolios of insurance companies earned higher rates of return without increased risk, a possibility permitted by more efficient diversification, British insurers would easily have been able to have increased their global market share in such a rapidly growing, price elastic field by means of a slight decrease in premiums. The closer involvement of banks with domestic technical advances would have permitted more active, more competent participation in the fostering of technological change abroad.

An indication of the substantial profitability of such ventures may be found in Riesser (1911 [reprinted 1977]: 472–526) where the activities of the largest German banks, all of them with close foreign connections based on the extension of domestic technological capabilities – most notably in electrical engineering – are discussed. The average yield from all German foreign investments may be estimated at 5.4% (Riesser, 1911: 546), whereas the average dividend pay-out of the German Great Banks were at least 8% of capital. The dividends of the Deutsche Bank averaged 9.1% between 1870 and 1908, while showing a sustained tendency to rise (Riesser, 1911: 480–481). While the Deutsche Bank was the largest and most successful of the German Great Banks, and hence its profitability would tend to be systematically greater than its domestic rivals, it also had an unusually large foreign involvement stemming from its support of the German export trade. Taking account of the practice of the largest German banks to follow a conservative policy towards the accumulation of reserves, and of the inherently higher risks foreign lending entailed, the yield on German foreign banking services may easily be estimated at no less than 8% of the resources ventured. Making allowance for the dominant position British financial intermediaries had secured for themselves in international markets by the mid nineteenth century, had they contributed more fully to economic development at home they would also, as a natural extension of those activities, have enlarged their markets abroad.

In Table 4.2, however, the greatest adjustment is shown to take place in Britain's exports of manufactured goods other than textiles. (See Table 4.3 for a detailed breakdown of the counterfactual expansion of trade in non-textile manufactured goods.) The export levels shown in Table 4.2 imply that Britain's

Table 4.3. *International trade in non-textile manufactured goods, 1899 and 1913*

	(1) British exports (£m) 1899	(2) British exports (£m) 1913	(3) Counter- factual British exports low variant (£m) 1913	(4) Counter- factual British exports medium variant (£m) 1913
1 Iron and steel	£19.539m	£37.507	£51.860	£51.860
2 Non-ferrous metals	4.591	7.694	10.948	10.948
3 Chemicals, etc.	12.649	24.039	25.114	56.258
4 Non-metalliferous materials (abrasives, glass, bricks, etc.)	2.364	5.279	5.279	5.279
5 Miscellaneous materials (hides, rubber goods, cardboard, etc.)	4.252	8.792	9.247	9.247
6 Industrial equipment (non-electrical)	16.220	30.364	42.853	51.041
7 Electrical goods	1.917	7.655	10.955	16.593
8 Agricultural equipment	2.116	3.748	5.919	8.637
9 Railways, ships, etc.	15.958	24.260	28.458	28.458
10 Motor-cars, aircraft, etc.	0.662	7.616	10.731	24.138
11 Spirits, tobacco	4.231	9.685	9.685	9.685
12 Apparel	10.802	22.006	22.006	22.006
13 Other metal manufactures	10.929	21.102	21.102	21.102
14 Books, films, cameras, etc.	3.547	8.419	8.419	8.419
15 Other finished goods	6.288	11.591	11.591	11.591
16 Not otherwise classified	1.663	1.849	3.357	3.357
17 British total	£117.728m	£231.606m	£277.524m	£338.619m
18 World total	£443.752m	£971.534m	£971.534m	£1,054.779m
19 British share of world total	26.53%	23.84%	28.56%	32.10%

Sources:
Column (1) – Tysznski (1951: Table I, row 1, p. 277).

Column (2) – Tysznski (1951: Table II, row 1, p. 278).

Column (3) – The estimates were obtained by holding constant the last row in Table II (Tysznski, 1951: 278), the row setting out total 'world' exports of non-textile commodities in 1913, divided into 17 groups, and calculating Britain's exports by the proportion of total exports in each category Britain held in 1899. For example in 1899 Britain's share of total 'world' exports of industrial equipment was 0.3958% (= £16.230m/£40.984m). In 1913, total world exports of industrial equipment was £108.28m; 39.58% of £108.280m is £42.85m, the entry in Table 4.3, column (3), row 6. This represents a conservative estimate of Britain's possible expansion of exports because it makes no allowance for the impact of improved British technological performance, and hence British export performance, on the level of world trade.

share of world non-textile manufactured trade, rather than falling from 26.5% in 1899 to 23.8% in 1913, would have risen to a level of between 28.6% and 32.1%, depending upon how the impact of Britain's increased export capacity is assumed to have affected levels of world trade. Such an expansion of Britain's non-textile manufactured exports could only have occurred if Britain had continued to expand her trade in most categories and had performed particularly well in those groups, most notably iron, steel, chemicals, electrical goods and industrial equipment which were growing most rapidly in international trade and consumption. (See Table 4.3.) Such expansion would have demanded vigorous

Notes to Table 4.3. (*cont.*)

Column (4) – These estimates make some allowance for the impact of improved British export performance on world trade as well as allowing in the categories of chemicals, electrical goods, agricultural equipment, and motor vehicles Britain's share of world trade to exceed the shares held in 1899. In those four categories British performance was already by 1899 falling markedly behind that of other developed countries. In chemicals Britain held only 22.85% of world exports; in electrical goods, 33.21%; in agricultural equipment, 34.96%; in motor vehicles, 24.13%, whereas in iron and steel, Britain held 49.29%; in railways, ships and other traditional forms of transport equipment, 56.50%; and in industrial equipment, 39.58%. The British share of 'world' exports in chemicals, electrical goods, agricultural equipment, and motor vehicles was set equal to Britain's share in industrial equipment, 39.58%, a proportion greater than that registered for those sectors historically but still well below the share held by Britain in the important areas of iron and steel or what Tysznski described as 'old means of transport', railroads and ships. In addition to this adjustment, total 'world' trade in five sectors (chemicals, industrial equipment, electrical equipment, agricultural equipment, and motor vehicles) was assumed to expand by the increment of Britain's increased output. The calculation was made according to the following formula:

$$y_i + z_i = n(m_i + z_i)$$

where $y_i =$ Britain's actual absolute value of exports of ith category (e.g. chemicals, electrical equipment) in 1913,

$z_i =$ the counterfactual expansion of the i export category (the variable to be solved for),

$n =$ the hypothesized share of total 'world' exports held by Britain in each of the five specified categories, set equal for each of them to 0.3958, Britain's 1913 share of total 'world' exports of industrial equipment,

$m_i =$ actual total 'world' exports of the ith category.

This procedure is justified by noting that in each of these five sectors technical change and the appearance of new and improved goods was particulary rapid and that, therefore, it is entirely reasonable to expect that, had Britain contributed more fully to the technological advance of the period, the resultant productivity gains and flows of new products would have created larger markets. Indeed, the extent of the hypothetical creation of new markets is conservatively estimated by the procedure outlined above. See text for further discussion.

ROW 18, columns (1), (2) and (3): Total value of 'world' exports of manufactured commodities *less* 'world' exports of textiles. The data are found in Tysznski (1951), Tables I and II, respectively. Column (3) is the same as column (2) by the assumption that improved British export performance had *no* impact on world trade levels.

ROW 18, column (4): This figure was found by adding the z_i calculated above to actual 1913 'world' export values for each of the five enumerated categories. The total was £83.245m, composed as follows: chemicals, £32.219m; industrial equipment, £20.677m; electrical equipment, £8.938m; agricultural equipment, £4.889m; and motor vehicles, £16.522m.

development of technological capabilities and their deployment with skill, but not to a degree unknown in other countries at the time.

Despite the sizeable balance of payments surplus (£67.5m) shown in Table 4.2, it may still be argued that balance of payments difficulties would have been possible had Britain's industrial structure changed more rapidly. These difficulties would most plausibly have arisen from two sources. First, the demand for British exports may have been adversely affected by the reduced level of British foreign investment implied in Table 4.2, where the counterfactual 1907 level of foreign investment (assumed to be equal to the balance of payments surplus) is only 41.7% of the actual 1907 level of £162m, while it is assumed that manufactured exports would rise by 38.1% over the actual 1907 value. A.G. Ford (1965: 22–4) has clearly shown that British foreign lending, directly or indirectly, stimulated British exports. The indicated increase in exports would thus have had to take place in a world trading environment which in some respects was less favourable than the one which existed historically. Second, reduced foreign investment would have tended to reduce supply capacity in those countries exporting heavily to Britain. Thus, British import prices, squeezed by higher demand and reduced supply, might have risen sharply; since demand for imports in important categories was generally inelastic, payments difficulties would follow sharp increases in import prices.

To counterbalance these pessimistic possibilities, however, four other factors must be considered. First, a very generous allowance for increased imports of food and raw materials has been made in Table 4.2, as well as conservative estimates of exports generally. The cushion of a balance of payments surplus can, therefore, reasonably be claimed to be more ample than has been allowed. In addition, a lower level of foreign investment, in the very short run, would have actually relieved the disruptive balance of payments strain which did arise periodically before 1914 as a result of vast sums of sterling being placed abroad in the course of British portfolio investment (Ford, 1965: 19).

Secondly, of more importance, is the stimulus to world trade which more rapid British growth would have produced. Trade was (and is) an important vehicle for the spread of industrialization. Increasing trade in the nineteenth century widened the markets for the goods which primary producing and newly industrializing countries were able to export and provided them, in turn, with the resources to accomplish further economic transformation themselves. The growth which this transformation generated was itself one of the most important reasons for sustained increases in world trade. More rapid growth in Britain, with its attendant increase in demand for imports, would have permitted a stimulus to world trade perhaps more durable and more potent than that which was possible through foreign lending of the kind which Britain actually conducted. In this view, the increased British demand for imports implied by faster British growth is a measure of the loss to the world economy caused by sluggish performance in its most important member and this loss may very reasonably be believed to be greater than any gain stemming from higher levels of the conservative foreign lending in which Britain so persistently engaged.

Furthermore, the actual extent of the stimulus to world trade administered by British foreign investment before 1914 may be questioned. Even before 1890, the direct relationship between British foreign investment and British exports had become tenuous.[4] After 1890 it was starkly obvious that the connection was very indirect (Hobson, 1914: 17–18). For example, in the massive wave of foreign investment which took place after 1903, British lending was heavily concentrated on Canada, yet the U.S. supplied most of the physical capital equipment. British lending at this time in Europe, on the other hand, was comparatively small, yet Europe absorbed well over one-third of all domestic British exports (Ford, 1965: 334–6). The impact which British foreign investment had on British exports operated in a complicated fashion through the overall level of world trade and faster British growth would have operated through world trade in a similar fashion. It is not clear that the increased stimulus from more trade would have been less successful than the stimulus from higher levels of British lending.

The third factor acting to strengthen Britain's balance of payments in a counterfactual Victorian world of faster British growth was Britain's small and falling share of world demand for primary products. It was the growth of the primary producing countries themselves which accounted for the great bulk of increased demand for these products (Olson, 1974). Increased British demand on a scale implied by Table 4.2 would not, of itself, given the magnitudes revealed by Olson's research, have been sufficient to push primary prices sharply upwards. For example, in the case of wheat, the most important of the internationally traded agricultural commodities in the Victorian period and the one where Britain's reliance on imports was greatest, amounting by 1914 to 80% of domestic consumption, Britain's imports in the years 1885–9 amounted to 9.7% of the total wheat production of the wheat exporting nations (Olson, 1974: 333). By 1909–14 this proportion had fallen to 8.1%, Britain's incremental increase in imports, despite falling British domestic production, taking only 6.1% of the incremental increase in the wheat output of the wheat exporting nations. Had British demand for wheat increased by 18.8%, the proportionate increase in retained food imports shown in row 1 of Table 4.2, Britain's imports as a fraction of the total wheat production of the wheat exporting nations would still have fallen, but to 8.6% rather than to 8.1%, with Britain's incremental import demand accounting for 7.2% rather than 6.1% of the incremental output of the wheat exporting nations. At the very most, this increased demand would have reduced, but certainly not eliminated, the contractionary pressures exerted on wheat growers everywhere in the early twentieth century. To assume otherwise would impute to Britain a share of world consumption which it did not in fact possess and could not conceivably attain.

The fourth factor, closely related to the third, concerns the role which British foreign investment played in increasing the world supply of primary products. That British foreign lending increased supplies, directly by investing in extractive activities and indirectly by investing in the transport networks needed to move raw materials, cannot be denied. Yet the aggregate yield on British investments was so low that the role of most of Britain's foreign investment could hardly have been indispensible. Because the bulk of British foreign investment was in relatively safe but unventuresome activities only 11% of British portfolio investments yielded returns as high as those obtained on the average domestic investment and yet these investments generated fully 25% of Britain's massive foreign investment income in 1913 (Kennedy, 1974: 432–33). Had any tendency for prices of primary goods to rise sharply developed, increased British foreign investments in the production of those increasingly valuable commodities would have shielded the balance of payments from any excessive pressure. By participating by direct investment in any foreign activity which Britain stimulated through her own import requirements, the balance of payments would become in an important sense self-balancing. The £120m allowed in Table 4.2 for the counterfactual yield on net foreign investments leaves ample scope for a pattern of British foreign investment more progressive than the one actually pursued. The counterfactual level of earnings required an increase of only 0.3%, from 4.7% to 5.0%, in the net yield of British foreign investment (see notes to Table 4.2). Much more could plausibly have been expected.

In fact it is easy to imagine, through a restructuring of foreign investments similar to the proposed counterfactual restructuring of the domestic economy, that earnings on foreign investments could have risen while the level of foreign investment fell. This restructuring of foreign investment would have required greater involvement with those activities expanding most rapidly. This meant manufacturing and American manufacturing in particular rather than world primary production, investment which (including related transport developments) was the hallmark of the foreign lending Britain actually made in the nineteenth century. Had such restructuring taken place, the world economy would have benefited in two important ways. First, the transfer of advanced technology from Britain would have remained at levels close to those of the mid nineteenth century in contrast with the dismal level of transfer from Britain which actually took place in the early twentieth century. Britain would have benefited, as occurred earlier with railroads, from the wider scope this transfer offered for further application of the technological progress achieved domestically in the course of faster growth. The rest of the world would have gained from more immediate access to the enhanced technology originating in the country at the centre of the international economy.

Secondly, it is only through technological advance, both in economizing on the raw material requirements of modern economic activity and in reducing the cost of initial extraction, that the upward pressures on raw material prices are contained. Greater concentration of British investment in areas of rapid technological advance would, therefore, in the long-run have played a more powerful, although more indirect, role in keeping raw material prices low than did actual British investment in nineteenth-century raw material production and transportation. Any bottlenecks created by the low supply elasticities of primary products would ultimately have had to have been altered by technological means if they were to be altered at all. A different pattern of British foreign investment, one involving more participation in the technological progress of the time, would very likely have ultimately yielded lower raw material costs than were achieved by the investment which Britain did in fact undertake.

It is possible, however, that a more aggressive pattern of foreign investment, one yielding higher mean rates of return, might have exposed Britain more fully to the dangers of greater fluctuations in income earned abroad. The strength of the British balance of payments in the period 1870–1914 rested not only on the size of the income earned abroad, but also on its stability. In reality, as in theory, low mean foreign rates of return were, in part, compensated by low variance of return. This danger, however, while real, should not be overstressed. First of all, the flows of British foreign investment implied by the counterfactual structural changes are not particularly small in absolute terms although they are much smaller than the actual flows in relative terms. Thus even in the counter-factual model the buffer provided by Britain's stock of foreign assets is quite substantial. Income from abroad would still have been, on average, quite large even with less foreign lending. Secondly, investments distri-buted among many different regions and industries offered great opportunities for diversification. So long as the covariances of yields on foreign investments were either small or negative, the variance of the yield from Britain's aggregate foreign portfolio could have been proportionately less than the variance of the individual assets which comprised the portfolio. Indeed, by failing to invest in the important new technologies and new industries as they emerged, particularly in the U.S., Britain's actual pattern of foreign investment was less diversified and thus riskier than it might reasonably have been, and hence a more aggressive and alert strategy of investment diversification might well have yielded both higher returns and greater safety, especially in the long-run. Third, the low variance of the rate of return on British foreign investment before 1914 was in part fortuitous. Much of Britain's foreign investment was in fixed interest assets and, therefore, highly vulnerable to inflation. Although the dangers of this situation did not become clear until mercilessly exposed by the inflation which accompanied World War I, they were clearly present – if generally latent – before 1914.

In summary, the faster growth which would have accompanied the structural changes set out in Table 3.6, would not, in all probability, have precipitated balance of payments difficulties. The proposed changes would have enhanced

Britain's ability to exploit rapidly and fully any changes in world export demand and to restrict efficiently, competitively and effectively import penetration in home markets. Even in a counterfactual world where foreign lending was substantially reduced, net income from abroad would still have been substantial and, depending upon the assumptions made concerning the distribution by area and activity of the reduced foreign lending, potentially better able to accommodate Britain's needs in a rapidly industrializing world than the foreign investments actually amassed. In no sense would faster British growth have inevitably spawned a balance of payments crisis; instead the likelihood of such a crisis would have been reduced. As it was, despite the appearance of massive solidity, Britain's balance of payments in 1913 rested perilously on the preservation of a very special, very fragile international economic environment. Once this environment was destroyed, and with it much of the very real advantage Britain had acquired as the world's first industrial nation, British balance of payments crises became endemic. These crises were all the more severe and intractable because of the pronounced inability to achieve quickly and effectively the domestic structural adaptation required by changing markets and technologies.

In addition to meeting greater import requirements by higher levels of exports – Table 4.2 indicates that £50.7m worth of additional commodity exports and £48.9m worth of net service exports would have been needed – a portion of the expanded capacity of the British economy would have had to have been directed towards capital formation within Britain. The medium growth model of counterfactual development would have required a higher rate of overall capital stock (including human capital) expansion than actually did occur. First, much of the resources invested abroad historically would have had been devoted to domestic transformation. Such a shift, had it diverted all foreign investment, would have doubled domestic investment in 1907. Furthermore, Kuznets has shown that both the U.S. and Germany invested a substantially larger share of GNP in the late nineteenth century than did the U.K. (Kuznets, 1961: 58–59, 64). If the proportion of income invested by the U.K. had risen to 25.8% (including stockbuilding) of hypothetical 1907 GNP, thereby reaching a level comparable with the investment rates of the other large technologically advanced economies of the period, rather than remaining at the actual, distinctly low, level of 15.5%, the total amount of investment required would have been £836.6m rather than the £322m actually invested at home and abroad in 1907. Allowing £67.5m for foreign investment (see Table 4.4, line 6 (b) ii) the counterfactual level of domestic investment in 1907 would have been £769.1m compared with the £160m worth of domestic investment (including stockbuilding) actually made in that year. Such a change would have increased domestic investment demand by £609.1m. Together increased exports and increased domestic investment would have raised expenditure requirements by

Table 4.4. *Estimate of consumption, 1907, in medium growth variant*[1]

1	Retained imports of industrial raw materials (CIF)	£287.5m
	(row 2 plus row 4, column 2, Table 4.2)	
2	Retained imports of manufactured and other goods (CIF)	175.4
	(row 3 plus row 5, column 2, Table 4.2)	
3	Retained imports of foodstuffs (CIF)	279.4
	(row 1, column 2, Table 4.2)	
4	GNP (row 25, column 3, Table 4.1)	3247.6
5	Total market value of product available in U.K.	£3989.9m
	(sum of rows 1–4)	
6a	Less: exports of goods and (net) services	£631.6m
	(sum of rows 6 to 10 plus row 11, column 2, Table 4.2)	
6b	Less: total capital formation	811.9
	(assumed equal to 25.0% of GNP)	
	(i) of which: domestic gross capital formation £744.4m	
	(ii) of which: net foreign investment 67.5	
	(row B minus row A, column 2, Table 4.2)	
6c	Less: domestic stock building[2]	25.0
6d	Sum of rows 6a to 6c.	£1468.5m
7	Total market value of product available in U.K. for private	
	and government consumption, medium growth variant	
	(row 5 minus row 6d)	2521.4
8	Actual 1907 market value of consumers' expenditure	
	and public authorities current expenditure on goods and	
	services (Feinstein, 1972: Table 2, column 1 plus column 2)	1974.0
9	Ratio of counterfactual consumption to actual 1907	
	consumption (row 7 divided by row 8)	1.277
10	Absolute counterfactual increase in consumption	
	(row 7 minus row 8)	£547.4m

Source: Tables 4.1 and 4.2, except where otherwise noted. The source is given in brackets beside entry.

Notes:

[1] Table 4.4 represents only one of many plausible representations of the distribution of counterfactual national income. Another very reasonable alternative would have been to assume more (less) rapid British importation of manufactured goods, holding exports of goods and services constant, thereby forcing down (up) the counterfactual level of British foreign investment. If the assumption that 25% of GNP was to have been invested at home or abroad is maintained, then the increase (decrease) in manufactured imports would be exactly offset by an increase (decrease) in domestic investment, causing the centre of investment activity to shift more (less) decisively to the British Isles.

[2] From Feinstein (1972: Table 2, column 4), the average value of stock building, here defined to include work in progress, was found to be £17.04m over the entire period 1870–1913. From Table 4.1, row 25, the expansion factor of counterfactual to actual output was 1.462. £17.04 × 1.462 = £24.91m. This figure was rounded up to the £25m estimate used above.

£709.0m. (From Table 4.2, column 2 minus column 1, row (11) and row for 'total exports of goods'.)

Finally, and most importantly, it must be shown that the counterfactual structure of output would have been capable of supporting a higher level of consumption, the ultimate object of all economic activity. This is done in Table 4.4. The sum of imports and value added arising from all British economic activity constitutes the market value of output produced in Britain which would have been available for consumption (including government consumption), domestic capital formation and export in the counterfactual medium growth variant of structural change. The levels of export and gross domestic capital formation have already been discussed. Note that in the counterfactual model, exports of goods and net services are equal to 19.4% of counterfactual GNP while imports of commodities (net of freight and handling charges) are equal to 21.1% of counterfactual GNP. In 1907, total exports of goods and net services were actually 23.9% and commodity imports (net of freight and handling charges) were 23.0% of GNP. Thus the relative importance of foreign trade is less in the counterfactual model than it was in reality. This arises because of the assumption of a comparatively low income elasticity of demand for imports of food and textile materials partially offsetting a rapid rise of raw materials and manufactured imports on the one hand, and, on the other, the assumption that while non-textile exports would rise rapidly, exports of textiles and raw materials would stagnate, the net result being a slower rate of growth of exports than of GNP. Therefore, taking imports and exports of commodities and services together, the counterfactual model shows an increase in domestic consumption arising from international trade equal to 2.6% of GNP, achieved by reducing the export surplus from 0.9% of GNP to − 1.7% of GNP. This increase was made possible by a fall in net foreign investment from 7.29% of (actual) GNP to 2.08% of (counterfactual) GNP.

The hypothesized increase in investment's share of GNP is large and such an increase directly acts to restrict consumption. Counterfactual 1907 domestic capital formation (including stock-building) is 23.7% of GNP whereas in 1907 domestic capital formation, including increased stockholding, was actually only 7.7% of GNP. The counterfactual model assumes that the bulk of British capital formation would take place domestically whereas historically this bulk increasingly tended to occur overseas as the U.K. accumulated financial claims on the rest of the world. It is this increase in domestic capital formation of 16.0% of GNP combined with a reduction in the relative importance of net property income from abroad, which accounts for the fact that counterfactual consumption increased by only 27.7% over the actual 1907 value of consumption while counterfactual GNP increased by over 46.2% over actual 1907 GNP.[5] Historically not only did Britain in 1907 invest a much smaller proportion of GNP than is shown in the counterfactual model, but of that investment foreigners contributed a disproportionate amount, as is shown by the actual relative importance in 1907 of net property income from abroad compared with its relative importance in the counterfactual model. Increased consumption is compatible with the higher rates of saving embedded in the counterfactual model because the capital stock that results from the more intensive investment would be, as it actually was in the U.S., sufficiently more productive to sustain a markedly higher level of consumption. While the increase in consumption is small compared with the increase in GNP, it is still impressive; the indicated increase yields a level of per capita consumption not equalled until the 1930's. Furthermore, the increase in consumption is conservatively estimated by setting the proportion of GNP invested fully 66.4% above its historical level in 1907, a level which was well above the overall average of 14.0% for the period 1870–1913 (see Table 4.7). The counterfactual model of structural change thus satisfies the requirement that in terms of end uses the pattern of output implied by the model is plausible.

A further check of consistency is set out in Table 4.5. The purpose of that Table is to confirm that the increased demands for investment, exports, and consumption can be met by the sectoral structure of output generated by the medium growth variant. Part A of the Table provides estimates – obtained by summing value added in successive stages of production – of the increased value of final output available to satisfy demands for investment goods, commodity exports, and consumer durables. The relevant sum is £561.1m. Part B provides estimates of the increased value of output available for current consumption, including government expenditure on goods and services but excluding all consumer durables. The total for Part B is £409.7m. Part C presents the calculations necessary to achieve a reasonable allocation of increased distribution and transport charges, equal to £227m, among the various categories of goods. Part D brings together the increased output produced in the medium growth variant that is available to meet the various demands made on that output by investment, export, and consumption requirements. In Line 16 of Table 4.5 an estimate of increased consumer durable production is given. It is only £72.1m, obtained by subtracting from the estimate of total increased consumption given in Table 4.4 (£574.4m) the increased net value of non-durable consumption goods produced in the medium growth variant. The increase in the net value of the consumption of durable goods is only 15.2% of the increase in the net value of non-durable consumption (which here includes the consumption of housing services).[6] This low proportion is a faithful reflection of the importance of food, clothing, public passenger transportation, personal services, and rent in Victorian consumption patterns, although it is a pattern that has become less typical as the twentieth century has progressed.

The medium growth variant shows production available for investment, commodity export, and durable goods production equal to £722.5m while the hypothesized structure of demand would have generated an output requirement of £732.2m, or £9.7m greater than the amount available. This discrepancy is small, and at 1.3% of the counterfactual level of increased demands as required by the medium growth variant, well within the margin of error inherent in the data available. Moreover, the discrepancy could have been eliminated by any one of a

Table 4.5. *Consistency check on 1907 sectoral output levels, medium growth variant*

A Value of increased output available for investment, commodity export, and consumer durables.

  1 Increase in manufactured output, value added (from Table 4.1)

Construction		£56.1m
Iron and steel production		27.7
Engineering		106.2
Electricity, telecommunications and scientific instruments		36.3
Brick, cement, glass		18.9
Chemicals (class (a))		25.8
Mining		55.2
Shipbuilding		9.5
Timber		8.8
Miscellaneous	168.1	
less: increase in imputed housing services (taken to be the difference between 6.6% of counterfactual GNP and 6.6% of actual 1907 GNP)	82.1	86.0
Total		£430.5m

  2 Increase in available imports of raw materials, non-textile (CIF at port of entry) (from row 4, Table 4.2)   85.7m

  3 Increase in available imports of manufactured goods (CIF at port of entry) (from rows (3) and (5), Table 4.2)   44.9

  4 Total (sum of rows 1 to 3)   £561.1m

B Value of total increase in current consumption (including government expenditure on current goods and services but excluding consumer durables).

5 Increased food availability		£90.0m
of which: imports (from Table 4.2)	£44.3m	
: domestic output (from Table 4.1)	45.7	
Increased value of personal services (from Table 4.1)		19.4
Increased value of domestic services (from Table 4.1)		− 16.5
Increased value gas undertakings (from Table 4.1)		− 4.1
Increased value of clothing (value added) (from Table 4.1)		22.9
Increased value of textiles (value added) (from Table 4.1)		12.5
Increased value of food processing (value added) (from Table 4.1)		20.7
Increased value of government and professional services (value added) (from Table 4.1)		73.4
Increased value of paper, printing and publishing (value added) (from Table 4.1)		73.5
Increased value of available imports of textile material (from Table 4.1)		12.8

Table 4.5. (*cont.*)

Increased value of consumption of passenger transport services (see Note 1)	23.0
Increased value of imputed housing services (see details in Line 1 above)	82.1
Total (sum of entries above)	£409.7m

C Allocation of increased value added in transportation and distribution.

6 Increase of value added in domestic wholesale-retail trade (from Table 4.1) — £173.1m

Increase in domestic transportation services (from Table 4.1)	£76.9m
less: passenger transport services (see note 1)	23.0
Adjusted increase in transportation services	£53.9m
Total (sum of entries above)	£227.0m

7 Value added from Section A passing through distribution and transportation system — £561.2

8 Value added from Section B passing through distribution and transportation system

Total from Section B	£409.7m
less: personal services	19.4
less: domestic services	−16.5
less: government and professional services	73.4
less: passenger transport services	23.0
less: imputed housing services	82.1
Total	£228.3

9 Total output (value added) passing through distribution and transport system (row 7 plus row 8) — £789.5m

10 Proportion of Line 9 attributed to Section A output (row 7 divided by row 9) — 0.711

11 Proportion of Line 9 attributed to Section B output (row 8 divided by row 9) — 0.289

12 Transport and distribution charges associated with Section A (row 6 times row 10) — £161.4m

13 Transport and distribution charges associated with Section B (row 6 times row 11) — £65.6m

D Distribution of increase in final output among ultimate uses.

14 Total value of increased output available for domestic capital formation, commodity export, and consumer durables (sum of rows 4 and 12) — £722.5m

15 Total value of increased output available for current (non-durable) consumption (sum of rows 5 and 13) — £475.3m

16 Value of increased output of durable consumption goods

Total increase in consumption (from row 10, Table 4.4)	£547.4m
Less: non-durable consumption (row 15 above)	475.3m
Total increase	£72.1m

Table 4.5. (*cont.*)

17 Required increase in output	
by: domestic gross fixed capital formation (row 6b(i), Table 4.4) less actual 1907 domestic gross fixed capital formation of £150m (Feinstein, 1972: Table 2, column 2)	£594.4m
by: domestic stockbuilding (row 6c, Table 4.4) less actual 1907 domestic stockbuilding of £10m. (Feinstein, 1972: Table 2, column 3)	£15.0m
by: commodity exports (from Table 4.2: sum of rows 6 to 10 column 2 less sum of rows 6 to 10 column 1)	£50.7m
by: consumer durable goods (row 16 above)	£72.1m
Total	£732.2
18 Discrepancy (row 14 minus row 17) (see note 2)	−£9.7m

Notes:

[1] From Data Appendix A (p. 16) the total net value added in the provision of passenger transport services was found to be £49.8m. This value was then multiplied by 1.462, the ratio of counterfactual to actual 1907 output, yielding an estimate of counterfactual net value added in passenger transport services of £72.8m. This procedure implicitly assumes that the income elasticity of demand for passenger transport services is unity. The total increase in passenger transport services is thus £23.0m(= £72.8m – £49.8m).

[2] The discrepancy shows the amount by which the increases in gross domestic fixed capital formation, domestic stockbuilding, commodity exports and consumer durables required by various assumptions (e.g. total investment equal 25% of GNP), exceeded the production of goods and services destined to satisfy these requirements. The discrepancy, under £10m, is within the error noted in Table 4.1 and may easily be explained by inaccuracies in a small, but admittedly difficult-to-measure sector such as stock-building. The important fact is that the counterfactual structural changes proposed in Chapter 3 did not imply a structure of output that could not plausibly satisfy the investment, export, and consumption, particularly of durable goods, requirements of a rapidly growing economy.

It should be noted that more accurate allocations of professional services (of architects and engineers for example) and of the value added in the sector of paper, printing and publishing would not alter the conclusions. To allocate such output to Section A from Section B would simultaneously increase the output available for investment, commodity exports, and consumer durables but at the same time increase the difference between the hypothesized level of total consumption and current, non-durable consumption. The main impact, therefore, of such shifts would be to increase the volume of consumption labelled 'consumer durables' and at the same time and by precisely the same amounts, increase the output requirements of those sectors and industries that would have to satisfy the durable consumption requirements.

A more precise specification of the main components of 'consumer durables' is made difficult because the sectoral output values are in terms of net value added, not in terms of the sales of final product of each sector, since such sales involve double-counting by including all intermediate goods. It may be hazarded, however, that much of the increase in spending on consumer durables would have number of re-specifications of the model, including a slight reduction in the high levels of investment, especially foreign investment, or in stock-building. Stock-building in particular is generously provided for in the medium growth variant because the improved communications, transport, and office equipment facilities implicit in the medium growth variant would have permitted more efficient and effective inventory control and disposition than was historically possible. It is interesting in this context to see the sharp proportionate fall in American inventory levels as the American transportation system was improved in the last quarter of the nineteenth century (U.S. Bureau of the Census, 1975: Series F-96; also Kuznets, 1966:257). The most plausible elimination of the discrepancy, however, would have required a slight modification in the specification of the medium growth variant to have permitted a slightly more rapid expansion of engineering, electricity, chemical, and telecommunications output. The medium growth variant was determined essentially by imposing a structure of manu-facturing output on the British economy similar to that which existed in the U.S. in 1909. A superior variant would have required a slightly greater shift towards the output pattern displayed in the high growth variant (see Table 3.9) in which sectors such as chemicals and engineering were held to have gained a larger share of final output than in the medium growth variant. Such a shift would have been more compatible with British resource endowments, which encouraged exploit-ation of organizational and technological skills to compensate for the reserves of natural resources that were substantially less ample than in the U.S. Furthermore such an output pattern would have permitted greater consumption of consumer durables without any reduction in production of capital goods, a change consonant with twentieth-century consumption patterns (Kuznets, 1966: 276–7).

Although a formal demonstration, under reasonable assumptions regarding consumer preferences and industrial production possibilities (including the specification of technical progress), that there existed a plausible vector of equilibrium prices supporting the counterfactually higher level of income would greatly strengthen the argument, it is clear that the medium growth variant cannot be rejected on the grounds of generating, as Meyer's model does, a counterfactual level of output which is unrealistic because the implied structure of output cannot be imagined or because a balance of payments constraint is violated. The hypothesized growth occurs, not by magnification of the existing economy, but rather by the more abundant provision of goods and services whose mass production was made possible (and highly profitable) by the new technologies of the late nineteenth century and whose demand was largely guaranteed by rising incomes.

Notes to Table 4.5. (*cont.*)

taken the form of transport equipment, especially automobiles and related goods, household fitments, especially for plumbing and heating needs, and goods like vacuum cleaners, refrigerators, irons and so forth that were beginning to appear in quantity in the opening years of the twentieth century.

Table 4.6. *Estimates of labour force productivity compatible with medium growth variant*[1]

(1) Sector	(2) Percentage change in sector's share of counterfactual output (value added)	(3) Actual labour force in sector, 1907 (000s)	(4) Counterfactual change in sector's labour force (000s)	(5) Actual net output (value added) per worker 1907	(6) Counterfactual 1907 output (value added) per worker[2]	(7) Actual American output per worker 1909	(8) Ratio of Col (6) ÷ Col (7)
1 Textiles	−31.90%	1,253	−400	£75.28	£125.28	£157.41	0.795
2 Domestic service	−48.92	2,098	−1026	35.41	53.92	49.03	1.100
3 Agriculture	−12.55	2,214	−278	66.85	100.12	86.20	1.161
4 Domestic wholesale-retail trade	−2.21	2,470	−55	165.13	240.50	262.82	0.915
5 Gas undertakings	−50.00	83	−42	207.30	316.40	460.62	0.687
6 Net property income from abroad	−44.86	(See note 3)					
Total change			−1801				
7 Construction	43.98	841	370	£74.10	£97.74	£184.92	0.528
8 Iron, steel trades	43.33	262	114	114.51	153.94	268.38	0.574
9 Engineering	86.29	648	559	106.48	145.18	241.67	0.601
10 Paper, printing and publishing	144.55	325	470	100.31	133.46	263.41	0.507
11 Electricity, tele-communication, scientific instruments	254.17	82	208	145.12	166.01	249.47	0.665
12 Brick, cement, glass	61.90	206	128	83.01	107.66	191.68	0.562
13 Chemicals: class (a)	85.25	126	104	159.52	197.08	320.28	0.615
Total change			1953				

Table 4.6. (cont.)

(1) Sector	(2) Percentage change in sector's counterfactual output (value added)	(3) Actual labour force in sector, 1907 (000s)	(4) Counterfactual change in sector's labour force (000s)	(5) Actual net output (value added) per worker 1907	(6) Counterfactual 1907 output (value added) per worker[2]	(7) Actual American output per worker 1909	(8) Ratio of Col (6) ÷ Col (7)
14 Mining	0.00%	965	—	£123.87	£181.04	£187.02	0.968
15 Shipbuilding	0.00	214	—	98.24	142.52	192.32	0.741
16 Food processing	0.00	372	—	119.97	170.70	259.06	0.659
17 International shipping	0.00	(See note 4)	—				
18 Clothing	0.00	807	—	61.71	90.09	190.97	0.472
19 Timber trades	0.00	215	—	90.15	131.76	172.78	0.762
20 Personal services	0.00	908	—	46.26	67.60	95.23	0.710
21 Professional and governmental services	0.00	1,668	—	95.38	139.41	142.89	0.976
22 Domestic transportation	0.00	1,364	—	122.25	178.67	206.38	0.866
23 International financial and commercial services	0.00	(See note 5)	—				
24 Miscellaneous[6]	0.00	3,024	—	120.34	175.88	314.16	0.560
25 Aggregate economy	0.00	20,145	—	110.30	161.21	172.78	0.933
26 Aggregate economy excluding agriculture	0.00	17,931	—	115.66	167.16	215.08	0.777

Sources:

Column (2) – column (3) of Table 3.6 divided by column (2) of the same Table. This yields somewhat different results than would have been obtained using the difference between columns (2) and (4) of Table 4.1, divided by column (2) of that Table, because the latter is concerned only with 1907 whereas the former is concerned with average differences over the entire period. The procedure used here tends to overstate labour shift requirements.

Column (3) – data Appendixes A and C.

Column (4) – column (3) × column (2).

Column (5) – output and employment data taken from Appendices A and C.

Column (6) – column (3), Table 4.1 divided by the sum of column (3) plus (4), Table 4.6.

Column (7) – data Appendices B and C.

Column (8) – column (6) divided by column (7).

Notes:

[1] Table 4.6 is not an attempt to estimate the most likely changes in employment levels induced by faster growth but only an illustration based on the assumption that employment changes would move in the same proportion as output shares.

[2] All calculations are made in terms of 1907 prices. Given the magnitude of the counterfactual changes, 1907 prices would very probably have been altered had faster growth occurred. However, even assuming relative prices would have changed, the calculations reported in Table 4.6 still yield a measure of the volume of real output implied in the medium growth variant even if the interpretation of the value of this new volume of output is not straightforward.

[3] No particular labour force can be identified with the flow of net property income from abroad. The earnings arising from the handling of foreign remittance to Britain by merchant bankers, coupon agents, solicitors, and other professional workers, along with their supporting clerical staffs, are included in the sector 'international financial and commercial services'. The impact of high levels of net property income from abroad on output per man is reflected in the global estimate of GNP per British worker (rows 25 and 26).

[4] Because the Census did not record British subjects engaged in providing international shipping services unless they were within the territorial limits of the United Kingdom at the time of the Census and because the British owners of ships engaged in international trade drew on an international labour force, no attempt has been made to estimate output per British worker in this sector. Output per man in the sector, however, is reflected in the global estimates presented in row 25 and 26 of this Table. Output per worker in domestic transportation (row 22) may be taken as a reasonable first approximation to output per worker in international shipping.

[5] No attempt has been made to estimate output per worker in this sector because of the difficulty of making a proper allocation of workers engaged in providing professional services domestically and internationally. Moreover, the conceptual problems in estimating output per man in this sector are compounded by the unusually large proportion of earnings within the sector that must be attributed to the financial resources deployed there in maintaining inventories, discounting bills of exchange, issuing commercial credit, providing insurance cover, and so on. To make no provision for output per worker in this sector over-estimates value added per worker in the sector 'professional services' (row 21). The significance of output in the sector is reflected in the global estimates presented in rows 25 and 26 of this Table, where domestic and international services are aggregated together. Also, rows 25 and 26 reflect the overall impact of the existence of sectors with substantial value added where labour earnings are relatively small.

[6] The relatively large size of output per worker in this sector in both the U.S. and U.K. is due most obviously to the inclusion in the sector of imputed income from dwellings.

Supply constraints may be accorded even less importance than the demand constraints just considered. Since much of the counterfactual growth is held to have taken place in the capital goods sector, the constraint of an inadequate capital stock would have been eased by the process of growth itself. This would have entailed greater, but not superhuman, saving. The argument has rested on the belief that a much more efficient allocation of resources was both feasible and desirable and has required at most only a moderate increase, relative to the other large, advanced economies of the time, in the proportion of GNP invested. The bolder application of electricity and the swifter utilization of new machine tools, communication equipment, and organizational methods by a better trained and educated labour force would have acted to ensure that diminishing returns in production would not have accompanied the subsequent increase in investment implied by the medium growth variant.

Nor would a shortage of labour have constituted an effective constraint to higher output in the medium growth variant. Table 4.6 indicates that if the labour force in each sector had gained or lost workers in the same proportion as the sector gained or lost in relative importance of output – a procedure that overstates labour requirements because it makes no allowance for the greater capital intensity and inherently greater labour productivity of most of the expanding sectors – the declining sectors would have lost 1.80m workers while the expanding sectors would have gained 1.95m workers. If account is taken of the fact that many of the workers released from the declining sectors – especially from domestic service – would have been women, who, judging from their earnings, possessed only limited skills and mobility, it would appear, superficially, that labour shortages might have been expected to hamper economic expansion. However, when labour productivity is considered, it may be readily realized that labour shortages could not have seriously hindered more rapid growth.

Using the mechanical procedure of altering sectoral labour inputs by precisely the same proportion as relative output changes – a conservative procedure that overstates overall labour requirements – yields only two instances of sectors where value added per worker in the counterfactual medium growth variant would be greater than value added per worker in the same sector in the U.S. This occurred in domestic services where the differential was 10% and in agriculture where the differential was 16%. The outcome for domestic service was produced by the fact that American productivity, as indicated by the low wages of American domestic servants, relative to other workers, was quite low and the proposed sectoral reduction in the U.K. was unusually large. The outcome for agriculture was also produced by the fact that productivity in U.S. agriculture, relative to the rest of the U.S. economy, was low and that American growth, and aggregate productivity, would consequently have developed more rapidly had the agricultural sector been able to contract more quickly. After all, aggregate American output per worker outside the agricultural sector was 2.50 times that of agricultural workers. Thus the relative productivity of American farmers, compared with productivity elsewhere in the U.S. economy, can be seen as the basic cause of the 'crises' which were endemic in late nineteenth-century American agriculture. There were simply too many farmers, too many of whom produced too little. It is not surprising, in such circumstances, that a relative contraction of British agriculture, accompanied by higher levels of industrial inputs such as steam ploughs, tractors, mechanical dairy equipment, and chemical fertilizers, would have yielded measures of British output per farm worker greater than those actually recorded for the U.S., which was slowly going through its own process of structural adjustment in agriculture. Elsewhere, in only three sectors, domestic wholesale and retail trade, mining, and professional and government services, was counterfactual output per worker as much as 90% of that in the comparable American sector. For the entire economy, including agriculture, counterfactual British output per worker was 93.3% of American, reflecting in full the deleterious impact of the large agricultural sector on the American economy. Excluding agriculture from both economies yields an aggregate British estimate of productivity in the counterfactual medium growth variant barely three quarters (78%) of that in the U.S. For all the sectors selected for counterfactual expansion, counterfactual British output per worker is at best no more than two thirds that of the comparable U.S. sector.[7]

The significance of the results reported in column 8 of Table 4.6 is unmistakable. Despite the great increases in output per worker generated by the counterfactual structural shifts, the implicit output per British worker is still systematically far below that of his or her American counterpart. Since the counterfactual structural shifts were predicted on an exploitation within Britain of the technological opportunities of the period comparable to that which took place in the U.S., it is clear that any possible bottleneck created by tight labour supplies would have been resolved through higher labour productivity. On average, counterfactual output per man could have increased by approximately a *further* third in Britain without requiring productivity per man greater than that which existed on average in the non-agricultural sectors of the American economy. In general, had British product per worker, in most sectors at the end of the nineteenth century, simply been no less than that of Britain's most progressive industrial rivals, output per worker would have been substantially greater than that set out in the counterfactual medium growth variant, which was in turn 46% greater than the actual British output per worker in 1907. Had Britain been able to sustain the favourable productivity differentials at the end of the century that had been established by mid century, counterfactual output per worker would have been higher still.

At this point, it may be objected that the medium growth variant gives the appearance of feasibility by 'smuggling' implausibly high productivity levels into

Table 4.7. *Estimates of capital intensity compatible with medium growth variant*

	(1) Gross domestic fixed capital formation (as % of GNP)	(2) Net investment abroad (as % of GNP)	(3) Stock- building (as % of GNP)	(4) Totals[1] (sum of cols. (1) to (3))
1 U.K., 1907 (actual)	7.2	7.8	0.5	15.5
2 U.K., average 1870–1913 (actual)	7.9	5.0	1.2	14.0
3 U.K., 1907 (counterfactual)	22.9	2.1	0.8	25.8
4 U.S., average, 1869–1911	18.6	−0.3	3.1	21.4
5 U.S., average, 1907–1911	19.0	0.1	1.5	20.6

Sources:
U.K. GNP (actual): Feinstein (1972: Table 4, column 5 plus Table 3, column 6, [compromise estimate of GDP plus net property income from abroad]).
U.K. Gross Domestic Fixed Capital Formation (GDFCF) (actual): Feinstein (1972: Table 39, column 6).
U.K. Net Investment Abroad, (actual): Feinstein (1972: Table 15, column 16).
U.K. Stock-building (actual): Feinstein (1972: Table 2, column 4).
U.K. GNP 1907 (counterfactual): Table 4.1, column (3), row 25.
U.K. Investment Levels (counterfactual): Table 4.4 rows 6(b) and 6(c).
U.S. GNP: U.S. Bureau of the Census (1975), Series F-71.
U.S. GDFCF: U.S. Bureau of the Census (1975), Series F-80 plus F-85.
U.S. Net Investment Abroad: U.S. Bureau of the Census (1975), Series F-97.
U.S. Stock-building: U.S. Bureau of the Census (1975), Series F-96.

Note:
[1] Row sums may not equal row totals due to rounding.

the counterfactual results through the capital stock rather than the labour force data. As may be seen in Table 4.7, however, the medium growth variant of the counterfactual changes not only makes full allowance for the capital intensive nature of late nineteenth-century technical change but also implies a lower level of capital productivity than that actually reached in the U.S. Counterfactual U.K. gross domestic fixed capital formation (GDFCF) measured as a proportion of GNP, is assumed to be 123% of the U.S. average of GDFCF as a proportion of GNP over the period 1869–1911 and 120% of the U.S. average for the period 1907–11. Total U.K. counterfactual investment (see Table 4.7, column 4) is assumed to be 120% of the comparable average of U.S. investment to GNP over the period 1869–1911. By capturing the impact of modern transportation and communication networks on stockbuilding requirements, the averages for the period 1907–11 are more indicative of capital requirements than are those for the longer period. For 1907–11 the average counterfactual rate of British capital formation (measured as a proportion of GNP) is 125% of the comparable American investment ratio. Thus taking aggregate capital and labour productivity together, the medium growth variant of the counterfactual structural shift implies total factor productivity well *below* that recorded in the U.S. The higher output in the medium growth variant of structural shift is in no way achieved by assuming a greater British technological capability than that obtained in the U.S. Had the counterfactual shifts been determined by equating productivity levels in the two countries rather than equating relative sector sizes by the procedure described in Chapter 3, the increase in output would have been far greater than the 46% increase generated by the medium growth variant of structural shift.

While the productivity estimates of Tables 4.6 and 4.7 are highly revealing, they must not be pressed too far. They are intended to provide a general indication of relative productivity levels, not precisely reliable estimates. Three important complications may be identified. First, the check on total factor productivity is crude. No attempt has been made to allocate capital formation in the counterfactual model across sectors. Instead a sufficiently large rate of capital formation was chosen to ensure that the counterfactual British capital stock in every sector could be larger than its American counterpart. This procedure is, however, at least fully consistent with the capital intensive nature of late nineteenth-century technical change and makes allowance for differences in natural resource endowments. The second complication arises because sectoral differences in output per worker may reflect differences in the competitiveness of output and input markets or productivity differentials due to the quality and quantity of available raw material inputs rather than differences in technological capability. Thus, for example, the finding of wider differentials between the U.S. and the U.K. in output per man in the iron and steel trades compared with the mining industry (see Table 4.6, columns 5 and 7, lines 8 and 14) may well be due to the fact that the highly concentrated, vertically integrated, U.S. steel industry had much greater bargaining power than its U.K. counterpart in determining prices for fuel and ore. Although such considerations greatly complicate the precise sectoral allocation of productivity differentials – witness the careful, data intensive procedure Robert C. Allen (1979) followed to identify a 15% difference in total factor productivity between the U.S and Britain in the production of iron and steel in the early twentieth century – they do not permit a reversal of the general implications of Table 4.6, since *all* sectors exhibit marked productivity differentials although the degree of difference does vary from industry to industry. International differences in industrial organization or raw material availability could at best account for only a limited number of the partial productivity differentials observed in Table 4.6, and certainly not all of them together.

The third and final complication arises because American output per worker, measured in dollars, is converted into sterling at the prevailing exchange rate of the period, \$4.86 to £1.00. To the extent that trade barriers and differences in the consumption of non-traded goods affected relative prices, the use of conventional exchange rates is misleading. This consideration suggests that comparison of British and American output using exchange rates based on purchasing power parity rather than prevailing market exchange rates would reduce the productivity differential between the two countries, since it was in the protected American markets that the higher levels of output per worker were observed. Without a more detailed investigation it is not possible to determine by how much U.S. productivity differentials are over-estimated by the use of prevailing market, rather than purchasing power parity, exchange rates, although it should be noted that there is some evidence based on detailed studies of income and expenditure in specific areas that real wages, especially among the least skilled workers, were nearly comparable in the U.S. and Britain in the early twentieth century (Shergold, 1976).

Productivity estimates based on purchasing power parity evidence, however, are not complete unless the final parity is one reflecting an underlying equilibrium condition. In the late nineteenth century the American labour force was growing rapidly due to both high (although falling) levels of native fertility and to large flows of immigration. This rapid growth of the labour force was accommodated with rising real wages. In contrast, the British labour force was growing much more slowly and providing a steady stream of increasingly skilled immigrants to North America while British real wage rates tended to stagnate. Moreover, as the sector growth rates of Table 3.3 indicate, important American industrial sectors were rapidly and profitably expanding employment and output while lowering output prices. In the circumstances of such changes, to find, temporarily, parity or near parity of real wages for some groups of workers indicates not parity in the underlying equilibrium but the much greater force of American productivity growth, a force that ultimately was reflected in greater occupational and social mobility in the U.S. The historical experiences of the American and British labour forces in the twentieth century strongly suggest that the millions of European emigrants who crossed the North Atlantic in the late nineteenth and early twentieth centuries seeking brighter economic prospects were not fundamentally mistaken in their choice of destination and their perceptions and experiences further suggest that, whatever the considerable difficulties of establishing precise productivity estimates, those presented in Table 4.6 are not basically misleading.

Despite the substantial productivity advances embedded in the medium growth variant, the counterfactual structural shifts would, however, have required a mobile labour force. British experience in the decades before 1914 reveals that labour immobilities could not seriously be considered an obstacle to more rapid growth. The large and persistent emigration and migration of British and Irish workers is a well-known feature of the U.K. economy in the nineteenth century. The rate of emigration from England and Wales in the decade of the

1880's was the fourth highest in Europe and the absolute number of emigrants tended to rise in the four decades before the war (Easterlin, 1961:339). This emigration demonstrated both considerable mobility and sensitivity to economic factors. The migratory response within Britain to evolving patterns of labour demand is equally impressive as evidence of mobility. This mobility carried clearly across industrial lines. The expansion of the already large coal-mining industry by over 60% between 1898 and 1913, with the increase in a single year of heavy inflow perhaps approaching 80,000 men (Taylor, 1968: 50–1), is one of the most notable inter-industry examples of labour transfer, but other examples are even more telling. In 1907 the U.K. automobile industry employed 70,452 people, or 0.35% of the labour force. The U.S. industry in contrast employed only 105,758 workers in 1910 or 0.28% of the U.S. labour force. The U.K. electrical apparatus industry employed 85,380 workers (0.42% of the labour force) in 1911 while the industry in the U.S. employed only 88,915 people in 1910 (0.23% of the labour force). (See Data Appendices A, B, and C.) The same results hold even more strongly when the comparisons are made using occupational data. Although both the automobile and electrical apparatus industries were substantially larger in terms of physical measures of output or of relative importance to GNP in the U.S., the industries in the U.S. were not as conspicuous as employers. This means, of course, that U.S. labour productivity was higher in the two industries, but it also clearly shows that the British labour market, whatever its imperfections, could supply labour easily to any sector capable of generating a sustained demand (Hunt, 1973: 149–53, 155–62).

In summary then, neither balance of payments constraints nor impossible technological demands, neither scarcities in input markets nor gluts in output markets, neither labour shortages nor labour immobility can account for the failure of the Victorian economy to achieve the structural changes that would have permitted more rapid growth and greater prosperity. The explanation for the failure must be sought elsewhere within the allocative mechanism of the Victorian economy. It is to that issue that we now turn.

5

Institutional obstacles to structural change:
British capital markets to 1913

If it is alleged that manufacturers and commerce find abundant [resources] for their successful pursuit [of expansion] in the hands of individuals in this country, I will answer – England cannot stand still.
Edwin Moss, *'Remarks on an Act of Parliament for the Formation of Companies with Limited Liability'* (quoted in Jefferys, 1938 (1856))

The social object of skilled investment should be to defeat the dark forces of time and ignorance which envelop our future. The actual, private object of the most skilled investment today is 'to beat the gun', as the Americans so well express it, to outwit the crowd, and to pass the bad, or depreciating, half crown to the other fellow.
John Maynard Keynes, *The General Theory of Employment, Interest, and Money* (1936)

The problems of market segmentation

The coincidence of systematic Victorian neglect of technologically promising investment possibilities at home with the commitment of huge investments abroad naturally focuses attention on the mechanisms of Victorian capital allocation. In order to examine these mechanisms systematically, it is first necessary to establish the most crucial aspects of their operations. Perhaps the most fundamental questions that can be asked about Victorian (or any other) capital markets concern their ability to indicate equally clearly to all potential borrowers and lenders the trading opportunities that existed at any given time. While the equal dissemination of information may not be a sufficient condition to surmount the obstacles to allocational efficiency discussed in Chapter 1, it is certainly a necessary condition and one upon whose fulfillment the resolution of deeper and more subtle difficulties depends.

Failure to disseminate information uniformly results in market segmentation, a condition in which a larger market area is partitioned into sub-divisions allowing differences in marginal factor payments to exist. Such differences clearly violate one of the most fundamental implications of the analysis of rational resource allocation – that factor payments be equated at the margin in all alternative uses. The larger the set of differentials which the economic system in given conditions allows to persist, the greater is the departure from the optimal allocation permitted by resources, preferences, and technology. A reduction in capital market segmentation increases the probability that most lenders – given their preferences for risk and return – will find more attractive assets to purchase and that most borrowers – given their prospects – will obtain resources at a lower cost. In some cases, such a reduction in segmentation may permit an expansion in the set of feasible projects, allowing the system to attain an equilibrium position greatly preferable to the one initially reached.

Segmentation arises most commonly because all participants in markets do not share the same information and all cannot acquire the same degree of knowledge, and act upon that knowledge, with equal ease. The information requirements for rational decision making under uncertainty, assuming that risk and return are the relevant considerations, are prodigiously extensive. It is necessary to have an informed estimate of the expected mean rates of return on all feasible projects, as well as an estimate of the expected variance of the distribution of possible yields and of the relationship of all the covariances of yield of all projects with each other.[1] A central implication of this analysis is that no investment project can be valued in isolation from all others. This is true in general and not only in the obvious case where one project is directly dependent on another, such as might be the case where the successful sale of electricity depends on the successful manufacture of lights and other equipment that use electricity. Even if all projects whose yields are perfectly correlated with one another's are treated as being effectively one project, the value of relatively uncorrelated projects can only be efficiently determined simultaneously.

The ramifications of this argument might be made more clear with a simple example suggested by Mossin showing how a financial system initially in equilibrium would adjust to a disturbance (Mossin, 1973: 133–35). Suppose that firms specialize in production so that all firms are not identical but are exposed to different circumstances. Consider a firm which faces a borrowing rate of 10% on its outstanding debt in a perfect capital market through which all members of the economy may equally accurately assess the firm's prospects in terms of a distribution of possible outcomes of the firm's risky activities. Since everyone is assumed to have identical knowledge but not perfect foresight and to interpret this knowledge in the same way, everyone agrees on what the distribution of possible outcomes is and what it is worth. Let the riskless rate of time discount be 4%. Suppose that the firm then suddenly discovers an investment opportunity which only it can take up but which was previously unanticipated by the firm's management or anyone else and which will yield 8% return with certainty.[2] Mossin shows that the addition of this new opportunity to the firm's activities alters both the feasible borrowing rate and the default risk. Most importantly, because the project is certain in its yield, inclusion in the firm's activities reduces the overall expected variance of the firm's total earnings. Since the intrinsic value of the firm depends on the yield and variance of its activities, the value of the firm is altered and the firm should, for efficiency, convert (and be encouraged to convert) its outstanding debt from a rate of 10% to a rate of, say, 9%. This new borrowing rate is still higher than the yield on the new opportunity at 8% but the reduction applied to *all* of the firm's existing debt, not only to the part incurred to secure the new opportunity. For concreteness, assume that the initial debt of the firm was £1500. At 10% interest, the firm was obliged to promise to pay its debt-holders a total of £1650. Let the new, riskless opportunity cost £250. If undertaken the principal of the firm's debt would be raised to £1750 but, if correct recognition of the reduced default risk caused by the addition's low variance is made, the firm's borrowing rate would drop to 9%, making the amount to be paid, both principal and interest, £1907.50 (£1750 × 1.09) which is an increase of £257.50 over the original debt position of £1650. Note that the effective interest rate on the new project, because it allows a reduction in its previous debt by reducing the default risk, is precisely 3% (£257.50 − £250 = £7.50; £7.50/£250 = 0.03). Mossin (1973: 134–5) concludes: 'Thus, the effective *marginal* borrowing rate is 3 per cent, and it is not surprising that the proposed investment should be considered profitable.' (Emphasis added.) In order for the investment to be undertaken, however, the impact of its addition to the firm's activities must be known by all potential investors. If it is not known the firm will incorrectly reject the project as too expensive and the firm and the economy, under the assumptions of the model, will be worse off than if the refunding of the firm's debt took place.[3]

The level of capital formation can thus be seen to be sensitive to the degree of segmentation which exists in an economy.[4] Risk is an intrinsic characteristic of capital formation for capital goods themselves are generally use-specific and the resale of used equipment is difficult, only infrequently admitting inexpensive adjustments to unfulfilled expectations. If investors are risk averse, as introspection and observation strongly suggest, the possibility of efficient diversification of risk in order to avert complete disaster is essential if substantial amounts of risk are to be borne. Segmentation, however, restricts the opportunities for effectively bearing risks.

Diversification is not a function which must be performed through formal institutions. Important examples of diversifying behaviour can be found in the histories of both firms and individual entrepreneurs. Diversification at the firm level – in order to ensure efficient use of the firm's quasi-fixed resources – is an important element of management's duties. However, diversification is most effectively carried out on a large scale, for there are important economies of scale in this activity. In the first place, the costs of gathering and interpreting information on alternatives are incurred only once for each institution. Similarly, transaction costs for trading and managing big blocks of assets are smaller on a per-unit basis than for trading and managing small blocks. Therefore, the greater the volume of investing and transacting done by an institution, the lower average fixed costs.[5] Secondly, as Mossin's example above indicates, risk can only be optimally interpreted within the context of the widest possible array of choices. The larger a portfolio the more opportunities that exist for laying risks off against each other; that is, the set of optimal feasible choices may be more favourable for large portfolios than for small ones, even ignoring transaction costs. Closely related to this point is the frequent existence of thresholds in the process of physical capital formation, such that the ability to complete a project, even when serious unexpected difficulties arise, is an important element of eventual success. Therefore, the greater the total resources relative to the largest project undertaken, the better the prospects that every worthwhile project will be undertaken despite the potentially discrete nature of some undertakings.[6]

These considerations offer a persuasive rationalization for the proliferation of financial intermediaries. The cost of capital is not uniquely determined for all firms but varies for each firm, depending on the structure of each firm's portfolio of risks and changing with every investment decision and environmental change that alters the characteristics of the distribution of possible outcomes which each firm faces. Projects which are unacceptable to one firm may be highly desirable to another identical in managerial skill and resources simply for the reason that the second firm's existing structure of risks is improved by the opportunity while the first's is not. Such possibilities emphasize the critical importance of the institutions that gather, transmit and act upon the information relevant to investment decisions.

The significance of institutional arrangements can be further highlighted by consideration of one of the more serious consequences of the failure to achieve equitable distribution of important information. The issues involved can best be seen in an example due to George Akerlof (1970). The example concerns the trading of a particular type of financial asset, perhaps the domestic industrial equities of new or expanding firms, where 'insiders' – assumed here for concretness without loss of generality to be sellers of the assets – know much more accurately than buyers the intrinsic value of each of the different assets being traded. For simplicity, buyers are assumed to be unable to distinguish good equities from poor ones (designated 'lemons') of the same type – new electrical engineering firms for example – although the argument essentially requires only that buyers can discriminate among such equities less well than can sellers. A situation similar to that proposed in the example would exist in the case of a closely held firm going public for the first time or in the case of a company selling a fresh issue of financial instruments where public disclosure of the firm's affairs is incomplete or ineffective. That there are some owners of the assets as ignorant of relevant information as potential buyers will not alter the analysis as long as substantial opportunities for the exercise of privileged 'inside' information exists. It is assumed that the projected value of the financial assets being traded – here taken to be new domestic industrial equities – may be characterized by a particular probability distribution such that the true value of each asset would lie somewhere between utter worthlessness (with a value equal to zero) and complete worthiness (with a value equal to p^*, the present discounted value of the accurately anticipated income stream of the best possible issue of the specified class) with the probability of each outcome for each equity determined objectively. It follows from these assumptions that buyers will know only the *average* value of assets of a given type, but not the intrinsic value of any *given* asset whereas sellers will know reasonably accurately the intrinsic value of each particular asset they offer to the market and will be able to exploit this superior knowledge while conducting sales.

Consider the trading of the equities of a particular firm at a moment when the ruling price for firms of that type is p, where $0 \leqslant p \leqslant p^*$. Owners who believe their equities to be worth exactly p would be just indifferent between selling them or not and may be assumed to make this decision randomly, perhaps by tossing a coin. Owners who believe their equities to be worth less than p, that is owners of all equities who value their own holdings at between nothing and p, would be only too glad to sell, owners of worthless and near worthless equities being the most eager of all. Owners who believe their equities to be worth more than p would, if they had a choice, refuse to sell at price p, although, if for some reason the price were to rise, more sellers of high quality equities would voluntarily enter the market and average quality would thereby rise. The average value of equities traded in this market would clearly depend upon the distribution of quality, but for any distribution owners of the lowest quality equities fare best (Wilson, 1980: 130).[7] If the probability distribution characterizing the quality of a particular class of equities is, following Akerlof, the uniform distribution, in which the probability of any given outcome is the same as that for any other possible outcome, the average value is very easily calculated – it is just the average of the highest and lowest values possible for the equities being traded. In the illustration the highest value would be the current ruling price, p – since owners of more valuable equities worth between p and p^* would not trade – and the lowest value would be zero, yielding an average realized value of $p/2$. Clearly, an average realized value of equities equal to only *half* the price paid for them constitutes a powerful disincentive to continued trading. In these circumstances, only if buyers value the utility of possessing equities of any given quality at least twice as highly as do sellers will trading continue even though the gain in utility achieved by trade taking place in conditions where buyers and sellers share the same information – information that need not be perfect but only equally available – may be great. If the probability distribution characterizing the quality of a particular type of equity is more concentrated about its mean value than is the uniform distribution, the average realized value of equities traded would be nearer the sum paid for them than is true in the uniform distribution case. Nevertheless, as long as information is asymmetrically distributed in sellers' favour, price will be greater than average realized value and at best the volume of trading in such a market will be suboptimally low. At worst, no trading at all will take place.

The argument so far has been conducted in static terms, with the assumption that there exists available for trade a fixed stock of equities with a given distribution of quality. Markets, however, may be under an even more fundamental threat arising from dynamic influences. Recall that in the illustration, when the given class of equities were trading at price p, owners of low quality equities had a particular incentive to sell. If this situation persists for any length of time, an entrepreneurial response is very likely to bring more owners (or fabricators) of low quality equities into the market to sell. When this happens, the average quality of the equities traded will fall, and consequently prices will fall as well, the process continuing until, in the limit, the market disappears *regardless* of how advantageous informed trade is. Trade can only be preserved or expanded with institutional support – defining the 'rules of the game' – of considerable sophistication and subtlety. Without that support markets are only too likely to collapse. Ignorance and suspicion nurtured by the painful experience of market collapse can in this manner create and sustain extreme forms of market segmentation. Even if yield differentials are correctly perceived, traders will lack the market channels to effect arbitrage.

From these considerations of the vital informational role that institutions must play in order to ensure the efficient allocation of resources, it is clear that failure to fulfil that role adequately could sustain yield differentials sufficiently large, sufficiently pervasive, and sufficiently persistent to account for the difference between what the counterfactual structural changes discussed in Chapter 3 show to have been feasible and what was actually achieved. The issue now becomes one of determining just how well British capital markets performed their momentous tasks.

Capital market evolution in the nineteenth century: an overview

From this brief discussion of the requirements of information on yield returns, variances and covariances minimally necessary to ensure efficient allocation of resources under uncertainty, it is clear that in reality no capital market is now, or ever has been, free from the distortions of substantial segmentation. The segmentation of markets is thus a universal problem. It is not a new problem. There was, of course, a strong incentive in all developing economies in the nineteenth century, as there is now, to reduce segmentation. Capital markets in all the advanced countries in the last century have changed constantly in an attempt to offer their users more beneficial choices. The institutional history of these markets may be interpreted as a search for improvement, and the growth in the capability and scope of financial intermediaries is an indication of progress. Yet the various national paths towards improvement have differed sharply and it is only to be expected that the consequences of the improvements achieved would differ as well. The course which financial market evolution took in Britain bore little resemblance to that taken in either the U.S. or Germany and changes in the latter two countries did not closely resemble each other.

These divergent trends resulted in national markets which performed certain tasks with marked differences in proficiency. By 1914, Britain had created a short-term money market of unrivalled efficiency and had supplemented this with elaborate institutions, also unmatched, specializing in the trade of first-class securities. In these two functions neither the U.S. nor Germany approached the level of performance Britain attained by 1914, although both had progressed far beyond their circumstances in the mid nineteenth century. Germany and America were compensated for their deficiencies in short-term and high-grade securities markets, however, by a superior ability to concentrate resources in areas strategic for rapid development at moments crucial to the evolution of new products and techniques.

The reasons for this ability were notably different for the U.S. and Germany. The U.S., with a rich resource base relative to a rapidly expanding population and benefiting from a tradition of mechanical tinkering tempered with respect for scientific knowledge, needed only intermittent support from a crisis-prone financial system to achieve rapid, but not optimal, exploitation of new possibilities. Railroads and some New England textile mills depended on funds raised on organized capital markets but the vast majority of industrial firms had little access to them before 1914 (Navin and Sears, 1955). When large financial intermediaries did become involved in industrial affairs, it was usually for the purpose of reorganizing an industry already in existence where both the buyers and sellers were generally well informed about each other's businesses through prior commercial contact. For example, the large American mergers in the late 1880s in distilling and flour milling took place when distributors bought out their suppliers and created a vertically integrated organization conducting everything from raw material purchase to the final marketing of output, whereas earlier most of these activities had been carried out by separate organizations. In a few isolated but critical cases, notably in electrical engineering (Chandler, 1977: 426–433) and automobile manufacture (Seltzer, 1928: 30–69), formal financial intermediaries – J.P. Morgan in the creation of General Electric and Detroit banks as a group in the support of the inevitably large inventories of rapidly expanding automobile manufacturers – played a vital role in linking industry insiders wishing to borrow on a grand scale with industry outsiders seeking a reliable means of investing in projects widely believed to have bright prospects.

Other than these important instances, although most firms did depend on bank loans in the initial stages of their development, the numbers of people and sums of money involved in individual transactions were generally small. Most firms capable of attracting continual, large-scale bank support were soon able to sustain further growth from internal sources (Davis, 1967a). Thus success in the scramble to employ new techniques, offer new products, or penetrate new markets often depended initially on favourable access to external finance. This often led at least temporarily to a monopolistic position for the successful firm. Subsequently it was often only the fear of further entry or the sheer momentum of the logic of a particular form of technical progress which maintained development in some industries, for one of the outstanding features of the emergence of new U.S. industries in the late nineteenth century was the large size and small number of firms which comprised them (Chandler, 1962: 23–36). These firms, giant-sized by the standards of the time, may be usefully viewed as affording an improved means of reducing geographical and industrial segmentation. By routinely operating over a larger territory than firms were previously able to do, the new firms could reduce the dangerous dependence on the prosperity of a single region or area and could participate more quickly in new opportunities. By applying a common technology to several industries or to several markets simultaneously – an option particularly attractive to makers of capital goods such as steel or electrical equipment – the new firms could reduce dangerous dependence on the prosperity of a single industry or market while more fully exploiting any technological advances they were able to make. Although these developments certainly did not eliminate segmentation, which could still be extensive between firms or even between different divisions of the same firm, the new giant firms did constitute, especially when their ambitious plans of expansion brought them into direct competition with each other, improved arrangements for resource allocation.

Ramshackle as it was, the system was capable of concentrating resources sufficiently to launch before 1913 a number of new, rapidly growing industries in electrical manufacture, chemicals (especially petroleum based chemical products), automobiles, communications, steel and food processing. In a sense, because of the greater level and wider distribution of wealth and the generally buoyant economic environment which this created, formal financial markets were less necessary in the late nineteenth century in promoting a given rate of economic growth in the U.S. than in Europe.

Germany, in contrast, was poorer than both Britain and the U.S. before 1914. Without the abundant natural resources of the U.S. it was less easy for individuals and small, local banks to preside unaided over the creation of entire industries. The German banking system, therefore, provided much more elaborate formal facilities for concentrating financial resources than either their U.S. or British counterparts. English financial authorities were well aware of both the hazards and the rewards of this concentration and often wrote favourably of the German system. Thus Lavington (1921: 210) wrote:

An organization of this kind, [an investment bank] intermediate between the sources of enterprise and the sources of capital must evidently possess machinery for investigating business ventures, financial strength adequate to sustain the heavy risks to which it is exposed and the reputation and business connexions necessary for the efficient sale of securities to the public. An organization such as the Deutsche Bank possesses these qualities to a high degree. Its practical administration [in 1914] is in the hands of a body of nine managers, all of them men of wide business knowledge, one or two of them admittedly of exceptional ability. It has a distinct staff of some eight or nine industrial experts, usually drawn from industry itself, and a highly developed department of information, while its system of unsecured advances keeps in the closest touch with the position and progress of business concerns. It is easy to see that, with able management and machinery of this kind, the risks of industrial banking are greatly reduced; business ventures in need of capital can be thoroughly investigated and the development of the more pioneering enterprises may be promoted with a reasonable prospect of success.

Clapham (1936: 390) concurred with the tenor of Lavington's argument, approvingly quoting a principal officer of one of the largest German banks:

'In Germany', said Herr Schuster of the Dresdner Bank in 1908, 'our banks are largely responsible for the development of the Empire, having fostered and built up its industries. It is from 1871 that our real development dates and it is since that year that our great banks have been organised.' 'To them, more than any other agency', he added with pardonable complacency, 'may be credited the splendid results thus far realized.' If his historical summary was not literally accurate, it was accurate in substance.

Moreover, the German Great Banks operated on such a scale as to enable them to overcome even well entrenched market segmentation. An important and illuminating example of this ability can be drawn from the development of the German electrical engineering industry in the late nineteenth century (Kocka, 1978: 558–63). The family controlled electrical engineering firm of Siemens and Halske had, by the early 1890s, achieved a position of dominance in the German industry just as important new possibilities arising from increasing understanding of alternating current generation and transmission were becoming available. Werner Siemens wished to exploit these opportunities only slowly in order to avoid dilution of family control, since rapid exploitation would have exceeded even the substantial internal resources of Siemens and Halske. However Werner Siemens was not to be left peacefully to expand in such a leisurely fashion. Emil Rathenau, the salaried chief executive officer of the AEG (Allgemeine Elektrizitäts – Gesellschaft) embarked, with substantial bank support, on an aggressive and successful programme of expansion by both merger and internal capital formation. By 1897, in order to avoid complete eclipse by the AEG, the owners of Siemens and Halske had been forced to counter Rathenau's strategy by aggressive expansion of their own. In this manner, and against their will, the owners of Siemens and Halske were compelled by external market forces to lower the internal rate of return on their company's assets and contribute more fully to the development of the electrical engineering industry. The opportunities, while risky, were so great that despite aggressive expansion by both firms rapid growth and high profits were maintained right down to the First World War. In Victorian Britain, however, banks, as will be argued below, played a different role that did not place such competitive pressures on family owned firms.

In a similar manner, in the development of the electricity supply industry, as distinct from electrical engineering, German capital markets offered opportunities for the sharing of costs, control and profits among joint stock companies and municipal authorities in such a way as to avoid the sterile and, in the presence of substantial economies of scale, debilitating conflicts that arose in Britain over the issue of whether companies or municipalities alone should be responsible for the public provision of electricity (Hannah, 1979: 52–3). Thus, with one notable exception, Victorian electricity was provided by plants of suboptimal scale while German joint stock companies enjoyed cheap public loans to build larger and more efficient plants in return for sharing profits and control with municipal authorities. Of course, the German engineering firms benefited fully from the buoyant demand for their products that arose from the availability of cheap electric power supplies.

The success of German and American financial intermediaries in concentrating resources in technically and commercially promising activities should not be interpreted as a claim that this vital task was accomplished without difficulties or costs. To the contrary, throughout the nineteenth century, significant regional differences in interest rates on short-term commercial paper and mortgages existed in the U.S. (Davis, 1965).[8] The yield differential on more complex, more risky assets was correspondingly greater. Although a national short-term commercial paper market had begun to appear by 1900, differentials on mortgages narrowed more slowly (Davis, 1965: 137–8). The economic development of the Southern part of the U.S., favoured by climate and resources, was probably greatly retarded by capital market imperfections (Davis, 1965: 150–2). Similar differentials appeared in Germany. Because the Great Banks 'did not care for that class of business' represented by local deposit banking and the extension of commercial credit to small traders, historians have argued that serious misallocation of resources occurred in Imperial Germany (Clapham, 1963: 394–5; Neuberger and Stokes, 1974). In contrast, these marked regional and, to some extent, sectoral differences in interest rates on mortgages and short-term commercial credit largely disappeared in Britain no later than the 1860s (Davis, 1966: 669).

Furthermore, concentration invited monopolistic abuses in both the U.S. and Germany (Davis, 1965: 680–2; Clapham, 1936: 394). The tendency to concentrate control of the nation's railroads in the hands of a small syndicate of financiers has not aided in halting the decline of a viable U.S. rail network. Morgan's colossal creation, U.S. Steel, has not been a dynamic, innovative organization; chaotic management and technological conservatism have relentlessly contributed to the firm's unceasing loss of market share since its creation. The pre-eminence at U.S. Steel's creation of financial concerns at the expense of production and marketing must bear a major part of the explanation of the firm's subsequent performance. The costs in terms of welfare and foregone growth of these departures from optimality must be of similar magnitude in Germany. If the Great Banks are to receive much of the credit for stimulating technical change in Germany, they must be held accountable for the failure of industries with great export if not domestic market prospects – such as the automobile manufacturing industry – to emerge as rapidly as in Italy for example. It is obvious, therefore, that economic performance in both the U.S. and Germany was far from equalling that permitted by resources and technology. Yet it also appears to be true that, with all their documented imperfections, capital markets in the U.S. and Germany, by making resources available to a large group of technologically progressive industries on a scale unequalled in Britain, account for much of the difference in the economic growth performance between those two countries and Britain in the half century after 1865. Quite obviously, British capital markets were not purposely intended to produce results markedly inferior to those obtained by other advanced industrial nations. Rather the difficulties of British markets can be most readily comprehended as emerging from a complex process of institutional evolution whose fundamental mechanisms were not readily controlled, or even understood, by contemporaries.

The development of the British capital market in the nineteenth century

The evolution of Britain's system of financial intermediaries was very much a product of her early industrialization. The British system in its formative years in the eighteenth and nineteenth centuries had to cope with the fact of growth achieved, not with the desire to redress manifest relative backwardness. The financial institutions that evolved in these circumstances tended to favour stability above other considerations, an emphasis that became distinctly less appropriate as the need for further development became more urgent. As late as the 1790s commerce and industry needed as much funding for stocks and inventories as for fixed capital formation (Crouzet, 1972: 33). By 1835, the fixed capital needs of commerce and industry were still only three times that of inventory requirements (Crouzet, 1972: 32). It was natural and reasonable then to fear the effects of commodity 'speculation' and to regard fixed capital formation as a largely self-regulating, self-stimulating process best nurtured under a regime of sound money. For these reasons the Bubble Act was preserved for over a century as a monument to prudence.

The quickening pace of economic development, the increasing demands for long-term capital formation, the heightening sensitivity of the entire economy to fluctuations caused by good harvests and bad, buoyant exports and slack, formed the background for fundamental institutional reform in 1844. The purpose of Peel's Bank Act of that year was to eliminate economic disturbances arising out of the 'unwise' actions of the Bank of England (Hughes, 1960: 229–31). A rigid division of the Bank's activities into an Issue Department and a Banking Department was stipulated; the Issue Department exchanged notes for gold and gold for notes and the Banking Department made loans on the basis of its reserves of notes thus rigidly controlled. Three crises in the twenty years after the Bill's passage were required to educate the Bank's Governors in the means of translating the formal mechanism into a device capable of exercising increasingly delicate control over the economy. But as experience in regulating bills of exchange and bank deposits grew, the original objectives of the Bill's authors were increasingly realized and the Bank became a massive force for stability (Hughes, 1960: 283–4). Stability of the Bank's reserves and the exchanges remained the Bank's objectives until 1914 (Sayers, 1936: 116–17). The state of the Bank's reserves before all else dictated policy. After 1890, the Bank increasingly tried to accommodate business conditions when taking steps to protect its reserves or to anticipate trouble but the Bank's objectives were never widened to encompass actively and continuously the maintenance of full employment or the promotion of growth (Sayers, 1936: 125–6).

The Bank of England, as it slowly began to fulfil the duties of a central bank, increasingly came to influence profoundly the tenor of British banking operations. The Bank's gradual articulation of its role coincided with a fundamental change in bank lending practices in which the strengthening bond between the banking system and industrial long-term finance, which had grown up in the early nineteenth century, was severed. As industrial fixed capital requirements had grown steadily through the early nineteenth century, banks had begun to play a major role in local industrial affairs. By the middle decades of the nineteenth century, the banking system at a local level was playing a role strikingly similar to that played at the end of the nineteenth century by the German Great Banks on a national level (Jefferys, 1938: 142). The unremitting increase in the size of plant demanded for efficient use of the complex technology evolving in many lines of production, however, began to outstrip the ability of most local banks to respond safely to these new requests for funds. The rash of mid Victorian bank failures can be attributed directly to banks' becoming too closely linked with local firms and over-lending as these firms attempted to expand (Jefferys, 1938: 17; Davis, 1966: 670). These failures reached a crescendo with the failure of the City of Glasgow Bank in 1878. This marked a final watershed for British banking before 1914. A point had been reached where the entire system had either to be reorganized to withstand the greater risks of steadily enlarging industrial requirements or the system had to withdraw from long-term industrial involvement. The system withdrew. After 1878, no longer would banks become willingly involved in the long-term financing of industry.[9] Industrial firms, to the extent that a partnership could not raise the funds and that short-term, limited bank support would not suffice, would, in the future, have to resort to the means made available by limited liability. Jefferys summarized this evolution thus:

But the shock of these failures in 1878 and the resulting turn toward timidity and amalgamation in banking, and the adoption of limited liability by industry, which lessened the demand for long term loans, brought to an end in the 'eighties, this formative period of British banking... (1938: 18)

The banks were by the 'eighties no longer showing such a readiness to act as partners in industrial concerns. They were moving further and further away from the concept of long term loans and were concentrating on an efficient national short term credit system. (1938: 119)

Thus, as the largest and most developed of Victorian financial intermediaries, the banks, amalgamated, thereby growing larger, stronger, and more diversified and, therefore, in principle better able to take bigger risks with less danger, they simultaneously reduced their long-term involvement with industry just as industry's demands were growing in response to advancing technological possibilities and foreign competition. To be sure, British banks after the mid nineteenth century continued to provide industrial accommodation, and, as Philip Cottrell (1980:210–36) has recently shown, examples can be found of loans or overdrafts made for periods longer than a year. Such accommodation was vital in helping firms both to overcome temporary difficulties and to devote their own resources to fixed capital formation. However, the intentions that lay behind this evolution of British banking practice were unmistakably clear – long-term risks and rewards were not to be lodged in bank portfolios as they often had been in the period of the classical Industrial Revolution, but were increasingly to be borne by borrowing firms and their owners. As long as firms could offer adequate collateral – enough for banks to avoid comfortably any imminent threat of a 'lock-up' of their resources in a borrower's business – well-run Victorian banks could be relied upon to lend (Goodhart, 1972: 154, 161–4). But further than this, actually to participate directly in the rewards and penalties of deliberate risk-bearing, banks were neither prepared nor willing to go. Consequently, the potential scope offered by the banking system's massed deposits and vast accumulation of commercial intelligence for the efficient diversification of meaningful risks was made progressively less available to the British economy. Although this behaviour produced, as it was intended to do, a banking system of great stability, it was a stability achieved not by efficiently sharing carefully evaluated risks but by systematically avoiding them.

Just as generals are often guilty of preparing to fight the next war as if it were a continuation of the last one, so British bankers in the late nineteenth century perfected a system of capital formation more appropriate to the age that was passing than to the age that was coming. In the new conditions of increased scale, complexity and competitiveness, efficiency required more complete, accurate and timely information than had been necessary or even possible previously. The effective withdrawal of banks from close and risky involvement with industrial and commercial firms removed an important element of personal contact that had earlier permitted richer flows of information and had created tighter bonds of mutual interest than were subsequently to be typical. The bureaucratized and amalgamated Victorian banking system, with its rigid limitations on the initiative of the local bank managers who knew their borrowers best and with its equally inflexible requirements that loans be amply safeguarded by collateral (Goodhart, 1972: 162–165; Cottrell, 1980: 236–39), not only wasted information prodigiously but also acted to stifle any impulse to change this condition.[10]

During the same period that the banks were amalgamating and drawing away from long-term industrial finance, the brief, tentative foray of the discount houses into this activity also abruptly ended. In 1863, the General Credit and Finance Company of London Ltd was launched with impressive financial support, including that of the most prestigious London and Paris banks. The aim of this company was to act as a Credit Mobilier type of bank, taking long positions in industrial projects. However, despite a very successful start in which an annual yield on invested capital of 17.5% was recorded (King, 1936: 232), the board's nerve broke during the panic following Gurney's collapse. Despite a strong reserve provided by a call on share-holders, the firm went into voluntary liquidation in November, 1866, reforming into a new company the following January with the well-announced intention to hold only short-dated assets (King, 1936: 257). With the retreat of the General Credit and Finance Company, an exploratory period in the history of the discount market ended. The discount houses became unrivalled specialists in short-term accommodation and provided the institutional basis on which the Bank of England was to exert such delicate control over British finances. However, as long as the discount houses of the later Victorian period successfully met their avowed objectives and distinguished between bills and mortgages, they did not become a source of long-term loans.

The withdrawal of the banks and discount houses from involvement in long-term capital formation left the burden of this task solely to the mechanism of limited liability. There were two main ways in which this mechanism was used. The first, easily the most common and most customary as far as industrial investment for most firms was concerned, used the company law to reduce the risks incurred in the course of investment by friends, relatives and business acquaintances. Reliance on close associates for investment funds was a tradition well-known before the last quarter of the eighteenth century, long before the active intervention of banks in industrial affairs and even longer before the advent of general limited liability. Postan (1935: 2–5) has written:

There were enough rich people in the country [England] to finance an economic effort far in excess of the modest activities of the Industrial Revolution... but... new enterprises, in their search for capital, were not much assisted by the fact that England happened to be at the time the richest land in Christendom. That in founding their enterprises the pioneers of the factory system had to draw almost entirely on their private savings, or on the assistance of friends may not strike us as strange or non-modern. But that throughout their subsequent operations, even after their ventures had proved successful, they should still have found it impossible to raise new capital, except among acquaintances and friends, is very significant. Arkwright obtained his first funds from a publican friend.

Limited liability, by eliminating the worst consequences of investment, reduced the risk of participating in commercial and industrial ventures, thereby enhancing the efficacy of the time-honoured practice of trusting savings to those one knew well. So well did this practice continue to develop that as late as 1904, 3068 of the 3477 new companies registered in London in that year were private rather than public companies (Lavington, 1921: 201). Private companies were those wishing, of the facilities which incorporation allowed, only the advantage of limited liability; in return for exemption from the requirements to publish income statements and balance sheets, private companies were required to make no public issue of their shares, to limit the number of share-holders and to restrict the transfer of ownership. Although many of these firms were small since the larger ones availed themselves of the flexibility of public ownership, the preponderance of private companies is a telling indication of the preference for finance through private negotiation.

Thus, as had been the case in previous centuries, most industrial capital formation in Britain, probably between 60% and 70% in a typical year of the last quarter of the nineteenth century, was carried out by small, segmented groups of men who were well acquainted with each other through personal or business contacts. Private British groups, usually acting without large institutional facilities for collecting information and for diversifying widely and efficiently, achieved the great bulk of the not inconsiderable capital formation and structural change which occurred during the late Victorian and Edwardian eras. Perhaps the most important way in which systematic, organized change occurred in Britain after 1870 was through the diversifying behaviour of established, viable firms with proven technical capabilities and trade connections. These firms accomplished change by using their cash flow from profits and depreciation either to alter the character of their activities by creating new product lines or to enlarge the firm as it was by expanding existing profitable operations. In any event, whether change occurred within firms or through the creation of new firms, it was accomplished by tapping relatively small, highly segmented pools of savings. In this respect, Britain, in the late nineteenth and early twentieth centuries, differed from the contemporary U.S. and the Britain of four or five decades earlier only in the refusal of the banks to play an important, conscious role in long-term capital formation. This was a crucial difference, however, for when private or internal resources were insufficient and short-term bank accommodation was too limited and risky, British firms and entrepreneurs were forced to turn to the stock exchanges.

The stock exchanges were the means by which the other main utilization of limited liability was achieved and, after the withdrawal of the banking system from the methodical provision of long-term capital, were the only avenues available for overcoming the pervasive segmentation spawned by networks of highly localized business contacts. Provincial exchanges, which had been established during the railroad booms of the 1830s and 1840s, were essentially an extension of the close circle of local associates, since those who traded there were generally well aware through personal knowledge of the circumstances of the quoted firms (Thomas, 1973:137–9). Provincial exchanges were an important means of providing liquidity for investors in local business but apparently accounted for raising no more than 5–10% of the annual amount of gross domestic capital formation in the years immediately preceding the war (Lavington, 1921:208). Provincial exchanges thus reduced segmentation, but the reduction was nevertheless sharply limited. The London capital market dwarfed those of the provinces and was much more important as a source of new funds, accounting for perhaps as much as 23–8% of the annual amount of gross domestic capital formation in 1911–13 (Lavington, 1921:200–6). However, the main functions of the London capital market were concerned with government issues, foreign loans, and railroads or other public or semi-public utility securities rather than with domestic industrial finance (Morgan and Thomas, 1962:Chapters 5–8).

There are good historical reasons for why this was so. Although the London market was an amazing mechanism of great capacity and flexibility, it operated in a legal environment which greatly amplified the information problems that are familiar features even of mid twentieth-century capital markets. This, of course, produced distortions. The extent to which incomplete or misleading accounting conventions and requirements has caused the observed prices of securities quoted by a capital market to be displaced from the complete-information equilibrium cannot be known, but there is evidence that the distortion is large even for markets well provided with communication links, a vigorous, inquisitive financial press, and binding legal requirements for extensive disclosure of business activities. For example, Marc Nerlove (1968), in a detailed econometric study of the performance of 271 firms quoted on the New York Stock Exchange for which complete, comparable financial records were available between 1950 and 1964, has found substantial differentials in rates of return *after* allowing for risk and transactions costs. Nerlove, who found rates of return most readily explained by a firm's growth of sales and level of retained earnings, attributed this result to the superior perception of investment opportunities within the firm. The management of a firm, he argued, despite legal disclosure requirements, has a much better perception of the opportunities and dangers within the scope of the firm's activities than do outsiders. This, of course, means that the level and structure of investments will be suboptimal; managers will know only if internal investment will yield higher returns than some 'market rate', usually the rate on short-term commercial loans, rather than whether, of all possible investments, the ones within their firm offer the best return for the risks involved. More ominously, the asymmetrical distribution of information deeply embedded in these arrangements makes it highly probable, as Akerlof has argued, that there will be critical, crippling gaps in the market channels needed to arbitrage effectively those yield differentials that are perceived.

What is true of the recent past is even more relevant to earlier periods, where in both the U.S. and Germany as well as Great Britain, business disclosure requirements were enormously more relaxed than at present. The early days of the corporate form of business organization were noted for the infinite legal, let alone illegal, elaborations of the art of concealment and manipulation. The legal requirements governing managerial behaviour and the disclosure of company affairs were so minimally drawn as to place the company's directors in virtually unchallengeable and unchecked possession of the company's assets. In Victorian Britain, the extent of the ignorance of shareholders and creditors without direct access to a company's internal accounts may be estimated by the fact that not until 1900 was an annual audit made obligatory for all companies registered for limited liability and not until 1907 were companies compelled to file publicly a balance sheet. Since the 1907 Act failed to specify that the published balance sheet be current, some public companies seeking secrecy for a variety of reasons chose to file the same balance sheet year after year (Edwards, 1981: 3–4).[11] This casual approach to the disclosure of company affairs no doubt stemmed in large part from the incomprehensibility of contemporary published accounting information. Even after repeated gestures towards reform it was still possible for a company chairman as late as 1938 to be quoted as saying: 'We bring into our accounts as much... as will enable us to pay dividends we recommend and to place to general reserve or add to carry forward just as much as will make a pretty balance sheet' (Hannah, 1974b: 70). In fact, it was not until after the 1948 Companies Act that the asymmetry in information possessed by company outsiders and insiders was reduced to a level that made uninvited company takeover bids a realistic prospect (Hannah, 1974b: 70, 75). While the possibility of contested take-over bidding is not sufficient to ensure efficient use of resources in situations where ownership is divorced from control (King, 1977: 144–52;

Hannah, 1974b: 75–76)[12] – there is not even now agreement on what the precise rules for efficient take-over bidding should be (Grossman and Hart, 1980)[13] – it is clear that it is a necessary condition, and the absence of an effective take-over sanction before 1914 merely served to heighten minority shareholders' sense of ignorance and helplessness, thereby critically eroding and distorting market channels. Only with a painful slowness, periodically prodded by sensational scandals, did the institutional framework necessary to make decentralized risk sharing work acceptably, if not efficiently, begin to appear (Cottrell, 1980: 54–75).

Thus in 1887 *The Statist* could report that 'an honest accountant's certificate honestly applied is one of the rarest features in an industrial prospectus'. (Quoted in Jefferys, 1938: 402.)

The situation did not improve in the next decade. In 1900, a judge commented on the great rise in 'ornamental directors' whose function was to reassure the less informed of the worth of a firm; these directors were, not surprisingly, often most prominent when there was much that required reassurance for 'the tempting facilities offered by this modern machinery [of limited liability] now attracts classes that in the past had not tested the flexibility of their consciences in the subject of accounts and balance sheets'. (Quoted in Jefferys, 1938:423.) The published data in Britain before 1914 were sufficiently bad that J.B. Jefferys (1938:409–10), in his careful study, concluded: 'The control exercised by the shareholders was mainly of a personal character, and the security of the investor lay in his knowledge of the men whom he elected to the Board of Management and the financial and personal interest these latter had in the concern. Shareholders' protection committees were rarely considered in these companies.'

While such evidence suggests that the arrangements for the public disclosure and review of company affairs in late nineteenth-century Britain were perhaps unusually susceptible to manipulation and abuse, similar difficulties were experienced to some degree in all countries. In Germany, for example, the Director of the Deutsche Bank in the 1890s, Georg Siemens, had such a low regard for the standards of public disclosure as to argue that only by securing a position of real discretionary power on a borrowing company's Board of Directors could a lender have a clear picture of the company's financial position, even if the company were controlled by his cousins as was the giant electrical engineering firm Siemens and Halske (Siemens, 1957: 154–7). What was unique in Britain was not the existence of imperfect sharing of risk and control among those with a stake in corporate ventures but rather the unusually slow development of recognition of the extent of the problem and of effective means to rectify it.

In light of the inherent informational weaknesses in British capital market operations, it is not surprising that the money ventured through them went very largely to the purchase of 'known' securities. There were a number of ways in which securities became 'known'. They might be the oldest securities traded on the exchange, government stocks. The price of these could certainly vary, but the instrument itself was well understood and obeyed known laws of behaviour. In the first quarter of the nineteenth century the securities of foreign governments began to appear in London in large quantities. Their number grew rapidly and at first they tended to be indiscriminately confused with domestic government stocks, but this was quickly changed in the 1820s as governments and firms began to be more rigorously classified according to their past record. The same evolution occurred in the marketing of home railroad securities which had by the late 1880s become thoroughly respectable as the memories of the excesses of the 1830s and 1840s faded under the impact of a long succession of dividend and coupon payments reliably made. The unmistakable sign of acceptance was extended to selected home railway debentures in 1889 when they were accorded trustee status (Morgan and Thomas, 1962: 110). The next group of securities gradually to win a favoured place in London were foreign rails, with colonial issues most preferred, followed by the issues of proven North and South American lines. Domestic non-rail companies began to appear in the 1860s; most of these issues represented established coal, iron, steel and heavy engineering firms taking advantage of the new provisions for limited liability to ease the burden of their relatively large fixed costs. These issues, too, were attended by unscrupulous promotions but the prudent Victorians who made up most of the investing public seldom strayed for any time from familiar securities. Finally, there was throughout the nineteenth century an accumulation of other foreign securities, primarily those of land, finance, and investment companies, mining and other raw material extracting concerns, and a few industrial and commercial enterprises. What is striking in the great rise of the London exchanges is not that

Table 5.1. *Approximate distribution by risk class of the value of outstanding home and foreign securities held in the U.K. in 1870*[1]

Safest	
1 British government funds	0.39
2 British (municipal) corporations	—
3 Dominion, provincial and colonial governments	0.01
4 Indian, colonial and foreign (municipal) corporations	—
5 Indian railways	0.03
6 Dominion and colonial railways	0.01
(subtotal)	0.44
Moderate risk	
7 Home railways	0.19
8 Foreign government	0.18
(subtotal)	0.37

Table 5.1. (*cont.*)

Risky

9	Home companies	0.04
10	American railways	0.02
11	Foreign railways	0.08
12	Non-domestic companies	0.04
	(subtotal)	0.18

	Total amount	£2266m

Approximate distribution by risk class of the value of outstanding home and foreign securities held in the U.K. in 1913[1]

Safest

1	British government funds	0.13
2	British (municipal) corporations	0.04
3	Dominion, provincial and colonial governments	0.09
4	Indian, colonial and foreign (municipal) corporations	0.02
5	Indian railways	0.02
6	Dominion and colonial railways	0.04
7	Home railways	0.17
8	Foreign government	0.04
	(subtotal)	0.55

Moderate

10	American railways	0.08
11	Foreign railways	0.06
	(subtotal)	0.14

Risky

9	Home companies	0.17
12	Non-domestic companies	0.14
	(subtotal)	0.31

	Total amount	£7884m

Source: Edelstein, (1970: 235–7).

Note:

[1]The definition of risk class is based on *ex post* evaluation of the variability of money payments on debt in each class. Hence all securities bore an interest rate risk, but British government securities were virtually certain not to default from the nominal payment. Not all foreign government securities were of equal quality although by 1913 London was accepting very few doubtful issues. American railways and companies of all regions were a mixed lot; the bulk of their issues were fixed interest rather than variable and most were well established. If anything, the division into classes probably overstates the variability of the expected yields by 1913. The division here accords with Lavington (1921: 193–4): 'It seems reasonable to assume that the investor has fairly adequate bargaining knowledge when he enters the market to buy, let us say, the stocks issued by a Colonial Government, a reputable foreign state or a large municipality or the debentures or preference shares offered by a railway of proved earning capacity... Let us make an exceedingly rough division of the whole series of securities offered in the English market, placing on the one side stocks and shares of the kind just described and on the other a large mass of less well-known securities whose main constituents are the stocks and shares of new joint stock companies, formed under the Companies Act.'

spectacular frauds occurred but that they were of such small magnitude compared with the volume of securities purchased. The Victorians circumvented remarkably well, although at a high cost of lost opportunities, the dangers which tenuous control of managers and unreliable information imposed upon them by buying selectively (see Table 5.1). In this they were aided by a set of institutions comprising investment trusts, insurance companies, company promoters, stock-brokers, and merchant banks and performing almost a pure intermediary function of a special sort while undertaking, with rare but notable exceptions, almost no managerial responsibility.

The manner in which these institutions functioned, combined with the withdrawal of the banking system from long-term industrial capital formation, had two far reaching implications for the overall efficiency of financial intermediation in Britain. First, it meant that there was no institutional means of forging tighter links between owners and managers. In Germany, and to some extent in the U.S., banks acted to evaluate managerial performance by rewarding good results and punishing bad ones, in short acting as a very large shareholders' protection agency, of which the banks were the major but not sole beneficiary. In addition the extensive commercial intelligence of large banks provided the management of client firms with information both of relevant production and investment decisions taken elsewhere and of possible investment or marketing opportunities while providing the banks with a ready measure of their clients' successes and failures. Financial intermediaries closely linked to industrial concerns by ownership and creditor status thus often were in a position to play an informational role of great significance at a time when data publicly available were so often deliberately misleading. Intermediaries did not play such a role in Britain however.

Intermediaries also failed to play a second role in Britain, which operationally must have been of equal significance. This role was the systematic provision of the facilities for efficient diversification whereby investors could be sure, for any level of *ex ante* risks they took, that they would obtain the highest possible return the system as a whole was capable of affording. Although diversifying institutions in the form of investment and finance trusts did indeed appear, their activities were too small relative to the volume of traded securities to have seriously affected the prices of securities, accounting for only £90m of the £7900m of securities traded in London in 1913, and furthermore, of more importance for the analysis of domestic capital formation, holding portfolios that were almost completely composed of foreign assets (Jefferys, 1938: 365–6; Burton and Corner, 1968: 46).

The first important investment trust, called significantly the Foreign and Colonial Government Trust, had appeared in 1868 (Burton and Corner, 1968: 15). Similar institutions multiplied and grew rapidly in spite of the well-known difficulties in making informed choices. They obviously served a clearly felt need. But even in the middle of the 1890s, a decade of little foreign investment, a typical trust such as the International Investment Trust with assets valued at about £3.5m in 1896 had only 22.4% of its holdings in domestic securities; 44.8% were in North America, 26.6% in South America, and 6.2% elsewhere abroad (Burton and Corner, 1968: 39–40). Furthermore, only 30% of the portfolio was in ordinary or preferred shares. The reluctance of investment trusts to have large positions in domestic issues can most readily be explained by two factors. First, most trusts appear to have acted as vehicles for conservative clienteles and, therefore, restricted their own purchases to high grade securities. Secondly, information costs involved in holding domestic industrial issues were prohibitively high. The most efficient means of gathering information on industrial firms was undoubtedly that employed by the German banks, unsecured short-term advances (Lavington, 1921: 210–11). Because investment trusts were not also banks, they were not able to use this profitable information-gathering device which the banks had constructed through the laborious process of amalgamation. Their preference for large, prestigious issues is, therefore, readily explained. The most favoured foreign issues, as their early succession to respect on the London exchanges suggests, were close but not perfect substitutes for well-known domestic counterparts. Hence, the preferred foreign assets, in terms of increasing expected risk, were colonial governments, selected foreign governments, colonial rails, American rails, other foreign rails, and finally, foreign company issues. Investment trusts selected the best portfolio, then, not from among all assets but rather from a subset of well-known securities. By substituting the foreign equivalent of a well-known domestic asset, expected yields could be raised with the least increase in expected risk. The investment trusts were undoubtedly a valuable financial innovation but their impact on domestic capital formation was distinctly limited.

Nor was the institutional gap left by banks, discount houses and investment trusts filled by insurance companies. They too faced problems of information through lack of steady flows of commercial intelligence and were guided above all by a sense of prudence and caution (Supple, 1970: 330–348; Dickson, 1960: 234, 262–3). Thus when the yields on the mortgages and government stocks they relied upon to construct their portfolios fell in the last decades of the nineteenth century, the insurance companies moved into foreign government securities and into proven foreign debentures but not in any substantial way into ordinary corporate equity. The cult of equity was to be a mid twentieth-century phenomenon and the undeniable emergence of life-insurance companies as important and forceful critics of corporate management has only recently begun. As Table 5.2 indicates, before 1914 the insurance companies as a group had extremely small holdings of ordinary stocks and shares and, while they held appreciable quantities of debentures, the failure of the Royal Exchange Assurance, a large, well-run company, to earn an average yield on its portfolio of more than 4% from 1895 to the outbreak of the First World War indicates that the increased debenture

Table 5.2. *Percentage distribution of assets of all insurance companies established in the U.K., 1880–1913*

End of Year	Total assets (£m)	Mortgages	Loans on British national and local government securities	Loans on policy and personal securities	Other commercial and municipal securities	Foreign government and municipal securities	Debentures
1880	155.1	45.2	15.8	5.8	4.6	2.8	6.8
1885	179.3	42.2	16.0	5.3	6.3	2.3	7.4
1890	211.3	39.3	13.8	5.0	6.1	1.7	11.0
1895	251.3	33.2	13.5	4.6	6.8	2.2	14.0
1900	311.1	27.4	13.1	4.6	6.2	3.5	19.3
1905	384.4	25.2	14.3	5.3	5.2	3.0	18.8
1910	467.3	21.9	8.3	5.9	8.1	6.3	23.2
1911	491.3	21.8	7.4	5.7	7.9	6.8	24.1
1913	530.1	21.5	6.9	5.9	7.9	7.4	24.8

	Preference and guaranteed stocks	Ordinary stocks and shares	Land insurance, property and ground rent	Other assets, residual
1880		3.7	5.2	8.1
1885		3.5	6.4	7.9
1890		5.1	7.5	9.6
1895		6.4	8.2	9.1
1900		6.2	9.6	5.0
1905		8.1	9.7	7.7
1910		11.3	9.5	7.2
1911	6.0	11.0	9.1	7.5
1913	5.8	9.6	8.7	7.6

Source: Sheppard (1971: 154–6).

holdings were not enterprising to the point of offering yields sufficient to restore the profitability levels of earlier years (Supple, 1970: 334–5).

With the established Victorian institutions removed from an active, direct role as either managers or risk-sharing agents in private industrial capital formation, savers were left to bear the risks of such investments individually. As the first wave of conversion of private partnerships took place in the late 1860s and 1870s, intermediaries appeared which helped otherwise ignorant investors to discriminate among issues. The success with which these first intermediaries fulfilled this role helped to convince prudent men of the worth of the innovation of limited liability. The most famous of such intermediaries between the owners of established firms who wished to liquidate part of their holdings or to expand a profitable operation and a public willing to bear reasonable risks was the firm of Chadwick, Adamson, and Collier (Jefferys, 1938:298). As early as the 1870s, Chadwick's had established a clientele of perhaps 5000 wealthy subscribers willing to invest in companies promoted by the firm (Davis, 1966:671). The operations of Chadwick's, however, differed sharply from the operations of the promoters and stockbrokers who were to take over home industrial issues during the 1880s and after. Chadwick's did not seek out firms to promote but rather offered their services on a selective basis when requested to do so. Their services consisted of a knowledgeable financial and technical check of the prospective company which they presented to their clients together with an assessment, occasionally over-optimistic, of the firm's future. The amount of 'new' money they raised was typically only 25–30% of the value of the issue, the remainder being the value of the vendor's or issuing group's assets (Jefferys, 1938:298–9). Furthermore, Chadwick's stayed with the company it had formed as auditor (Chadwick was an accountant) thus providing a vital reassurance to those whom it had encouraged to invest.

These services were generally astutely and cheaply rendered; Chadwick's failure rate by 1877 was but one firm in ten and the commission was only 1% of the issue, and this for companies with a capital as small as £100,000 (Jefferys, 1938:320, 309). By the 1890s, the standard rate for less responsible and discriminating services was at least $2\frac{1}{2}\%$ and often more. But promising as the line of development pioneered by Chadwick's was, it was not long pursued. Apparently for reasons of personality – Chadwick had a disconcerting tendency to involve himself in acrimonious litigation with former partners (Cottrell, 1980:114) – Chadwick's firm did not survive the difficult transition from conversion work to new issues. Moreover, once the bulk of eligible established businesses had been converted from partnerships to limited companies, the task of company promotion became more demanding and complex. It was one matter – manifestly not without its own problems – to assess the value of an established enterprise; it was another matter, even less tractible, to estimate objectively the future earnings of an untried venture and to ensure, somehow, that the new venture actually got underway in some rough accordance with its published prospectus. Consequently, firms such as Richardson, Chadbourn and Company; Alfred Whitworth, Clemesha and Company; Joshua Hutchinson and Company; and George White's of Bristol continued in the same broad tradition as Chadwick's but without ever matching its stature, importance or volume of business. Other successor firms such as George Gregory and Son and the Investment Registry Limited arose to serve clients seeking a higher rate of return than could be had with perfect security but they, as did the investment trusts, concentrated their attention on foreign debentures and bonds, steering clear of common stock. George Gregory, for example, centred its promoting efforts in the

1890s in the West End of London, in Brighton and in Hastings, as far in distance as in investment intent from the turmoil of industrial activity in England (Jefferys, 1938: 365).

While the intermediaries most closely linked to sustained long-term industrial capital formation remained small, select, and local and thus highly segmented, investors were not without other, wider-reaching facilities to aid them in disposing of their funds. By the 1890s the age of the company promoter, often working with stockbrokers, had clearly begun. The promotion activity of the 1890s, however, involved a commitment of much shorter duration and responsibility than Chadwick's promotions of a decade or two before. The promoter now was often offering a chance for a bonanza, and bonanzas by their nature were more a matter of vision than of a reality which could be certified by an accountant, especially one given to asking awkward questions. Thus, Lavington (1921: 213) has characterized the British capital markets of the last quarter century of peace before 1914:

In the absence of strong intermediary agencies with machinery available for the investigation of industrial propositions and the organization requisite for the efficient marketing of their securities, the work of selecting profitable new ventures, of capitalizing their prospects in terms of securities and of selling these securities to the public, falls mainly to the company promoter; while that of marketing further issues of existing companies is undertaken by the companies themselves.

The trouble with this system, for new companies or old, however, was the promoter; Lavington (1921: 213) again noted:

The promoter is not a very definite kind of person. He may be a parent company engaged in the formation of a subsidiary or allied business enterprise; he may be, and very often is, the vendor of the assets purchased by the new company; or he may be a financier whose contact with the new company ceases when he had completed its flotation and sold any shares which may have been alloted to him. But whoever he may be, his interests *as promoter* are quite distinct from those of the company he forms. (Emphasis in the original.)

It is no surprise then that, despite the ability of some promoters, underwriters and stockbrokers consistently to launch successful new companies, the stock exchanges as a whole had a distressing tendency to launch new issues, especially for firms in new industries, disastrously.

Victorian capital markets in operation – three illustrations: electrical engineering and electricity supply, automobiles, and chemicals

These three industries – electrical engineering and electricity supply, automobiles, and chemicals – encompassed many of the most important technological developments of the late nineteenth century. Their financial histories reveal, in rather different ways, the manifold short-comings of Victorian capital markets in effectively concentrating and utilizing resources in vital areas of economic development.

The early financial histories of the electrical engineering and automobile industries were surprisingly similar. Both represented instances where technical change created a sharp discontinuity in industrial development, making it difficult for firms previously in existence to play a dominant role in the subsequent growth of the industries. In both cases the resources for successful expansion could not be drawn from a single established, well-defined industrial base but had to be drawn from the wider economy. In both cases, in a manner strikingly similar to Akerlof's (1970) analysis of markets for 'lemons', early and calamitous financial mobilizations severely crippled subsequent development and the funds necessary for expansion, when they finally did appear, almost invariably did so too slowly to exploit the periodic booms in demand.

The electricity industry was the first to pass through this cycle. It is important to note that early British experiments in the application of electricity to lighting – the first large-scale practical use of electricity – were many and vigorous. Joseph Swan's independent invention of a practical incandescent lamp, demonstrated to the Newcastle-on-Tyne Chemical Society in December 1878, is most easily understood as an extension of a rich technological tradition dating back at least to Sir Humphry Davy's experiments, disclosed to the Royal Institution in London as early as 1802, with both incandescent and arc lighting. Michael Faraday had invented the dynamo in 1831 and, during the middle years of the century, James Clerk Maxwell had worked out the fundamental scientific basis upon which the practice of electrical engineering – and much else besides, such as long distance communication – would eventually develop. By 1882, electrical lighting in England was widespread – wealthy magnates intrigued their house guests with it, theatres and football grounds operated at night with it, MPs in the House of Commons deliberated under it (Hannah, 1979: 3–4). Into this technological and commercial ferment the Stock Exchange intruded in 1882 with devastating effect. In that single year, at least £1.5m were raised by promoters of various lighting schemes (Hannah, 1979: 5–6). This was a vast sum for the time, amounting in 1882 to more than one tenth of one per cent of GNP. A comparable sum in 1978 would come to £190m, nearly four times the amount committed by the Labour government of the day – private firms refusing to take the risk – to establish a domestic capacity to mass produce powerful integrated electronic circuits. The results of the 1882 flotations were, however, only to transfer money from eager investors to a wide variety of promoters, lawyers, and owners of dubious, fraudulent, and useless patents (Byatt, 1979: 17–21; Hannah, 1979: 6–7). In this manner, the financial assets of the electrical engineering industry were firmly established as 'lemons' and, perhaps not coincidentally, Britain was never again to be so prominent in the theoretical development and practical application of electricity as in the decades preceding the early 1880s.

The consequences of this ruinous start became clearer as time passed. The industry struggled through the continuous technical change of the mid 1880s with a tarnished financial record. Capacity grew slowly, often as a result of mechanical engineering firms opening a line of electrical manufacture. Profits in the industry did not start to become impressive until the boom from 1888 to 1891. Yet as demand surged ahead and output trebled in three years, firms still found it difficult to expand fast enough. The factor perhaps most responsible for hindering rapid advance then was the borrowing constraint; at a time when conditions justified ploughing all firms' net operating receipts into more capacity, electrical companies could not use the equity market but, because of their past record, were forced into the debenture market if they could borrow at all. Equity financing was preferable at this stage, however, because it relieved firms of the need to meet regular debt payments when conditions for expansion were unusually favourable. Yet electrical engineering firms attempting to raise money found it necessary to signal continuously through high payout levels the soundness of their current affairs at the expense of their long-term development. Thus, Brush, the largest British manufacturer of the late 1880s and possessed of unusually good City connections through stockbrokers Foster and Braithwaite (Morgan and Thomas, 1962: 111), was unable, despite considerable effort, to meet the boom after 1888 by selling equities and was forced at this time to raise nearly two-thirds of its funds for expansion in the debenture market (Byatt, 1962: 342–3). Crompton, one of the most innovative firms, was not even this lucky. Its second bond issue during the boom in the summer of 1890 failed with only £10,800 of a £25,000 issue sold by March, 1891. Another bond issue and a preference share issue also were not well received. By March, 1895, only £83,000 of a £100,000 bond issue of February 1894 had been sold (Byatt, 1962: 343). The strain clearly showed in Crompton's management. Elaborate experimentation was to be halted and a general manager, 'not a member of the Board [of directors], but open to every possible criticism and under the most complete control', was to oversee technical development (Byatt, 1962: 350).[14] R.E.B. Crompton, who had been a prolific innovator, was repelled by this atmosphere and as the 1890s wore on took progressively less part in the affairs of the company which bore his name.

Unfortunately for the British electrical industry, the boom starting in 1888 was prematurely damped down in the aftermath of Baring's embarrassment with Argentinian securities in the autumn of 1890. (A more detailed analysis of the important relationship between foreign investment and the development of the domestic electrical engineering industry is given in Chapter 6.) Difficulties, already present before the crisis, became much worse, as the events at Crompton showed. Expansion in the industry slowed to a crawl and the major developments of the period, polyphase a.c. motors and traction motors were ignored. The liquidity problems of the manufacturers were augmented by the behaviour of their biggest customers, the new supply companies, who were also pressed for cash and paid for plant in illiquid and depreciated securities which they themselves could not sell on open markets. The industry and the economy were temporarily depressed. The industrial potential of electricity, however, was too great to be long stifled and by 1895 the great home boom ushered in the beginning of an electrical boom that lasted until 1903, when foreign investment once again became extremely popular and sharply curtailed housebuilding, the driving stimulus behind much traction construction, which in turn was the largest prop of Britain's electricity industry at the time.

The liquidity problems of the early 1890s, however, had left an indelible mark. When the boom and the profits anticipated in 1882 and 1888–90 finally arrived the British industry was exhausted from thwarted anticipation. It had neither the capacity nor the technology to meet the boom and the long-sought gains were reaped largely by foreigners who poured in exports and finally followed with high levels of direct investment in the industry. The established British electrical firms were illiquid and by 1895 in the hands of cautious men who used the affluence which the boom brought to restore their companies rather than expand them (Byatt, 1962: 369–70). Thus of the increase of £4.1m in the value of fixed assets in the British electrical industry between 1896 and 1904, 67% was supplied by foreign firms. The industry, especially the new foreign arrivals, faced difficult times as domestic investment, and with it the demand for electrical equipment, fell by a third between 1903 and 1908 (Feinstein, 1972: Table 40, column 6; see also Table 5.3).[15] Yet as Britain once more fell behind foreign technology, the foundation for a catch-up spurt was once more laid; the upturn duly came in the three years just prior to the war. Foreign firms were then still in their dominant position.

One might go farther and argue that many of the peculiar, generally debilitating characteristics of the British electrical engineering industry were closely associated with a segmented financial system which concentrated resources for risky domestic ventures only with difficulty. A notable drawback of British arrangements was that electrical manufacturers did not have a dominant holding in supply companies, although in the early 1890s the struggling manufacturers were often paid in the shares of the struggling new supply companies, which typically did not add general electrical engineering to their burdens. Unlike the situation in the U.S. and Germany, where the financial control of manufacturers and suppliers was frequently unified, often through a bank or interlocking shareholding, the practice of inserting an independent consulting engineer became established in Britain. These engineers were frequently considered by contemporaries, probably correctly, to impose need-lessly rigid and unique specifications on manufacturers, thereby raising costs (Byatt, 1962: 471–2), although this did not always happen. Charles Merz, consulting engineer for the Newcastle Electric Supply Company, for example, followed a very enlightened policy of close co-operation with manufacturers

(Byatt, 1962: 471–2), but Merz was *sui generis* and his ability to make his talent tell was magnified by family connections. His uncle, Wigham Richardson, a prominent Tyneside shipbuilder and power user, had substantial interests in one local electricity supply company and his father was a prominent director of another (Hannah, 1979: 28–9). Thus, once Merz could demonstrate before such a receptive audience the extent of the economies of scale in electricity supply he had a free hand to realize them, thereby avoiding the fragmentation of supply operations that distinguished the rest of the British industry. There is obviously much to be said for institutional arrangements that can systematically act as a substitute for talents and circumstances that occur all too rarely by any standard.

Failure to concentrate resources, to expand manufacturing facilities and technological capability, especially during recessions, and to ensure low cost electricity supply to customers, meant that British firms were always caught short of capacity and backward in products when the booms came and generally faced less buoyant markets than their more successful counterparts in North America and Europe. Since it was recognized by the perceptive no later than the early nineties that electricity was the power of the future, the only explanation of the poor state of the industry in the boom beginning in 1896 was the inability to translate the force of technological convictions into physical capital, a risky business but one in which the rewards were correspondingly high. Furthermore, the reluctance to commit resources to investment until a boom had materialized, when widely practised, was ultimately self-justifying and guaranteed the lengthening of recessions. This reluctance on the part of such an important supplier of inputs to the rest of the manufacturing sector had implications far beyond that implied by the size of the electrical engineering industry. The drawbacks, furthermore, were cumulative; when most of the innovations in electrically powered equipment were made abroad, British firms, especially the smaller ones for whom electricity was to mean an added flexibility which ultimately offered great hope for the future, became aware of the potential of such equipment more slowly than their foreign counterparts. The slow spread of power equipment limited the growth of the demand for electricity, the supply of which enjoyed substantial economies of scale. High electricity supply prices, already raised by fragmentation among supply companies, then further discouraged the spread of electricity usage. The failure to break this vicious circle satisfactorily was in large part the failure of financial intermediaries to find the successful men, and to back them with resources sufficient to weather the inevitable recessions. This failure meant that domestic firms could rarely compete with foreigners on equal terms and lacked the financial stamina to win the potentially lucrative domestic markets that only attractively priced, reliable goods could capture.

The lamentable financial circumstances of the launching of the electricity

industry were repeated less than half a decade later for automobiles. S.B. Saul's concise description (1962: 22) has a familiar ring:

The first British motor company was launched in 1896 by a group of financial speculators, headed by Harry J. Lawson, almost as an appendix to their disastrous speculations with the cycle industry, though by that time the automobile industry was already well established in France. The first five years were unrewarding in many ways; little positive progress was made, companies such as Daimler and Humber had to struggle for years to overcome the burden of watered stock imposed upon them by Lawson, and the public soon became shy of investing in the industry as a result.

The subsequent development of the industry also parallels that of electricity. The industry consisted of a host of small producers intermittently facing financial difficulties. After a bad beginning, the industry, now believed to be dangerously riddled with 'lemons', could not easily again obtain capital market support until 1904–7. (See Table 5.3.) Then, beginning in 1904, with many successful foreign examples before them and the extent of the home market sharply outlined by burgeoning imports, new money did flow into the industry. Output began to rise, although this was a product as much of new entry as of established firms expanding sharply. The burst of well-supported expansions,

Table 5.3. *New issues offered in London for selected domestic industries, 1899–1913*
(£000s)

	Electric lighting	Engineering	Electrical manufactures	Automobile manufacture
1899	661	2246	1174	20
1900	1968	4150	1374	20
1901	1576	1821	880	30
1902	1356	1145	1611	119
1903	2662	957	155	—
1904	1449	1171	25	75
1905	1233	1134	393	404
1906	1265	1324	591	1104
1907	710	501	50	772
1908	1473	1121	665	75
1909	866	400	159	—
1910	359	442	720	—
1911	297	480	397	231
1912	649	542	427	426
1913	1450	2168	115	1443

Source: G.L. Ayres (1934: Table 13).

however, was short lived. In 1907, overseas troubles, this time in the U.S., once again suddenly disrupted the market, forcing several firms into liquidation. This disruption was even worse for the automobile industry than the Barings crisis of 1890 had been for electricity for a world-wide boom in automobile production was under way. Output in the U.S. was barely affected by the crisis, which resolved itself with unusual speed, and output there more than trebled between 1908 and 1913.[16] Yet during most of this feverish world-wide boom, the domestic British industry could not use the stock exchanges. (See Table 5.3.) Little was raised in 1908 and nothing at all in 1909–10. Imports poured in, and by 1911, as the stock market showed signs of recovering its nerve, Henry Ford had settled in to dominate the lower end of the market with the Model-Ts gushing from his Trafford Park plant.

The episode from 1907 to 1913 caught the defects of the British capital markets in a harsh glare. The exchanges were then (and are now) extremely fickle with a notoriously high implied discount rate. Thus, flickers of doubt and subtle intimations of difficulties could choke off the flow of funds; while the boom roared on after 1907, the expansion had to come with painful slowness from within the car firms, not from without. On the other hand, when resources were flung into the industry by the market, it was often done without coherence and discipline. With no shortage of potentially successful automobile manufacturers, the three firms on which the market lavished funds most readily were the most unprofitable in the industry. Saul (1962b: 32, 40) was surely too generous in his judgment of the stock exchange's provision of funds to the industry. What was required was a steady, rational, courageous effort to distinguish promising firms from 'lemons' in an industry which had technical troubles and dangerous inventory requirements but also a huge market. What it got was waves of money carelessly supplied, mostly to 'lemons', followed by an equally unreflective withdrawal when problems appeared, problems magnified by the previous carelessness. Thus, the electricity industry's experience was repeated in considerable detail. The industry struggled through slack periods and was unprepared for the booms. By the time domestic investment did manage to exert itself, foreign competition was thoroughly entrenched making the investment ultimately less profitable (although still fabulously profitable) and more risky for domestic producers. In the automobile industry, as with electrical engineering, it was not so much that the slumps were severe but that the booms were so badly exploited. As international markets became more lucrative, the rewards for financial concentrations in the right industry at the right time grew; the penalties for not concentrating soon enough or effectively enough grew also.

The experience of the chemical industry varied considerably in detail from that of electrical engineering and automobiles. Chemical manufacture by 1870 was already a large and important business, capable of generating within itself most, if not all, the resources needed for exploitation of the dramatic new opportunities the scientific and technological advances of the period opened up. Moreover, many of the established firms in the industry had over time formed links with financial intermediaries, who, for their part, developed an understanding of the unique needs and problems of the chemical industry. But as in automobile manufacture, those resources that did come through formal capital markets were lavished on the least capable firms in the industry while the most successful firms were unable to attract formal capital market support until they were so manifestly flourishing that they could grow without it. In this manner British capital markets made an indispensable contribution to a situation where a British industry, which had been a world leader in 1870, stagnated until thoroughly overshadowed in almost all areas of production by foreign, particularly German, rivals.

The key to this stagnation lay in a system of market behaviour in which external support never acted to reward and propel forward the dynamic firms but instead served to prop up moribund ones. This system suppressed the normal competitive pressures that would have sustained the industry's growth by transferring resources quickly from incapable to capable hands and by placing on technological prowess sooner the market valuation eventually shown to be warranted. To be sure, while competitive pressures were greatly attenuated, they were not eliminated altogether. The weak gradually sank into insignificance while the strong registered growth to the point where their expansion alone represented net growth for the entire British industry. But this process took decades and meanwhile, as technological advances radically widened the horizons of industrial chemistry, the British industry as a whole stagnated, suffering serious losses in its technological acumen and in its ability to respond to new opportunities.

Thus, two of the most successful firms in the British industry, British Dynamite Company (later renamed Nobel's Explosives Company) and Brunner, Mond, were established without any help from financial intermediaries.[17] Rather the makeshift arrangements of the classical Industrial Revoluion, relying upon finance from personal contacts, were employed to launch the two firms. Although Alfred Nobel sought in London to secure financial backing for his plans for explosives production, the barriers between financiers and industrialists in the capital were sufficiently durable that Nobel could not elicit support through his own efforts and, for their part, the financial intermediaries took no notice of Nobel. Glasgow, an industrial not a financial centre, ultimately proved receptive to his ideas and Nobel was able to raise sufficient money, £24,000 in April 1871, from local industrialists to launch his enterprise without further difficulty. Once the enterprise was established and profitable it was possible to obtain further finance, even in large amounts, comparatively easily.

John Brunner and Ludwig Mond were not able to solve their early financial problems so neatly and decisively. They could not manage to tap a circle of wealthy, discerning backers at the outset and their early operations were marked by a constant struggle for funds which they obtained in small amounts from diverse sources. In 1872, their business got under way with £5,000 from their own resources and another £5,000 advanced by a boyhood friend of John Brunner. Subsequently, they depended upon bank overdrafts secured against assets and upon a series of small loans from the Solvay family of Belgium, also their main technical advisers. William Reader (1970:49, 52) has summarized Brunner, Mond's early financial experience thus:

In the most advanced industrial country of the world, they [Brunner and Mond] could find no access to any but local sources of capital – London was no help to them at all – and they had no institutional support whatever.... They evidently found it almost impossible to borrow without property to pledge, and until they could borrow they could acquire no property.... The early financing of Brunner, Mond, sound enough though it turned out in the end, has an air of desperate improvisation about it.

Clearly, what was needed but was so difficult to find in Britain was what Dr Herbert Levinstein, the son of the founder of perhaps the most successful firm in the minuscule Victorian dyestuffs industry and himself an industrial chemist of wide experience, called 'educated money'. Levinstein argued that:

the application of knowledge requires finance and the capacity on the part of those who control finance to judge the value of a scientific discovery. The main cost of industrial research is not in the laboratory but in the application to the large-scale.... Who in England was going to find money for this? In Germany, the banks would and did find it. We [in England] suffered and have always suffered from a lack of 'educated' money. (Quoted in Reader, 1970: 261.)

The contrast between the creation of Nobel's Explosives Company and Brunner, Mond on the one hand and the formation of the Salt Union Ltd and the United Alkali Company on the other could hardly have been greater. The Salt Union and United Alkali were both large-scale, multi-firm mergers and both proved to be monumental 'lemons'. The Salt Union boasted at its creation that it controlled 90% of the United Kingdom's salt output, a major raw-material of the chemical industry. United Alkali represented a merger of all the major British manufacturers of alkali employing the Leblanc process. Powerful support by financial intermediaries made it possible for the two companies to raise millions of pounds publicly (Cottrell, 1980: 171–2). The Salt Union raised approximately £3m from the public in 1888 while United Alkali, despite a combination of the Baring Crisis and press opposition, secured £1.3m in cash from public issues in 1891, a time when the entire electrical engineering industry was spurned. The total nominal capital for the Salt Union was approximately £4m and that of United Alkali about £8.2m, making them for a short while the undisputed global chemical giants of the day. Also in contrast to Nobels and Brunner, Mond, however, this vast capital was mobilized on behalf of obsolete technologies that within a short span of years could no longer support dividend or even interest payments. The disparity between the ample profitability of those firms that had not raised substantial sums publicly and the penury of those that had was not lost on the minority shareholders of the stricken firms. These shareholders, however, could do no more than vent their frustrations by impugning, with good reason, the competence of managing board members at the firms' Annual General Meetings. In all, it was a sorry spectacle.

The giant flotations in the chemical industry had two enduring consequences, one of significance for the entire economy, the other of particular importance to the development of the chemical industry. Because of their size, the large chemical issues exerted a greater demonstration effect, and touched directly more people, than any other single issue by firms operating in technologically advanced sectors of the economy during the Victorian period. By exposing an unusually large number of people to the dangers of dealing in markets for 'lemons', the abysmal performance of these issues made an unusually large contribution to the hostility and suspicion subsequent ventures in new technologies faced from the investing public at large. In the long run the losses were not confined to the hapless shareholders of the Salt Union Ltd and the United Alkali Company, but were also apportioned among less culpable entrepreneurs, offering not 'lemons' but worthwhile proposals, who could not gain a ready public hearing because of the earlier failures.

The consequence for the British chemical industry was the removal of any real competitive pressures for a more vigorous response to the technical changes of the period. By facilitating the merger of all the firms engaged in the entire Leblanc soda industry into two huge incompetent entities, British capital markets acted to stifle any impulses for rejuvenation that might have existed within that branch of the industry. And because, until the turn of the century, United Alkali was large enough relative to Brunner, Mond to determine effectively prices in Britain, Brunner, Mond, with their greater productivity, were enabled to earn super-normal profits at virtually no risk. At any price level United Alkali could bear, Brunner, Mond could make good, often very good, profits. If market demand slackened, the brunt of excess capacity fell on United Alkali, not on Brunner, Mond. It is no wonder, then, that Brunner, Mond became increasingly solicitous about the future of United Alkali as soon as it became clear that the larger firm constituted no real threat. This cosy situation, however, engendered over time a complacency that served progressively to weaken the British chemical industry. Unlike their counterparts within the Solvay groups in Belgium and Germany, Brunner, Mond did not feel compelled to monitor carefully the full range of technological changes that could affect the alkali industry. Thus Brunner, Mond remained surprisingly undiversified in their operations right up to the First World War, although by 1914 the firm was beginning to feel uneasy about the situation. The threat of technological advance by competitors, which was a very real force in many of the highly structured, carefully controlled markets in Western Europe and which was sufficient to keep the members of even well-disciplined cartels constantly searching for new areas of innovation, was conspicuously absent in Britain, for there, unlike elsewhere, once Brunner, Mond had achieved market dominance there was no other source of potential challenge. Thus while the Solvays and their German allies were anxious to incorporate the manufacture of chlorine into their product cycle, Brunner, Mond could afford to be oblivious to the problem. Brunner, Mond in Britain faced no pressure comparable to that faced by Siemens in Germany, where an alert, aggressive financial system quickly mobilized the resources to force a wider sharing of super-normal profits in a technologically demanding industry. While such security was highly satisfactory in the short run, no matter how disadvantageous it might have been for the economy as a whole, Brunner, Mond was building problems for the future, although such was the company's strength and so stable were the pre-1914 international chemical cartel arrangements, that it took a World War to shake Brunner, Mond loose from its comfortable niche.

Biases in Victorian capital markets

British stock exchanges did not always perform as badly as they did in the launching of the electrical and automobile industries or in the transformation of the chemical industry. In some instances, as David Chadwick has shown, they could offer valuable means of raising money for domestic ventures and for affording investors greater liquidity than would otherwise have been possible. The yields on even a partial relaxation of segmentation were often high and some promoters such as H. Osborne O'Hagen, often in conjunction with stockbrokers Panmure, Gordon and Company, launched companies that were fully intended to be – and often were – viable. Nevertheless, without stronger, better informed, and more vigilant intermediaries the exchanges could never have significantly reduced segmentation. The most obvious means to achieve this end was, as in Germany, through bank involvement in long-term capital formation. Had banks been thoroughly committed to underwriting, and had they been responsibly involved subsequently in the management of the firms they launched, their financial and informational resources would have offered much greater reassurance to outside investors than the words of loose, uneasy coalitions of under-capitalized promoters and stock brokers. But such involvement was foreclosed in the course of bank evolution in the nineteenth century. As has already been stressed, the banking system gradually broke the local links that had bound it to the long-term fortunes of British industry and instead fashioned for itself a relatively trouble-free relationship based on short-term loans and well-secured advances. This is not to deny the undoubted skills of many late Victorian bankers, but only to stress that those skills were deployed within an institutional framework that systematically sought to exclude responsibility for long-term capital formation from bankers' tasks.

As a consequence of these institutional developments, an important bias operated in British capital markets, though the bias was not the one most frequently cited, that towards foreign investment. Rather the bias was towards safe, well-known securities in general, a great number of which were foreign, and away from riskier, smaller, but ultimately from an economy-wide viewpoint, much more profitable ones. Furthermore, the neglect which the organized markets showed towards the riskier ventures was reinforced by a lack of adequate facilities for diversification which would have made the burden of risk and uncertainty lighter. Because diversification possibilities for the most dangerous domestic ventures were so limited, their riskiness was made to appear more stark than necessary. The imbalance created by the clear articulation of the characteristics of selected issues easily and confidently traded in London and the ignorance and suspicion surrounding the issues of most provincial industrial concerns gave a pronounced foreign orientation to British capital markets. It was not that foreign assets as such were more highly esteemed than their intrinsic earning capacity would warrant. Far from it, other things being equal there is every reason to believe that domestic assets were preferred to foreign ones. But other things were not equal. Britain could not generate the same volume of secure government debt issue, of profitable railroad construction, of public utility operation that the rest of the world generated. Had the huge flows of Victorian savings been constrained to these activities at home, the rate of return would have fallen unacceptably low. The crucial point is that the foreign counterparts to the safest and best-known domestic assets were markedly preferred over domestic (and even more so over foreign) industrial issues by all but a small subset of unusually well-informed and well-placed domestic investors – most of whom were isolated from each other – whose wealth constituted a woefully small proportion of all British wealth. A very different type of capital market, supported by a much richer, more capable information network permitting much wider patterns of portfolio diversification and facilitating more informed control of corporate managers, would have been required in order to produce a market environment in which domestic industrial ventures could compete on even terms with the trusted, staple vehicles of Victorian investment among which foreign issues were so prominent.

The London stock exchange offered perhaps the best choice of essentially *safe* securities available anywhere in the world. As a consequence, less knowledgeable risk taking (in the sense of domestic, industrial capital formation in areas of advanced technology, the real risks) took place in Britain than in any of her advanced competitors. A classic problem of the second best appears to have operated in Britain before 1914. A part, but only a part, of her set of capital markets operated better than anyone else's. Had Americans or Germans had the facilities to obtain such high yields with such low risks as did Britons, particularly Londoners, perhaps they too would have taken fewer of the risks which their own imperfect capital markets forced upon them. But Americans and Germans did not have such effective facilities as near to hand and they did bear, collectively and successfully, the risks associated with later nineteenth-century technical change. As a consequence their growth rates were substantially higher than Britain's as their levels of per capita wealth surpassed or rapidly approached that of Britain.

Michael Edelstein (1970, 1971, 1974, 1982) has made the first systematic investigation of bias within the U.K. capital markets. Although the pricing model he uses to detect bias is a general one which could, in principle, be applied to any asset, the data base which he has constructed for his test consists only of high quality securities (Edelstein, 1970: 238–75). Since his data base is quite broad in range of industries, the dividends and coupons paid reflect to some extent conditions within the industries in his sample. On the other hand, Edelstein's sample of securities is obviously placed in a special category by the absence of an effective takeover sanction and the requirement that the securities must have exhibited regular pay-out patterns (although equities were permitted to fail to pay dividends for short periods without losing their first-class status). The assumption that all expectations *ex ante* were fulfilled further reveals the special nature of his sample because his selection of high quality securities clearly demanded care *ex post* with large numbers of securities rejected.[18] Therefore, Eldelstein's conclusions are relevant, not for all assets but only for a restricted subset of assets. Thus, for example, much of the explanation Edelstein offers for a narrowing in rate of return differentials among the comparable securities in his sample must arise simply from increasing market familiarity with assets whose history has been traced for some time. By the time the select group of assets which Edelstein chose largely on the basis of their similarities to each other had been observed for twenty or thirty years, price differentials must have moved in such a way that rate of return differentials were largely eliminated. Pre-selection also helps to account for his failure to detect directly evidence of regional or scale bias in the period 1870–1913 (Edelstein, 1971: 98–103).

It is, therefore, entirely consistent with Edelstein's results that although within the sample group no evidence of bias towards foreign issues appears, the capital markets were in fact deeply biased away from favouring most home industrial projects, particularly those in risky areas of new technology. Furthermore, some of Edelstein's findings confirm the existence of bias even within his special sample. Edelstein's 1974 study of the determinants of U.K. purchases of U.S. railroad securities does not confront the possibility that British capital markets systematically undervalued most domestic industrial securities. Nevertheless, without directly confronting this issue, Edelstein does report a low cross-elasticity of British demand for U.S. railroad bonds with respect to yields on comparable

British home securities. While this cross-elasticity remained low throughout the period, it did rise over time but never became elastic. Therefore, even for his restricted sample, Edelstein finds that trading in Australian, Indian and home long-term negotiable debt instruments remained partially isolated (segmented) from dealings in their U.S. counterparts. In view of the complex changes taking place in both the U.S. and the U.K. during the period, the interpretation of the increase in the cross-elasticity of demand between the U.S. and U.K. which he does find is not straightforward, but it seems clear that only a small proportion may be explained by a heightened British sensitivity to domestic yields induced by the appearance and spread of large scale U.K. corporate enterprise after the 1880s. U.K. home industrials, despite the increased demand for resources induced by the major technological advances of the late nineteenth century, do not seem to have been the beneficiary of the weakened reception of American securities after 1895. In the nineteen years from 1895 to 1913, U.K. capital markets were concerned intensively with internal financing only from 1895 to 1899 and from 1902 to 1905. From 1899 to 1902, the financing of the Boer War dominated the market and by 1905 the greatest surge of foreign investment ever mounted by Britain was well under way, although the U.S. was by then not so well favoured as had been true earlier.

Therefore, Edelstein's conclusion appears to be only partially valid. The U.K. capital market surely improved but at best by reducing segmentation *within* the classes of established securities, leaving the segmentation between these securities and the newer, less familiar, often riskier, issues of domestic firms unchanged or even increased. This segmentation, as argued at the beginning of the chapter, ensured that only inadequate market channels, or even none at all, existed to arbitrage the differences between the yields created by the application of new technologies abroad and those earned by the same technologies in Britain. Despite some limited aspects of efficiency in Britain's capital markets, efficiency which has impressed many historians, such qualities seem in retrospect only incompletely to compensate for the growth which others, but not Britain, enjoyed.

6

The economics of British foreign investment in the late nineteenth century

As regards the absorptive capacity of the English [electrical equipment] market, I do not at all share the optimistic views which were current, more particularly, several years ago, and which doubtless induced the American Westinghouse Co. and B.T.H. [British Thomson-Houston] to establish large factories in England. A great deal is spoken about the extraordinary wealth of England. This may be correct, but it is not the case that this wealth is invested in industrial undertakings from which we can expect to receive orders. Some time ago Government statistics came to my notice, according to which 55 Milliards of Marks of English Capital are invested abroad, to a great extent in foreign Government loans and in English Colonial Administration, in shares or loans in foreign railways, in foreign, especially South African, gold and diamond mines, in Colonial Companies, etc.

Without a doubt, England is very extensively industrialised; it is characteristic, however, that as compared with Germany and America these industries have undergone little development [recently]...German Industry as a whole has multiplied several times over, whilst Industry in England has hardly grown at all. It is these new undertakings in Germany, however, which provide our Workshops with work.

Karl Köttgen, Managing Director of Siemens Bros. Dynamo Works in a report to the headquarters of Siemens and Halske, Berlin, circa 1909. (Quoted in Siemens, 1957:313–14.)

Introduction

The distortions and malfunctions that characterized British capital markets in the half century before 1914 did not simply prevent investment resources from reaching promising but risky ventures. Capital market imperfections were also central to an economic process that served to justify an increasingly peculiar pattern of resource allocation in which important activities – not least technical education – highly profitable in other advanced economies proved to be much less so in Britain. At the heart of this debilitating process lay the fact that Victorian capital market imperfections did not occur in a vacuum. If it were more difficult in Victorian Britain than in almost any other advanced country of the day to participate efficiently in the exploitation of new and risky technological and commercial opportunities, it was also easier there than anywhere else to deal in certain types of relatively secure and well-known financial assets. If British capital markets were poor places to buy and sell industrial securities they, especially in London, were very good places to buy and sell government stocks, railroad securities and municipal and public utility bonds and selected other issues, such as those of mining and real estate enterprises, many of them foreign. Foreign industrial assets, however, were traded in Britain with, if anything, even less success than their domestic counterparts (Patterson, 1976:88–102). Economies of scale made large flotations – usually issued on behalf of governments, railroads, public utilities, and municipalities – highly profitable for the investment houses that handled them and thus caused the attentions and efforts of the most reputable, prestigious, and perhaps most capable, houses to be concentrated on them (Edelstein, 1971:85–7; Cottrell, 1980:179–81). It would have taken 50 issues of £200,000 each, a substantial size for a domestic industrial flotation, to equal the £10m or so that would be raised for a single substantial foreign railroad. And it would only be reasonable to expect, even disregarding the possibility of fraud or deception, that some of the 50 small issues would yield only losses whereas, although a large rail system financed in London could certainly disappoint its backers, it was highly unlikely, so discerning had the specialized London market for railroad securities become, that it would fail completely and irrevocably.

In this manner, British foreign investment came to represent a search for security of a type that a fiscally frugal, heavily industrialized Britain – where the major rail lines and the most conspicuously needed public utilities had already been built – could no longer provide. The heavy foreign investment spawned by the urgent, unceasing pursuit of assets that were acceptable substitutes for the favoured investment vehicles of the middle Victorian years imposed certain crucial adjustments on the domestic British economy. The most important of these were the expansion of traditional export industries at the expense of more technologically advanced industries and the accommodation of a vast, progressively rising influx of imports.

The evidence for this argument is developed in two stages. The first consists of the demonstration that Victorian foreign investment was generally cautious and risk averse. The second considers the means by which technologically progressive activities in Britain were rendered unattractive or unprofitable by the huge surges of conservative foreign investment that the Victorian economy sustained.

The characteristics of British foreign investment, 1870–1913

The conservative nature of British foreign investment, revealing a marked preference for low variance of returns at the cost of foregoing high yields, may be seen in an examination of three characteristics: (1) the infrequency of defaults on foreign investments; (2) the preponderance of fixed-interest securities in the aggregate portfolio of British foreign assets; and (3) the relatively low rate of return as compared to estimates of the yields on the British domestic real capital stock.

However, in no sense was British foreign investment, especially after 1880, thrown away. British investors got very largely the returns they paid for and generally enjoyed capital gains as well. This is in marked contrast to the nineteenth-century French experience with foreign investment. The countries in which Britain invested were friendly to British interests. Growing countries such as the U.S., which was the largest single recipient of British foreign investment, had the means to honour their debts and the incentive to maintain their credit; British civil servants in the closely governed parts of the Empire saw to it that defaults in areas of their jurisdiction did not occur. Little was lent to bankrupt princes and insolvent potentates. By 1913, the experienced dealers in the London capital market had become so skilled in steering their clients away from bad loans that a close, contemporary observer of British foreign investment, R.A. Lehfeldt (1913a: 200–1), could treat defaults as a vanishing phenomenon. Cairncross (1953: 229) estimated that for the decade 1870–80, which stands out as a particularly bad period for foreign investments, the yield in dividends was 5.4% and aggregate foreign investments actually appreciated by 0.7%. Defaults were apparently never severe enough to reduce significantly the aggregate rate of return.[1] After 1880, and particularly after 1890, this record improved. The majority of British investors never pursued high yields to the point where, in the worst years, defaults radically reduced the realized return. It is not surprising then that yields, even in the best years, were not breathtaking either.

That British foreign investments exhibited a low variance in their yield becomes more easily understood with the realization that the preferred instrument of foreign investment was the fixed-interest security rather than equities. The careful, prudent choice of foreign assets protected the British investor against default, but for most foreign investments there was no way for them to share fully in capital gains, for the yields were fixed. R.A. Lehfeldt (1913a: 199) in a study of British foreign investments between 1888 and 1911, observed that for large issues, which usually accounted for between one-half and two-thirds of the total amount raised by overseas borrowers, 'the first point that stands out is the insignificance of shares.' For the medium-class issues, those between £900,000 and £200,000, which he examined in the years 1911–13, Lehfeldt (1913b; 1914: 434) observed: 'Again the preference for loans, as compared with shares, which is so marked a feature of the "large" investments, is reproduced in the "medium", though not quite so intensively – share issues constitute about one-eighth of the large, one-fourth of the medium class.' Although his coverage is not complete since he is dealing with only about 75% of the total money calls as calculated by Simon (1967), Lehfeldt probably presents an accurate picture of the division between shares and fixed interest securities as instruments of long-term British foreign investment. In fact, because Lehfeldt covered the period of the heaviest British foreign investment which occurred before the war, a time when equities were more widely purchased than they had been in earlier decades, he undoubtedly overstated the share of the equities in the entire fifty year period.

Lehfeldt's conclusions regarding the predominance of bonds are borne out by a study conducted by G.L. Ayers (1934: 52) of foreign investment in the important years 1899–1913. Ayers found that only in 1910 did sales of ordinary shares, carrying no guarantee of nor limit to yield, exceed £30m. Annual purchases of foreign shares were usually below £20m; only in the years 1909–1912 was this level broken for the period 1899–1913. For the period 1899–1913 total money calls for foreign investments averaged £125m.[2] The figure for 1910 was £198m. Towards the end of the period ordinary industrial shares appeared in the aggregate British portfolio of foreign investments, but they were neither representative nor particularly venturesome.[3] The nature of British foreign investment is well captured by C.K. Hobson. In a sharp contrast with American foreign investment in Canada, Hobson (1914: 28–9) wrote:

Americans come into Canada and buy a lumber proposition, a commercial enterprise, or a branch of some of their own enterprises in one of the provinces. In these cases they go to the country themselves and look after the business in which they are interested. British investors, on the other hand, remain quite satisfied if their moderate interest and dividends are forthcoming at the proper time and their loans are met at maturity. There has in recent years been an extensive movement of British capital into Canadian industrial enterprise, but even here there is a distinction between British and American capital investments, as in mines which have frequently been first developed by Americans, and subsequently sold to British buyers.

Hobson's findings of 1914 have been more thoroughly investigated and broadly reconfirmed in a recent study by Donald Patterson (1976: 96–8).

The average rates of return which the British portfolio of foreign investments yielded are consistent with a description of the aggregate portfolio as bond-laden, conservative and chosen to suit the tastes of discriminating rentiers. The most detailed studies made of the earnings of the aggregate portfolio are those of George Paish (1909). In that year, he made a thorough examination of the returns to Britain from foreign investments with the aid of the Reports of the Commissioners of Inland Revenue. These reports detailed the incomes to British taxpayers from Indian, colonial and foreign government stocks, municipal securities and railways. Paish supplemented this partial information on overseas earnings by examining the statements of 2172 public companies which had raised money through the English capital market. His comprehensive study, however, had one significant omission which must be kept in mind in the following discussion. It covered only foreign portfolio investment; he did not include direct private investment abroad, which he guessed to involve £300m to £500m or 7.5% to 12.5% of total foreign investment (Paish, 1909:490; 1911:191). Direct investment generally brought with it direct control over foreign assets. Only the best informed and least risk averse of British investors made such investments; the yields on these investments were correspondingly expected to be higher. (See Appendix E, Part I.)

Paish's study of foreign portfolio investment showed that in 1907, 38% of total British foreign holdings of £2692.7m earned between 3% and 4% interest; 42% earned between 4% and 5% interest; only 18.5% of total holdings earned more than 5% and, of this amount, 11% earned more than a 10% rate of return. (See Appendix E, Part I, for sources.) The British holdings yielding more than a 10% return accounted for a full quarter of Paish's estimates of total British portfolio income earned abroad. These figures, of course, are only average rates of return. Between 1907 and 1913, Paish calculated that British foreign portfolio investment, already large, rose by a further 38% to £3714.7m. This massive flow of new investment did not substantially alter the sectoral distribution of British portfolio investment. Railroads in 1913 accounted for 40.9% of total portfolio investment, whereas in 1907 they had accounted for 44.5%. Commercial and industrial investment rose to 3.9% in 1913 from 2.9% in 1907; municipal bonds rose from 2.2% in 1907 to 4.0% in 1913. Despite this massive investment in roughly the same pattern as the previous holdings, there is no evidence of a sudden alteration in the rates of return on foreign investments. The marginal rates of return within large categories, at least as shown by the increase between 1907 and 1913, were approximately equal to the average which obtained in 1907. Moreover, not only was the British aggregate portfolio heavily weighted towards foreign fixed interest securities, but there is also evidence that these securities were valued, relative to equities, more highly than their actual realized earnings warranted. Michael Edelstein (1982:131–5) has found, for his study of long-term rates of return on 566 first and second-class securities cited earlier, that the preference and debenture issues, both foreign and domestic, were systematically over-priced (that is, exhibited a lower risk adjusted rate of return, where the measure of risk used was the covariance of security yield, defined as the sum of *ex post* capital gains plus annual coupon or dividend payments, with the yield on the market portfolio) compared with equities, indicating a willingness by British wealth-holders to pay heavily for the additional security offered by the terms of preference and debenture issues.

The price of foregone potential yield with which the typical British investor bought his stable foreign income can be estimated by a contrast with aggregate private rates of return on domestic real capital. The yield on the gross domestic capital stock for the years 1910–14 can be shown to be 10.6%; the yield on the private, gross domestic capital stock (excluding dwellings) can be approximated at 11.3%.[4] These are, again, only average private yields and not the marginal yields upon which investment decisions depend. However, aggregate profit figures, which are closely correlated to yields, show much more fluctuation over the business cycle than they show over variations in the rate of investment; the effect of shifts in the capital demand schedule apparently dominated movements along the schedule. Indeed, to the extent that the rate of technical change accelerated, economies of scale existed, or new markets were opened, the marginal yield on many investments may have surpassed by a wide margin the average yield. In any event, there is no evidence of sharply decreasing returns to investment indicating that marginal rates of return were well below the average.[5] To the extent that private yields on investment were less than social yields, the true difference is under-estimated even further.

In the aggregate, then, since British domestic investments as a group yielded a higher private return than did the assets which comprised the bulk of the British foreign portfolio, domestic investments, assuming rationality and reasonable foresight, were believed to be riskier. Colonial and foreign investments were not perfect substitutes for the safest domestic securities, a fact reflected in the higher yields apparently earned on colonial and foreign securities when compared with the yields earned by domestic securities of the same type. In the eyes of many savers, however, foreign and colonial railroad bonds must have been better substitutes for the safest domestic bonds than were domestic industrial equities. Only a small proportion, no more than a quarter, of total British foreign investment, including both direct and portfolio investments, earned a yield as high as the average earned on domestic real capital in manufacturing, mining, construction and financial services. The yield on some of the more venturesome projects in British industry, despite a pronounced lack of success in the most technologically advanced sectors, must have been far higher than average.

The consequences of British foreign investment, 1870–1913

The tendency of the British economy to sustain high levels of foreign investment influenced in three important ways the performance of British entrepreneurs: (1) it acted to maintain a pattern of demand which discouraged structural change within the economy; (2) it acted to reduce aggregate capital formation for the long periods of time when foreign investment was out of favour; (3) it acted to increase the cost of domestic capital formation.

First, foreign investment affected export demand (Ford, 1962). An understanding of the precise relationship between foreign investment and exports is complicated because of the intricate network of multilateral trade flows which had developed by the end of the nineteenth century. British loans increased liquidity abroad and relaxed a constraint on foreigners' import flows. Those imports however often did not come directly from Britain even when the loans did. Nevertheless, a cessation of foreign investment almost invariably meant a decline in exports. Directly or indirectly, large amounts of foreign lending were translated into extensive orders for exports. Because of the higher levels of transactions costs involved in trading over long distances, the variety and diversity of exports was considerably less than that of British manufactured goods in general. For example, in 1907, a year rich in data as a result of the Census of Production, 46% of British commodity exports were comprised of coal and textiles while domestic consumption of those goods amounted to only 17% of the total value of traded goods both produced and consumed in Britain. (See Appendix E, Part III.) Since the beneficiaries of increased demand for exports were generally well-established industries, foreign investment reduced the incentive to diversify through the creation of new lines of goods because the new lines usually depended on domestic markets for their initial development. In this regard, the patchy performance of the British capital goods industry in developing new products, especially new types of machine tools and electrical equipment, is a measure of the domestic impact of foreign investment.

The importance of domestic demand for the development of the capital goods industry is well known (Saul, 1968a: 209–37). The home investment boom of the 1890s played a crucial role in firmly establishing new machinery techniques, especially the use of millers and turret lathes, often of American design (Saul, 1968b: 29, 41). The critical importance of domestic demand stems from the nature of information flows concerning capital goods. British firms were almost invariably more familiar with British engineering equipment than were foreigners. Foreign investment switched demand for capital goods from domestic customers, with a high propensity to use British equipment, to customers with a lower propensity; this was especially true of the newest types of equipment. This argument can be illustrated by considering the varying levels of foreign investment, capital equipment export, and domestic fixed capital formation. In the years of very heavy foreign lending 1910–13, when net foreign lending exceeded Gross Domestic Fixed Capital Formation (GDFCF) by *more* than 40%, domestic expenditure on plant and machinery averaged £45.5m annually whereas a decade earlier, 1900–3, when net foreign lending averaged barely 15% of GDFCF, the level of comparable expenditure was £54.5m although the price index of capital goods stood at 91.0 compared to 94.4 in the later period. Had the level of domestic investment as a proportion of GNP remained during the years 1910–13 at the level reached in 1900–1903, that is at a level of 10.6% of GNP rather than only 6.2% and had the proportion of GDFCF made up of plant and machinery remained at the 1910–13 level, the value of the domestic installation of plant and machinery in current prices would have averaged £77.0m during those years, an increase of 69.2% over the actual value of £45.5m.[6]

Whereas coal, cotton, steel and ships responded markedly during periods of heavy foreign investment, plant and machinery exports were more exogeneously impelled by the tendency for international trade in such equipment to grow more rapidly than total trade as industrialization spread and accelerated (Maizels, 1970: Tables 7.7 and 7.8). Thus, even when foreign lending collapsed completely as in the years 1901–2, Britain exported an amount of plant and machinery equal in value to over 40% of the value of such equipment installed domestically.[7] For the period 1894 to 1904, exports of plant and machinery amounted, on average, to 1.17% of GNP while at the same time net foreign lending amounted to only 28.5% of the value of gross domestic capital formation. The situation changed dramatically in the years 1905–1913 when net foreign lending amounted to 115.4% of GDFCF but exports of plant and machinery had still risen to only 1.56% of GNP, an increase clearly fuelled in part by the autonomous, long-term global increase in the demand for capital goods noted earlier. The same point may be illustrated by noting that while in the years 1905–1913, when more was lent abroad than was invested at home, exports of machinery amounted, on average, to only 74.5% of the value of machinery installed domestically. Thus if one assumes that *all* British exports of machinery were due to British foreign lending, British foreign investment generated a demand for capital goods at home equal to only 64.6% (0.745/1.154 = 0.646) of that generated by a similar amount of domestic investment.

However, this overstates the impact of foreign investment upon the demand for British capital goods for it makes no allowance for autonomous foreign demand.[8] It is more reasonable to assume that at most only the *difference* between the levels of machinery exports, measured as a fraction of GNP, during periods of high and low foreign investment should be considered due to the stimulus of foreign investment. Thus, for the two periods, 1894–1904 and 1905–1913 only 25.2% ([1.563 − 1.170]/1.563 = 0.252) of the level of machinery exports in the latter period can reasonably be attributed to British foreign investment. If at most only 25.2% of British exports of machinery is attributed to British foreign lending, then foreign investment resulted in demand for British capital goods which was only 16.3% ([0.745 × 0.253]/1.154 = 0.163) of that which resulted from a similar amount of domestic investment. In other words, by 1913 as much as £6 of foreign investment was needed in order to generate the same level of demand for plant and machinery as was generated by £1 of domestic capital formation. Earlier, when there were fewer alternative sources of capital goods' supply and when machinery made up a smaller proportion of foreign capital formation, an even greater volume of foreign investment was necessary in order to yield the equivalent stimulus to the domestic capital goods industry.[9] Thus, from 1870 to 1875, net foreign investment averaged 83.2% of the total of GDFCF whereas the ratio of the value of the export of domestic machinery to the value of domestically installed machinery was only 0.372, a ratio of 0.447 (0.372/0.832 = 0.447) as opposed to the similarly computed ratio of 0.646 recorded for the years 1905–13. From 1876 to 1883 net foreign investment averaged only 37.2% of total GDFCF while the ratio of the value of the export of domestic machinery to the value of machinery installed domestically actually *rose* from its previous level to 0.401, a ratio of 1.078 (0.401/0.372 = 1.078).

The failure of foreign investment to provide the same degree of stimulus as domestic investment to domestic capital goods producers helps explain why certain types of technically sophisticated investment, that proved highly desirable in other countries, appeared unattractive in Britain and why the increasingly fragile industrial structure described in Chapter 2 cannot be attributed to incompetence and timidity alone. The phenomenon may most readily be illustrated by the experience of electrical engineering but it was not restricted to that industry. As a result of the slow development of electrical engineering in Britain in the 1880s, foreign firms detected a substantial market opening which, during the British home boom of the 1890s, was tested, with highly encouraging results, by the absorption of high levels of imports into Britain (Byatt, 1979: 146–7). Direct investment followed in the late 1890s. This investment, however, never fulfilled the early promise held out by import penetration. There are a number of explanations for this. The foreign firms that attempted to establish sizeable subsidiaries in Britain – Westinghouse, Thomson-Houston (later part of U.S. General Electric), and Siemens – were breaking ground in the management of multinational enterprises that has since become commonplace but was quite unfamiliar at the time. Problems of establishing effective managerial control over remote operating units, of adapting to transnational patterns of labour relations that were new and confusing for both managers and workers, and of bringing onstream large foreign plant – British Westinghouse's facilities in Trafford Park were planned at one stage to be larger than those found at the parent company's Pittsburgh site (Jones and Marriott, 1970: 48–51) – all contributed to preventing or deferring the achievement of consistent profitability.

The most serious mistake, however, as Karl Köttgen, the talented engineer-manager of Siemens Bros. Dynamo Works quoted at the beginning of this chapter, learned to his cost, was to suppose that the aggressive expansion that worked well in the rapidly electrifying German and American home markets would be suitable in perverse British conditions where the firms that did best remained small, conservative and cautious (Byatt, 1979: 157, Table 34, Panel A). No sooner had the new arrivals in Britain neared completion of their plants than an enormous upsurge in foreign investment, beginning in 1903, heralded the end of the home investment boom. Installation of plant and machinery, measured in constant 1900 prices, fell by 37.5% between 1903 and 1912 (Feinstein, 1972: Table 40, column 3). Even in nominal terms, despite the inflation of prices in Edwardian Britain (Feinstein, 1972: Table 63, column 4), the peak level of installations in 1903 was not regained before the outbreak of war and for electrical engineering, where the pace of development was especially rapid, it has been estimated that the 1905 level, £7.7m, was not reached again until 1913, £10.0m (Feinstein, 1959: 97–98, column 2; see also footnote 15 of Ch. 5 above). It is, therefore, not surprising that over-capacity and low profitability should have characterized the operations of the British industry, affecting the freely spending foreign firms most of all. The relief that was provided by improved export demand for capital goods was not sufficient to compensate for the loss of domestic investment. Although the fall of 17.5% between 1903 and 1912 in the sum of British domestic installations plus British exports of plant and equipment was only half of the decline in domestic installations alone, the increased foreign demand did not benefit all capital goods producers equally. Instead – to the detriment of technical advance in general and to electrical engineering in particular – foreign demand was concentrated principally on those established products which Britain had traditionally exported – primarily boilers, steam engines, textile machinery, railroad equipment, and heavy machine tools (Saul, 1968: 227–230) – and which in the late nineteenth century were experiencing only minor improvements. To be sure, given the global effort to apply electricity, an effort manifested in the heavy issue of foreign municipal and public utility bonds on the London capital markets after 1905, (Ayres, 1934: 47–48, Table 17, columns 2 and 8), and given Britain's newly acquired supply capability, the British electrical engineering industry gained some benefits and succeeded in increasing exports markedly from 1903 to 1910 (Byatt, 1979: 152). These exports, however, went predominantly to less sophisticated markets in the Empire, Latin America, and Asia, earning profits considerably smaller than could have been anticipated by buoyant domestic demand (Byatt, 1968: 273).

By reducing the level of demand for British engineering goods and by deflecting what demand there was away from new lines, British foreign investment thus depressed the profitability and retarded the expansion and diversification of domestic engineering firms (relative to what might have been reached with more extensive domestic investment) and contributed to the incomplete development of the engineering industries before 1914 (Saul, 1972a: 142). This in turn raised the costs of those firms which used engineering goods as inputs; they either had to import the equipment or make do with less useful but readily available domestic goods. By this process the weaknesses in capital market operations, discussed in Chapter 5, that created difficulties in concentrating, monitoring, and controlling resources committed to new and risky sectors were systematically amplified by a hostile demand environment that left no room for errors.

Foreign investment, however, did more than alter to the disadvantage of capital goods producers the structure of demand facing domestic British industry. A second detrimental effect, which may be described as a systematic Keynesian reduction in the overall pressure of domestic demand, also operated to reduce capital formation, albeit in a more indirect manner.[10] By 1913 an astounding 8.2% of British GNP was being earned by the foreign investments accumulated over the preceding century and a half. Furthermore, the peculiarities of British financial intermediation were such as to produce a very conservative, stable portfolio of foreign investments with a remarkably low variance in earnings over the business cycle. Nothing less than a profound crisis like the First World War could undermine the inherent solidity of Britain's foreign investments. But such solidity meant that, in those periods of uncertainty and indecision which plague every economy where saving and investment decisions are undertaken by different people, the short-fall in effective demand did not tend to fall most directly on the foreign borrowers struggling to maintain their credit-worthiness under an implacable gold standard regime of fixed exchange rates, but instead on producers in the domestic economy caught in the double bind of finding their foreign markets reduced by faltering real income growth abroad and their domestic markets swamped with cheap foreign goods delivered in partial redemption of debt claims falling due continuously.

Most prominent among the debtors perpetually struggling to support their currencies against the perennial strength of sterling were the Americans, who had in the course of the nineteenth century borrowed more from Britain than from any other nation. Sir George Paish reckoned the British stake in America at the end of 1913 to be worth no less than £754m, or almost exactly half of America's total foreign indebtedness in June 1914.[11] The average yield on this vast British holding in America must have been of the order of 5%, which was typical of the municipal, public utility, and railroad bonds that made up the bulk of Britain's foreign portfolio holding. Such an average yield would have given Britain an amount equal in that year to 6.5% of America's total exports of goods and services or to 30.6% of America's exports of goods to the U.K. Of course, in the last half of the nineteenth century, American obligations to Britain for past borrowings did not have to be redeemed by goods and services exported directly to Britain. A complex system of multilateral settlement meant that sterling could be earned in almost any export market in the world. But American debts were enormous and Britain was one of the world's largest markets, inhabited at least temporarily by the wealthiest consumers in Europe and, perhaps above all, one of the most accessible anywhere. This accessibility, however, was the necessary and inevitable consequence of the massive foreign investment Britain had sustained throughout the nineteenth century and lay at the source of the persistently low demand pressure contemporary observers such as J.A. Hobson had noticed.[12] If Britain's foreign investments were to be profitable, British consumers and investors had, sooner or later, to absorb their yield of foreign goods and services. The longer absorption was deferred the higher the rate of investment had to be, given a constant propensity to consume, in order to maintain a constant level of domestic demand pressure in the face of ever mounting foreign debt repayments.[13] However, foreign, especially American, output was not only directly complementary to British production, supplying the foodstuffs and raw materials Britain could not, but was also directly competitive, supplying for investment or consumption manufactured goods which were close substitutes for the output of

British factories. And as the highly industrialized European economies became more prominent in the multilateral payments system, their industrial competition with Britain within that system also became more pronounced, both through their direct exports to Britain and through their growing exports to foreign markets once dominated by British exporters.

The accommodation of the yield from Britain's foreign investment took place in many ways. Real foreign investment could be achieved not so much by increasing Britain's exports, as had tended to occur in the 1870s, but by more frequently reducing the rate at which the burgeoning foreign earnings of previous investments were repatriated. Accordingly, exports as a proportion of GNP underwent a slow secular decline between the mid-nineteenth century and 1913 while the levels of foreign investment rose. Even after 1904, when foreign investment as a proportion of GNP reached unprecedented levels far above those recorded in the early 1870s or later 1880s, exports (measured as a proportion of GNP), while showing a great increase over the previous decade when foreign investment had almost completely collapsed, never regained the levels recorded in the early 1870s. Thus, between 1904 and 1913, exports averaged 31.4% of GNP while net foreign lending as a proportion of GNP averaged 7.17% whereas between 1870 and 1876 exports averaged 33.4% of GNP while net foreign investment averaged only 6.00% of GNP. Alternatively, real foreign investment could be accomplished with both exports and imports (as a proportion of GNP) falling as long as imports fell more sharply, as occurred in the late 1880s. Or the gains from foreign investment could be consumed by letting exports fall as a proportion of imports, as happened in the 1890s. However the accommodation took place, demand pressure on the domestic British economy was gradually reduced. The extent of the reduction can be seen most clearly by examining an index of demand pressure constructed from the movement of total exports, gross domestic fixed capital formation and total imports, all measured as proportions of GNP. The index is defined in equation (5.1).

$$D = \frac{TX + GDFCF - TI}{GNP} \times 100, \qquad (5.1)$$

where D = index of demand pressure,
TX = total U.K. exports of goods and services,
$GDFCF$ = gross domestic fixed capital formation,
TI = total U.K. imports of goods and services,
GNP = gross national product.

Current government expenditure on goods and services is ignored here for simplicity but would not greatly affect the results if it were incorporated. In peacetime the combined current accounts of public authorities before 1914 tended to a slight surplus and any balanced budget effect would be relatively small and would change only slowly compared to the multiplier effects generated by the components of the index. In a straightforward manner the numerator of the index captures the conventional sources of Keynesian demand pressure. In interpreting the index, it is assumed that the aggregate propensity to save remained constant throughout the period.

The index is at its greatest between 1871 and 1876 and at its lowest between 1891 and 1898. The demand pressure (excluding net government expenditure associated with the Boer War) generated in the years 1899–1913, produces an average index value of 7.14 which is only 69.25% of the index value of 10.31 registered in the years 1870–6. In the first half of the period, 1870 to 1890, the index stood at an average value of 7.93; from 1891 to 1913 the average was 6.23, or 78.6% of the index's average value for the previous period. Moreover, where the domestic economy experienced a secular decline in demand pressure stemming from the accommodation of the huge inflow of interest earned on previous investments abroad, Britain's debtors experienced a corresponding stimulation, principally of exports.

The foreign orientation of British capital markets not only generated huge flows of foreign goods and services that had to be absorbed by the domestic economy at the expense of domestic producers, but also caused great difficulty in productively deploying British savings during those occasional periods when foreign investment was out of favour. Movements in foreign investment dominated British capital formation. Twice in the period from 1870 to 1914 total British investment as a proportion of income dropped sharply below the long-term average. On both occasions, from 1876 to 1880 and from 1893 to 1898, foreign investment fell much more steeply than did domestic fixed capital formation. On the other hand, at those times when total investment rates were rising above the long-term average, as from 1870 to 1872 and from 1903 to 1913, foreign investment was experiencing a pronounced boom; when the total savings rates were approaching a pre-war high in the period 1905–13, domestic investment rates were falling. Only in the years 1894 to 1900 did domestic investment dominate the movement of total investment, pulling up total investment relative to GNP while foreign investment continued to decline. The inference drawn from these movements in investment behaviour is that the domestic capital markets could not channel productively into the domestic economy the massive levels of savings Britain generated; when foreign investment was out of favour, as it was from 1872 to 1877 and again from 1890 to 1901, rentiers either increased consumption or increased their holdings of money balances. Had they been willing and able to find domestic substitutes more readily, investment levels would surely have been higher. As it was, only when interest rates sank to record lows in the 1890s at the cost of deep depression, were sufficient substitutes for foreign investments found, often in mortgages, to reverse the trend of total investment without the stimulus of renewed foreign lending.

In a related consideration which also preoccupied J.A. Hobson, it is plausible to believe that the vast foreign investment of the half century before 1914 affected the domestic British distribution of income in such a way as to discourage domestic fixed capital formation. The income of security conscious rentiers would appear to have been raised at the expense of the earnings of both entrepreneurs and ordinary workers. Rentiers clearly benefited from the wide range of relatively secure investments which foreign investment made possible. On the other hand, the reduced proportion of national resources available to Britain's entrepreneurs at a time of technological ferment and rising foreign competition must have significantly constrained their domestic opportunities and ultimately their earnings. The situation regarding workers is equally clear cut. It is a staple result of conventional economic analysis that the level of wages depends, among other things, on the size of the co-operating capital stock: the larger and more productive the capital stock, *ceteris paribus*, the higher the wages. By reducing the growth of the domestic capital stock through sustained foreign investment, domestic real wage increases were restrained. To the extent that reduced levels of capital formation retarded structural change, wages were even more severely depressed. To be sure Britain's foreign investment benefited the domestic economy indirectly by acting to keep food and raw material prices lower than they would otherwise have been. While these were real benefits, however, they were globally shared and thus of second-order magnitude compared with the first-order magnitude of the losses to Britain stemming directly from reduced levels of domestic capital formation. The benefits of British foreign investment must also be set against its opportunity costs. A lower rate of growth in the British domestic economy in the late nineteenth century acted to lower world export demand, and Britain's failure to contribute as fully to the technological advances of the late nineteenth century as she had done earlier in the century made the world poorer in a very real way. The combined impact of sustained foreign investment on the distribution of domestic incomes served to increase the share of those unlikely to invest in the domestic economy or to demand to a high degree the output of the domestic economy.

A recent study by Robert Frank and Richard Freeman (1978: Chapter 8) of the impact of direct foreign investment by U.S. firms abroad on the American economy during the 1960s and 1970s lends support to these conclusions. Frank and Freeman found that direct foreign investment both lowered American national income and reduced wage rates and labour's share of national income. Although these losses, calculated in relation to a counterfactual situation where substantially less direct foreign investment took place, were small, this was due to factors not operating in the circumstances of Britain's foreign portfolio investment. In the American case it was assumed that the rate of return abroad was higher than at home because of American technological advantages and because direct foreign investment was often necessary to overcome transport costs and tariff barriers in markets where American firms were otherwise highly competitive. In contrast, a large share of the vast Victorian portfolio investment abroad, it has been argued above, was the product of institutional failures which prevented domestic investment projects from competing as effectively for available funds as their inherent prospects warranted and, therefore, the alternative domestic yields were at least as great as the largely fixed-interest investments actually made overseas. Furthermore, Frank and Freeman's analysis notes the possibility that the enhanced profitability of technologically progressive firms encouraged them to maintain higher rates of investment both at home and abroad than would otherwise have occurred without foreign investment and that this higher rate of investment further augmented the significance of these firms. But British portfolio investment was, to the extent that foreign and domestic investment moved inversely, at the expense of technologically progressive firms at home. Thus what in the recent American experience is seen as an influence marginally lowering domestic income and labour's share of national product can be seen in the markedly different circumstances of Victorian Britain as an influence producing a much more substantial impact, the exact dimension of which, however, must await a comprehensive general equilibrium analysis. But at the very least, this line of argument is at present complete enough to suggest that Hobson's turn-of-the-century concern over the distributive effect of British foreign investment was only too well founded.[14]

The domestic impact of British foreign investment was not restricted to the impact on the level and structure of demand. A third influence also operated. British entrepreneurs found the cost of obtaining domestic funds rising over what the cost would have been had the existing capital markets permitted and encouraged more efficient risk taking. It was not only a matter of high-risk domestic projects being unable to raise money at any price, or that the risks were overstated because of inadequate opportunities for diversification, but rather, the funds available for risky projects were fewer, and more dispersed, and less accessible than was feasible. The extent of the resources available to entrepreneurs in established industries such as textiles, iron manufacturing and shipbuilding, which were able either to borrow on the basis of proven earnings or to exploit an existing cash flow, were quite different from the extent of the resources available to entrepreneurs in newer areas such as automobiles and electrical engineering. This relatively easy availability of funds to established industries further reinforced the tendency towards over-commitment to the traditional staples. Similarly, industries which faced large, discrete investment decisions, thus giving the investment an all or nothing character, found borrowing more difficult than in the U.S. or Germany. The difference between the performance of the British bicycle and automobile industries may exemplify the contrast between the ability of small but venturesome projects to raise money and the difficulty of larger, riskier, but much more profitable ventures in doing so. By affecting the structure and terms of capital supplies available domestically to British firms, the level and structure of demand for the output of British firms, and the domestic cost of capital for risky ventures, foreign investment acted powerfully to freeze the structure of the British economy in the position seen to be so precarious in the inter-war period.

The structure of the Victorian economy was ultimately compatible only with slow growth and that only in the relatively favourable conditions of the nineteenth century. When those conditions were altered or destroyed by the First World War, Britain could not respond with the flexibility needed to meet adequately the successive shocks of the twentieth century. While the Victorian legacy of heavy foreign investment and a backward looking industrial structure created difficulties serious enough in the short-run, it was the institutions that had guided the investment and moulded the structure that were to prove even more durably intractable.

Appendices A, B, and C

These three data appendices provide the details of the sources and of the classification procedures used to determine the structure of output and employment in both the United States and the United Kingdom in the early twentieth century. A lack of space prevents them being reproduced here but copies may be obtained, as long as the book is in print, at cost from the author, c/o Department of Economic History, London School of Economics, Houghton Street, London, WC2A 2AE.

Appendix A: Distribution of Employment (1911) and Output (1907) in the United Kingdom (summary)

This appendix, presenting details of employment (1911) and output (1907) in the United Kingdom, consists of 21 pages. Only a summary of output in the construction, manufacturing, and mining sectors is given in Appendix A; the detailed breakdowns for these sectors are found in Appendix C. The data were drawn primarily but not exclusively from *The Census of England and Wales, 1911, Summary Tables* (Cd. 7929, 1915); *Report of the Twelfth Decennial Census of Scotland, Vol. II* (Cd. 6896, 1930); *The Census of Ireland, 1911: Provinces of Connaught* (Cd. 6052, 1912); *Leinster* (Cd. 6049, 1911); *Munster* (Cd. 6050, 1911); *Ulster* (Cd. 6051, 1912); *Census of Production: Final Report, 1907* (Cd. 6320, 1912).

Appendix B: Distribution of Employment (1910) and Output (1909) in the United States (summary)

This appendix, presenting details of employment and output in the United States in 1909, consists of 13 pages. As in Appendix A, only a summary of output and employment in the construction, manufacturing, and mining sectors is given in Appendix B, with the detailed breakdown deferred to Appendix C. The data on numbers employed were drawn primarily but not exclusively from United States Bureau of the Census, *Thirteenth Census of the United States, Volume IV: Occupational Statistics* (Washington, D.C.: U.S. Government Printing Office, 1914), Table VI, pp. 302–432. Output outside construction, manufacturing, and mining was estimated using a wide variety of sources, but for most sectors labour's share of value added was obtained by multiplying average sectoral income per worker by the average number employed in 1909. Total value added was then obtained by adjusting labour's share by an estimate of labour's share as a proportion of the total and multiplying accordingly (e.g. if labour's share was estimated to be 2/3 of the total, the value of labour's share was multiplied by 3/2).

Appendix C: Distribution of Employment and Output in Construction, Manufacturing, and Mining; U.S. (1909) and U.K. (1907) (summary)

This appendix, presenting details of employment and output in the sectors of construction, manufacturing, and mining in the United States in 1909 and the United Kingdom in 1907, consists of 22 pages. U.S. data were drawn primarily, but not exclusively, from United States Bureau of the Census, *Thirteenth Census of the United States, Volume VIII; Manufacturers: General Report and Analyses* (Washington, D.C.: U.S. Government Printing Office, 1914), especially pages 40–3, 507–17. U.K. data were drawn primarily but not exclusively from *Census of Production: Final Report, 1907* (Cd. 6320, 1912).

Appendix D: Calculation Procedures—Tables

Table D1. *Average sector size: U.K. (1870–1913)*

	(1)	(2) Relative sector size, 1907	(3)
	B	(% of GNP)	Column (1) × Column (2)
1 Textiles	1.049	0.0424	0.0445
2 Domestic service	1.389	0.0334	0.0464
3 Agriculture	1.459	0.0666	0.0972
4 Domestic wholesale-retail trade	0.961	0.1835	0.1764
5 Gas undertakings	0.589	0.0078	0.0046
6 Net property income from abroad	0.705	0.0648	0.0457
7 Construction	1.366	0.0280	0.0382
8 Iron, steel trades	0.887	0.0135	0.0120
9 Engineering[1]	0.796	0.0311	0.0248
10 Paper, printing and publishing	0.690	0.0147	0.0101
11 Electricity, telecommunications, scientific instruments	0.441	0.0054	0.0024
12 Bricks, cement, glass	1.366	0.0077	0.0105
13 Chemicals: class (a)	0.683	0.0090	0.0061
GNP	1.000	1.0000	1.0000

Sources:

Column (1): $B = \dfrac{\text{Sector Index (Average Index Number, 1870–1913)}}{\text{GNP Index (Average, 1870–1913).}}$

Column (2): Table 2.1.
See also text of Appendix D.

Note:
[1] Defined as engineering (excluding electricity supply), motor and cycle trades, road carriage, non-ferrous metal working in Table 2.1.

Table D2. *Average sector size: U.S. (1869–1913)*

	(1)	(2) Relative sector size, 1909	(3)
	B	(% of GNP)	Column (1) × Column (2)
1 Textiles	1.065	0.0227	0.0242
2 Domestic service	1.443	0.0164	0.0237
3 Agriculture	1.597	0.1637	0.2614
4 Domestic wholesale-retail trade	1.008	0.1711	0.1725
5 Gas undertakings	0.645	0.0036	0.0023
6 Net property income from abroad	a	b	b
7 Construction	1.008	0.0546	0.0550
8 Iron, steel trades	0.852	0.0128	0.0109
9 Engineering[c]	0.775	0.0416	0.0322
10 Paper, printing and publishing	1.052	0.0235	0.0247
11 Electricity, telecommunications, scientific instruments	0.572	0.0104	0.0059
12 Bricks, cement, glass	1.008	0.0118	0.0119
13 Chemicals: class (a)	0.881	0.0090	0.0079
GNP	1.000	1.0000	1.0000

Sources:

Column (1): $B = \dfrac{\text{Sector Index (Average Number, 1870–1913)}}{\text{GNP Index (Average, 1870–1913)}}$.

Column (2): Table 2.2.
See also text of Appendix D.

Notes:
[a] Greater than unity.
[b] Negative.
[c] Defined as engineering (excluding electricity supply), motor and cycle trades, road carriage, non-ferrous metal working in Table 2.2.

Table D3. *Differences in average sector size between the U.K. (1870–1913) and the U.S. (1869–1913)*

1 Textiles	− 0.0203
2 Domestic service	− 0.0227
3 Agriculture	0.1642
4 Domestic wholesale-retail trade	− 0.0039
5 Gas undertakings	− 0.0023
6 Net property income from abroad	− 0.0457[1]

Table D3. (*cont.*)

7 Construction	0.0168
8 Iron, steel trades	− 0.0011
9 Engineering	0.0074
10 Paper, printing and publishing	0.0146
11 Electricity, telecommunications, scientific instruments	0.0035
12 Bricks, cement, glass	0.0014
13 Chemicals: class (a)	0.0018

Source: Column (3) Table D2 minus Column (3) Table D1.

Note:
[1] Minimum difference.

Table D4. *Composition of counterfactual increase in aggregate growth rate*

	(1) Low growth variant	(2) Medium growth variant	(3) High growth variant
1 Acceleration effect (change in aggregate growth rate)	0.004111 (72.9)	0.007765 (73.8)	0.022703 (71.9)
2 Shift effect (change in aggregate growth rate)	0.000454 (8.0)	0.000719 (6.8)	0.001551 (4.9)
3 Interaction effect (change in aggregate growth rate)	0.001076 (19.0)	0.002043 (19.4)	0.007338 (23.2)
4 Total effect (change in aggregate growth rate)	0.005640 (100.0)	0.010527 (100.0)	0.031592 (100.0)

Sources:
Row 1: row 15, column (4), Tables 3.5, 3.8, and 3.11 respectively.
Row 2: row 15, column (5), Tables 3.5, 3.8, and 3.11 respectively.
Row 3: row 15, column (6), Tables 3.5, 3.8, and 3.11 respectively.
Row 4: row 15, column (7), Tables 3.5, 3.8, and 3.11 respectively.

Note:
Figures in brackets under each entry represent the percentage of the total growth rate change in each variant due to the effect listed in the left-hand column. See also text, Appendix D, III.

Appendix D: Calculation Procedures—Text

The calculations in Chapter 3 require an estimate in real terms over the years 1870–1913 of output growth in the various sectors selected for counterfactual expansion or contraction. For the U.K. most of this information was available in a series of index numbers recently prepared by W.A. Lewis and reported by Feinstein (1972), Tables 51–53 inclusive. Specifically, the index for textiles output was Table 52 column 6. That for domestic service was derived from the data for employment in private domestic service given by Feinstein (1972), Table 60, row 12(a) (1913 = 100); it was assumed that output in the sector was directly linked to employment. This would appear to be a reasonable assumption given the labour intensive character of the sector. Output growth was estimated over the period 1861–1911; inclusion of 1861 has the effect of increasing the measured growth rate of this sector and thus acting against the argument in the text. The index for agricultural output, 1870–1913, came from Feinstein (1972), Table 8, column 1. The distribution index's source was Feinstein (1972), Table 53, column 1. Output of manufactured gas was proxied by assuming that the growth of output of Feinstein's column 11, Table 51 – the combined sector of gas, electricity and water, over the years 1870–1902 – was similar to that of gas output growth for the entire period 1870–1913. This would certainly be reasonable for the period 1870–90 as long as the growth of water supplies was not markedly slower than that of gas. It is believed that the net impact of the various assumptions is to yield an estimate of the rate of growth of gas output which is biased upwards substantially.

The index of construction output was Feinstein (1972), Table 51, column 10, iron and steel output, Table 52, column 1; engineering output, Table 52, columns 3 and 4; output of paper and printing, Table 52, column 10; and the chemical output index was Table 51, column 4. The index of output of bricks, cement and glass was assumed to be identical to that of construction; this assumption very probably understates growth of the sector. Output growth of telecommunications services, electricity, and scientific instruments over the entire period 1870–1913 was provided by the growth of gas, water, and electricity output (Feinstein (1972), column 11, Table 51), over the period 1888–1913. This was the period when growth of electricity generation was most rapid.

Once an index of output for the various sectors was defined, the next step required calculation of an average index number of the sector over the period 1870–1913 and then comparison of the average index number for each sector with an average index number of

GNP for the same period. The index for GNP was obtained from Feinstein (1972), Table 5, column 10, GNP calculated at 1900 *market* prices. In most cases the average index number was calculated in the obvious manner of adding together the index numbers of output in each year and then dividing each series by 44. In the case of gas the average was arrived at by redefining the 1902 index number as 100, adding all the observation suitably altered (1902 = 100 rather than 1913 = 100) from 1870 to 1902 inclusive and dividing by 33. Electricity's average index was calculated by adding the numbers in Feinstein's Table 51, column 11 for the years 1888–1913 inclusive and then dividing by 44, yielding an average index number of 31.6. Dividing the observations from 1888–1913 by 44 yields an average index number smaller than the 'true' average index for output in the sector was not zero before 1888. The use of a smaller index number serves to bias downwards the importance of the sector which is overstated due to the inability to exclude gas and water supplies from the index. The comparison of the average index number of each sector with the average index number of GNP was necessary in order to convert the relative share of GNP arising in each sector in 1907 into an average relative share for the entire period. For example, in 1907 value added in agriculture accounted for 6.66% of GNP, yet agriculture had been growing much less rapidly than GNP. Hence the relative share of GNP arising in the agricultural sector before 1907 was higher than 6.66%. How much higher was determined by the ratio of the sector's average index to the average index for GNP. This ratio will be greater than unity for a sector which grew less rapidly than GNP and less than unity for a sector growing faster than GNP. The ratio will be unity for a sector which grew on average as rapidly as GNP over the entire period and which thereby maintained for the entire period the same relative importance as it held in 1907. The 1907 relative share of each sector is multiplied by the ratio of the sector's average index number to the average index number of GNP. These operations are set out above for the U.K. in Table D1.

Column (3) of Table D1 represents the average relative size of each sector over the entire period. Had systematic Censuses of Production been taken before 1907 the calculation of average relative size would undoubtedly have been more accurate since much less reliance on indices with inevitable shortcomings would have been necessary. At the very least indices with more frequent changes of bases would have been available. Nevertheless, the adjustments to 1907 relative sector size are plausible and in accord with other sources of evidence.

It should also be noted that when choices of growth rate estimates arose from the regressions run on the various indices, choices which could not be resolved on grounds of the obvious superiority of F-statistics or Durbin–Watson statistics, the choice was made so as to reduce the size of any counterfactual change. This was done by choosing higher growth rate estimates for contracting sectors, most notably domestic service and net property income from abroad, and lower growth rate estimates for expanding sectors. The only deviation from this principle arose in the estimate of output in the sector of paper, printing and publishing where the higher estimate was chosen. Although the Durbin–Watson statistic of the lower estimate was just on the statistic's upper bound, indicating positive autocorrelation, visual inspection of the residuals suggested that the CORC 2 estimate, with a much better Durbin–Watson statistic and only a very marginally inferior F-statistic was to be preferred. In any event, the unusually high standard error of the estimate serves as warning that the underlying data exhibited such high variance that inference may be expected to be difficult.

Column (5) of Tables 3.1, 3.6, 3.9, representing the index number of each sector's output in 1870, was calculated in the following manner:

(D1) $O(I) = A(I)(1 + G(I))^{-22}$
   where $O(I) = $ index of sector's output 1870
         $A(I) = $ average index number for period 1870–1913, assumed to equal actual sector output in precisely the middle of the period, 1 January 1892 (22.0 years from the beginning of 1870)
         $G(I) = $ estimated growth rate of sector's output.

The data in the sector listed 'rest of the economy' in Tables 3.1, 3.6, 3.9 was calculated as follows: column (2) – obtained by summing relative sizes of all sectors selected for counterfactual change and subtracting total sum from unity; column (3) – must equal zero by stipulation of no counterfactual change; column (4) – calculated by use of equation (2.1) in main text where the growth rates of all sectors involved in counterfactual change were known, as well as the average relative sizes of these sectors and the growth of GNP; column (5) – calculated using results of column (4) and solving first for average index number (where average index number for GNP is known and must equal the sum of the products of each sector's relative size times its average index number) and then, in the manner of equation (D1) solving finally for $O(I)$ rest, index of output for the rest of the economy in 1870.

Interpretation of the U.K. data required a standard of comparison. This was afforded by examination of the structural characteristics of the U.S. economy. The massive, careful work done by John W. Kendrick (1961), greatly aided preparation of the data presented in Table 2.2, but unfortunately, since most of Kendrick's disaggregated data series do not start until 1899, various other sources had to be employed. The index for textile output was constructed from a series representing raw cotton consumption reported in U.S. Bureau of the census (1975), series P-228. The growth rate of output implied by this index for the years 1899–1909 was checked with Kendrick's estimate of textile mill product output. The divergence this check revealed may very well have occurred because of increased finishing embodied in final textile products over time. The growth rate estimated from increased cotton consumption was, therefore, multiplied by 1.05 to bring it more fully into accord with Kendrick's data. Domestic service output in the U.S. case, as in the U.K. case, was estimated from employment data concerning people working in the sector over the years 1870–1910. Agricultural output growth was estimated from Kendrick's data on net farm output (Kendrick, 1961: Table B-1, column 1, pp. 362–363).

An index of value added in distribution was estimated from data found in Harold Barger (1955: especially pp. 74–79). Barger's figures were adjusted to exclude value added in food sales in restaurants, bars, hotels, etc. and to account for inputs into the distribution sector purchased from the rest of the economy, most importantly utilities, legal services, communications and construction. This latter adjustment was necessary in order to obtain estimates comparable with those of rest of the economy. His figures, after these adjustments were increased by 12% to allow for understatement in the retail census as identified by both Kuznets and Barger (see Barger, 1955: 124, 127). The resulting growth rate was only marginally lower than that of GNP and would appear to be an over-estimate. Using Barger's (adjusted) figures for sector net output and Kendrick's figures for GNP, the share of value added produced in the sector fell by 13.1% between 1869 and 1909 whereas the differences in growth rates reported in Table D2 imply a fall of relative share of only 7.7%.

The index of manufactured gas output available for census years only, was taken from Kendrick (1961: Table H-VIII, p. 594). Output of construction was taken from Kendrick (1961: Table E-1, p. 498); this series also was for Census years only.

The index for iron and steel was constructed from an index of ferrous mineral production (U.S. Bureau of the Census, 1975: series M-63) over the years 1880–1913. Since the period was one of rapid technological change in the U.S. iron and steel industry and since there was a pronounced tendency to use iron ore with a higher iron content and that the American industry was self-sufficient on American ore resources (see Robert C. Allen, 1977: especially Table 7), it would appear that use of an index of ferrous mining activity would conservatively measure the growth of value added in the industry. A comparison of the index of ferrous mining activity with Kendrick's estimates of blast furnace output over the period 1899–1929 reveals a tendency for blast furnace output to rise faster than mining activity, although this was not true for the decade 1899–1909.

An index of U.S. engineering output was constructed by adding together total sales, in current prices, of producer durables (Series P-352) and sales of selected consumer durables (Series P-336, 337, 345–349) and then deflating the resultant sum by a price index (1913 = 100, obtained from series P-373). (All Series numbers refer to U.S. Bureau of the Census, 1975.) This index over the period 1899–1909 yields a growth rate less than that implied by Kendrick's data for fabricated metal products and electric machinery, approximately equal to the growth rate implied by Kendrick's data for non-electric machinery, and somewhat more than Kendrick's series for transportation equipment output. This latter series, however, includes railroad equipment which is excluded from the definition of engineering used in this book.

This index of paper and printing output was the least satisfactory measure of American developments in the sectors selected for counterfactual change since the long-term index behaved over the decade 1899–1909 very differently from Kendrick's measure. During that period, Kendrick's data (1961: 471) indicates that output in paper and allied products and in printing and publishing more than doubled in the years 1899 to 1909 whereas the long-term index reveals an increase of only 45.0% over the same period. The long-term index, nevertheless, showed nearly a ninefold increase over the period 1869–1913, although much of this increase occurred between 1869 and 1879. Acceptance of the growth rate implied by the long-term index yields a higher average index number for the sector than would be otherwise warranted by a faster growth rate. On the other hand, the U.S. sector (1909) was relatively much larger than its U.K. (1907) counterpart (59.9% again as large, relative to GNP in the respective countries) and growth in both countries was more rapid than GNP. Hence any reasonable counterfactual argument would allow very substantial gains in relative size for the U.K. sector. The U.S. index was prepared from Series P-324 and P-343, deflated by Series P-370, a price deflator for perishable consumer goods. (All series numbers refer to U.S. Bureau of the Census, 1975.)

The index of output for electricity, telecommunications, and scientific instruments was derived by assuming that output of scientific instruments grew at the same rate as electricity output, an assumption warranted by the fact that much of the scientific instrument output of the period was devoted to devices for the measurement of electrical flows, and that electricity output and telecommunications output were given equal weight in the final index. Output of electric utilities is given by Kendrick (1961: 590), from 1899 onwards; output for telephones from 1879 onwards (Kendrick, 1961:585). These data were translated into an average index number 1869–1913 by assuming in both cases output was zero before the first observation. As in the U.K. case, these assumptions act to lower the calculated growth rate.

U.S. chemical output growth was conservatively estimated by using Kendrick's series for all manufacturing output (Kendrick, 1961: Table D-II, p. 465).

The index of U.S. GNP was taken from U.S. Bureau of Economic Analysis (1973: series A-1, pp. 182–83). These data were derived from Kendrick (1961).

II

It is important to stress once again that the calculations in Chapter 3 do not represent the growth rates potentially attainable had the British economy achieved optimal allocation of resources. Instead they represent the gains from the marginal shifts required to achieve a structure of output more compatible with satisfactory long term development. By assuming counterfactual contraction in sectors destined for long-term decline such as textiles, gas, distribution and net property income from abroad, but which over the period 1870–1913 nevertheless maintained respectable growth rates (relative to overall U.K. GNP growth) and by assuming counterfactual expansion in sectors such as construction and bricks, glass, cement which were unnaturally retarded in growth, the net counterfactual structural change is considerably reduced. Only in the case where the British economy was moving unambiguously towards a more viable structure with *all* of the sectors destined for long-term decline growing relatively slowly and with *all* of the sectors destined for long-term expansion growing relatively rapidly would the suggested counterfactual structural shifts act to maximize long-term growth. But of course before 1914, the British economy was certainly not moving unambiguously towards a more viable structure, as the very slow growth of construction output and the very rapid growth of net property income from abroad indicate.

III

Table D4 sets out the composition of the counterfactual increase in aggregate growth distinguishing among the acceleration, shift and interaction effects. In all cases the acceleration effect accounts for the greatest share of the total increase while the shift effect accounts for the least. Such relative importance among the various effects superficially suggests that structural change is relatively unimportant. This is quite wrong for each structural shift *also* implies a corresponding change in sectoral growth rates. The importance of the interaction effect reflects the significance, over long periods of time, of the faster-growing sectors gaining an ever larger proportion of the economy's resources while the slower-growing sectors occupied an ever smaller proportion of the economy's resources. This characteristic explains the fact that the interaction effect is almost always positive, the only exception throughout being agriculture which experienced a slight fall in the actual rate of output growth over the entire period.

These characteristics of the relationship between growth and structural change have been reported in recent studies of economic development. Thus T.P. Hill (1971:87), in his careful, disaggregated study of growth in post-1945 Western economies, found that difference in industrial structure alone cannot explain differences in GDP growth rates:

'Clearly, the effects on GDP growth rates of differences in the weights attached to particular industries in different countries tend to be negligible compared with effects of differences in the industry growth rates themselves'.

It is obvious that shifts in the weights of sectors are an integral part of the process of economic growth and that they account for differences in industry growth rates, although at any one time, over a short interval, the only indication of the significance of structural change is the differing sectoral growth rates. This description of the growth process explains another feature of modern growth which Hill (1971: 61–96) noted: there is little tendency for the degree of dispersion of sectoral growth rates in rapidly growing countries to differ from the dispersion found in more slowly growing countries, although the mean growth rates obviously differ. Rapidly growing sectors gaining in importance give a boost to aggregate economic activity in a way which allows declining sectors to maintain a substantial rate of growth while losing their *relative* positions in terms of value added. Declining sectors generally do not contract absolutely because the economy is growing as a result of their loss, but no matter how fast the economy grows, their relative share must fall.

IV

Although the numerical results obtained in Chapter 3 obviously depend on the particular data series described in section (I) of this Appendix, some series of which are clearly provisional, the broad conclusions depend only on the existence of substantial markets which were both growing rapidly and were comparatively neglected by British producers. A large number of runs of the algorithm with different data inputs indicated that the overall results were quite robust with respect to alterations for one or two sectors of relative size and growth rate. The broad conclusions can only be overthrown by showing *both* that the sectors selected for counterfactual decline were substantially smaller and growing more rapidly than shown in Chapter 3 while the sectors selected for counterfactual expansion were smaller and growing less rapidly than shown in the same chapter *and* that the structural differences with the American economy were less pronounced than indicated. Only if it were not possible to find strategic sectors markedly smaller than their American counterparts and exhibiting poor long run performance could it readily be claimed that the economy was operating near the historical limits of growth. While the precise size and rate of growth of the sectors examined here may be revised by future research, the orders of magnitude almost certainly will not be, in part because a conscious attempt was made to bias downward the impact of counterfactual shifts. Further research is at least as likely to reveal more substantial lags in development of important areas of the economy as it is to reverse the findings reported here.

V

Algorithm used to calculate impact of counterfactual structural shifts

```
        DIMENSION S(14), DS(14), G(14), O(14), G1(14), DG1(14), SUM(14),
    (1) SUM1(14), SUM2(14), SUM3(14)
        DO 1 I = 1,14
        READ(1, 2)S(I), DS(I), G(I), O(I)
```

```
2        FORMAT(4F)
         WRITE(3, 13)S(I), DS(I),G(I), O(I)
13       FORMAT(1H0, 4F)
1        CONTINUE
         READ(1, 3)BASE1
3        FORMAT(F)
         RN = 1.00/43.0
         E1 = 100.0
         DO 4 I = 1,1500
         WRITE(3,9)
9        FORMAT(1H0, 1HJ, 5X, 7HSUM1(I), 1X, 7HSUM2(I), 1X, 7HSUM3(I), 1X,
    (1)  6HSUM(I), 2X, 4HTSUM, 4X, 5HTSUM1, 3X, 5HTSUM2)
         TSUM = 0.0
         TSUM1 = 0.0
         TSUM2 = 0.0
         TSUM3 = 0.0
         DO 5 J = 1,13
         G1(J)((((100.0 + 100.0*(DS(J)/S(J)))/O(J))*(E1/100.0))**RN) − 1.0
         DG1(J) = G1(J) − G(J)
         SUM1(J) = DG1(J)*S(J)
         SUM2(J) = G(J)*DS(J)
         SUM3(J) = DG1(J)*DS(J)
         TSUM1 = TSUM1 + SUM1(J)
         TSUM2 = TSUM2 + SUM2(J)
         TSUM3 = TSUM3 + SUM3(J)
         SUM(J) = SUM1(J) + SUM2(J) + SUM3(J)
         TSUM = TSUM + SUM(J)
         WRITE (3, 8) J, SUM1(J), SUM2(J), SUM3(J), SUM(J), TSUM, TSUM1,
    (1)  TSUM2, G1(J), DG1(J)
8        FORMAT (1H0, I2, 9(1X, F9.6))
5        CONTINUE
         SUM1(14) = TSUM*S(14)
         SUM2(14) = 0.0
         SUM3(14) = 0.0
         TSUM1 = TSUM1 + SUM1(14)
         SUM(14) = TSUM*S(14)
         TSUM = TSUM + SUM(14)
         WRITE(3, 12) TSUM1, TSUM3, TSUM3, TSUM
12       FORMAT(1H0, 6HTSUM1 = ,F9.6, 3X, 6HTSUM2 = ,F9.6, 3X, 6HTSUM3
    (1)  = , F9.6, 3X, 5HT SUM = , F9.6)
         ANR = 1.0/RN
         E2 = BASE1*(((100.0/BASE1)**RN) + TSUM)**ANR
         X = ABS(E2 − E1)
         WRITE(3, 10)X
10       FORMAT(1H0, 2HX = ,F)
         IF(X.LT.0.001)GO TO 6
```

```
        E1 = E2
        WRITE(3, 11)I, E1
11      FORMAT(1H0, 5HLOOP, I2, 10X, 3HE1 = ,F)
4       CONTINUE
6       WRITE(3, 7)E2
7       FORMAT(1H0, 17CONVERGENT VALUE = ,F)
        WRITE(4, 7)E2
        STOP
        END
```

Note:
BASE 1 = 43.7. Base 1 is the index number of GNP at constant factor cost in 1870 (1913 = 100). The value is taken from Feinstein (1972: Table 7, column 7).

Appendix E

Part I. Characteristics of British Foreign Investment – Geographical and Industrial Distribution and Rates of Return

The most complete account of British foreign investments before 1914 appears in a series of three articles by George Paish (by 1914, Sir George Paish): (1909, 1911, 1914).

The figures for income from and total value of foreign investments are summarized in Paish (1914:84–5). The basis for these figures is Paish's estimate of foreign capital through 1907 (Paish, 1909:475–6). Paish (1911) extended the 1907 data, which were classified according to industry to include information on the location of various investments. The figures for 1907 were extended to 1910 and then to 1913 by calculating the new issues on London. Paish was careful to exclude conversion loans and shares issued to vendors; he calculated the value of new foreign issues bought by British wealth-holders at the price of issue. His figures, therefore, would represent the amount of sterling in the control of the foreign borrower. (See Paish, 1914:80–1.) Not all the investments bought in London, however, were made by U.K. citizens. Paish (1911:171) figured that £16m of £145,878,300 of foreign securities bought in 1908 in London were owned abroad; £22m of £181,831,646 in 1909; £24m of £189,151,137 in 1910. These latter totals in each case are carried over almost unchanged to the 1914 paper. Hence Paish's final figures include securities bought in London by foreigners and, therefore, do not represent British foreign investment. On the other hand, Paish does not include private (direct) investment, nor the deposits of foreign banks raised in Britain, nor the money used to finance trade (no short-term assets are included).

These estimates of annual investment after 1907 were used to update the comprehensive survey Paish had made in 1907. The only firm data he had for that survey were the incomes subject to tax derived from government, railway and municipality securities. By examining the statements of 2,172 companies which had raised capital in Britain and which had offices in Britain, Paish was able to supplement the government's official information on foreign investment and the income derived from it. These income figures are the most accurate information Paish presents. The estimates of the capital stock which generated these flows are sensitive to the specific assumptions made to relate the flows to the imputed stock.

But even the income figures have gaps. Paish does have a firm defence of the allocation of investments made by Britain when the issue was made in several markets simulta-neously. Only the incomes accruing to those liable for British tax are reported. No foreign security held by a Frenchman, say, would be liable for British tax and hence such securities would not be reported. The matter is different, however, in the cases where foreigners held an interest in a British company. The income of British firms subject to tax would be reported but all the income subject to tax would not accrue to British citizens. Paish (1909: 491ff) claimed, on the basis of private inquiries of informed tax officials, that the extent of the income from foreign investments *assessed* to income-tax in England but received by foreigners was 10% of the total income. There is no indication of the distribution of this foreign-held portion of British foreign investment either by industry, instrument (bond or share) or country. A guess would be that this foreign investment was concentrated in mining, rubber, oil and other raw materials because foreign government and railroad bonds were so easily available that there was no special incentive for foreigners to obtain such investments through a British company.

There are also certain problems in the coverage of the income statistics. Paish (1909: 469) wrote: 'In brief, the income which the (Inland Revenue) Commissioners earmark as coming from abroad is that received from Indian, colonial and foreign government stocks, municipal securities and railways, and the great additional income the country derives from its investments in a vast number of miscellaneous undertakings of all kinds is excluded.'

This description is not necessarily complete, for on the preceding page the Commis-sioners are cited specifically noting (1) 'income disclosed by *agents* [italics mine] for payment of dividends and interest of foreign and colonial companies and corporations (2) income disclosed by bankers and coupon dealers in connection with the realization of foreign and colonial coupons [this realization is apparently different from the income of common or preferred stock] (3) income declared by persons, firms, or public companies as received in respect of investments abroad without taxation at the hands of agents, bankers, or coupon dealers'. (This amounted to £6,947,484 and was the category most likely to be under-represented due to evasion.) (Paish, 1909: 468).

What was simply lumped under income of 'businesses, professions, etc., not otherwise detailed' was the income of 'concerns (other than railways) situate abroad but having their seat of direction and management in this country, e.g. mines, gasworks, waterworks, tramways, breweries, tea and coffee plantations, nitrate grounds, oil fields, land and financial companies, and etc.' (Paish, 1909: 469). The income of this category was estimated by Paish to be approximately £60,000,000. It should not be interpreted as representing direct investment. Many of the investments of a public utility nature such as tramways, electric lighting and power, telegraphs and telephones probably were represented by an office in London as a condition for borrowing money in London. The operation of these enterprises may actually have been effectively made abroad by foreigners whose only responsibility to London was to assure the prompt arrival of a portion of the realized earnings. However, this would represent a more direct control from London than in the case of coupon holders. It also points up the need to examine the earnings of British engineers, technicians and others working abroad who operated the investments. However, to the extent that their incomes were not captured in property income from abroad, they should have been recorded in current transfers.

A much larger element of direct control appears to have existed in the case of banks, mines and rubber. Again, it is important to emphasize that direct investment is excluded by Paish; he (1909: 490) gives only an estimate of its total amount, £500,000,000, with no indication as to country or industry.

Estimates of capital stock

Paish also tried to calculate the capital stock which generated the observed income flows. Paish (1911: 197) makes clear the method of assessment: 'With regard to everything else but government loans, he was obliged to take the nominal amount of capital. When he got the balance sheet, he had to take the capital raised by the company.'

There was a discrepancy, noted by A.W. Flux, of more than £25,000,000 between the two calculations of the total value of all foreign government loans. Paish indicated a change of method of calculation between his 1909 paper and the 1911 paper. In 1909, he had capitalized the income from government loans at the current rate of interest to get the value of the loans. In 1911, in order to achieve uniformity with the estimates for companies, he extended the practice of calculating only the nominal amount of capital lent to governments, i.e. the amount of the sterling loan outstanding, presumably excluding conversions and vendor's shares; Paish (1911: 197) only refers to the 'sum subscribed'.

There is a possibility that realized rates of return are under-estimated by Paish because he did not allow for capital gains on foreign government securities bought below par. Such under-estimates are unlikely to have been important, however. First, loans to governments became progressively less important after the 1870s (Feis, 1930:26–8), which means that the scope for unrecorded gains was greatly reduced by the twentieth century. Secondly, the gains must be set against all the defaults accumulated since 1870; Paish does not count foreign holdings which paid no interest. Finally, but most importantly, there is no evidence from the balance of payments figures that realized capital gains were an important element in the flow of earnings from overseas; if anything, the inward flow of foreign earnings as recorded by Paish is too high rather than too low, suggesting that the aggregate return on net foreign lending was less than Paish estimated.[1] For the years 1908–13, Paish sets forth the gross purchases of foreign investments. His figures may be compared with Matthew Simon's (1967) series of new British portfolio investment and Charles Feinstein's (1972) 'net investment abroad' series.

	Simon	Paish	Feinstein
1904	85.0		121
1907	116.3	89.4	162
1908	147.4	145.9	150
1909	175.7	182.4	142
1910	198.0	189.1	174
1911	169.2	164.0	204
1912	200.7	160.0	203
1913	217.4	196.7	235

Simon's figures are probably more accurate than Paish's; hence Paish tended to under-estimate British new foreign portfolio investment. There must have been serious gaps in both Simon's and Paish's stock estimates. Neither of them included private direct investment abroad nor did they include *sales* of foreign securities by British citizens. There is no indication of the nature of the sales in terms of industrial classification or location. The problem is important, for the presence of sales from the aggregate British portfolio may invalidate Paish's distribution of portfolio foreign investment by both country and industrial classification. Information on sales of previously purchased foreign securities may also affect Simon's conclusions regarding the nature of foreign investment in terms of both its geographical and industrial characteristics.

If Feinstein's figures of the major components of the current account on foreign trade, especially the series for property income earned and owned abroad are roughly correct, then the series that results, net foreign investment, should be roughly correct. The problem, therefore, is to identify the financial instruments which brought about this net foreign investment. The instruments are related as follows (the description of each category is interpreted as the annual figure):

[new foreign issues purchased by British firms or individuals (K)] – [sale of previously held foreign issues to foreigners (U)] + [purchase of outstanding foreign debt from foreigners (U)] + [direct British investment abroad (U)] + [short term lending (U)] – [short term borrowing (U)] = net foreign investment in any given year (K),

where: (U) series unknown,
        (K) series known.

It is reasonable to believe that in years of large purchases of foreign issues as reported by both Paish and Simon the sale of previously held foreign issues would be small and distributed differently from the composition of the new purchases. In years of low levels of foreign purchases, years usually characterized by distrust of foreign investment in general, it is not possible to make even such a rough estimate. For this reason, since his data related to a period of heavy foreign investment, Paish's figures on the industrial (and geographical) distribution of British foreign investments are more reliable, in the absence of further information of other elements of British international finances (especially information on the sale to foreigners of previously held foreign securities), than are Simon's figures. It is not especially revealing over a long period simply to add the annual gross purchases of foreign securities without, at the same time, making an assumption about the disposition of previous purchases. An estimate of the disposition of previous foreign investments remains to be done.

Overall, Paish's articles remain the best source of information on the nature and distribution of British foreign investment. They must be used with some caution, however, especially in the absence of more information on sales.[2]

Table E1. *Paish's estimates of capital stock held abroad in selected years*

Type of investment	End 1913 (£) 000s	End 1907 (£) 000s
Banks	72,909	54,101
Breweries and distilleries	17,980	17,205
Canals and docks	7,110	5,974
Commercial and industrial	145,332	77,610
Electric lighting and power	27,310	7,686
Financial land and investment	244,187	187,027
Gas and water	29,216	22,771
Insurance	246	—
Iron, coal and steel	30,535	12,956
Mines	272,789	230,430
Motor traction, etc.	1,059	—
Nitrate	11,623	10,903
Oil	40,579	14,268
Rubber	40,982	5,433
Shipping	794	—
Tea and coffee	22,443	21,399
Telegraphs and telephones	43,692	34,235
Trams	77,790	35,289
Railways		
Colonial	306,460	188,950
Indian	140,796	123,341
American	616,581	600,000
Foreign	457,177	286,700
Total rails	1,521,014	1,198,991
Municipal	147,547	58,901
Governments		
Colonial	675,494	531,559
Foreign	284,059	167,000
Total	£3,714,690	£2,693,738

Sources:

For December, 1913 data, Paish (1914:85).

For December, 1907 data, Paish (1909:475, 476).

The total of American and foreign railway holdings reported at the end of 1913 in Paish (1914:85) is less than the sum of the holdings at the end of 1907 (Paish, 1909:476) and the new subscriptions for foreign issues taken up in the intervening years (Paish, 1914:82–83). The difference is of the order of £40m and would apparently represent British sales of the debt issues of American and foreign railways to foreigners.

Table E2. *Rate of return in 1907–08 earned on capital invested in each category*

Type of investment	Rate of return (percentage)
Banks	13.6
Breweries and distilleries	4.2
Canals and docks	19.9
Commercial and industrial	6.3
Electric lighting and power	4.2
Financial, land, and investment	3.3
Gas and water	7.2
Insurance	—
Iron, coal, and steel	3.9
Mines	11.1
Motor traction, etc.	—
Nitrate	15.0
Oil	4.5
Rubber	8.2
Shipping	—
Tea and coffee	8.4
Telegraphs and telephones	6.5
Trams	5.1
Railways	
Colonial	4.0
Indian	3.9
American	4.5
Foreign	4.7
Total rails	4.4
Municipal	4.5
Governments	
Colonial	3.6
Foreign	4.8
Total government	3.9

Source: Paish (1909: 475).

Table E3. *Percentage of total portfolio comprised by various components*

Type of investment	Percentage of total held in Dec. 1913	Percentage of total held in Dec. 1907
Banks	0.0196	0.0200
Breweries and distilleries	0.0048	0.0063
Canals and docks	0.0019	0.0022
Commercial and industrial	0.0391	0.0288
Electric lighting and power	0.0073	0.0028
Financial land and investment	0.0657	0.0694
Gas and water	0.0078	0.0084
Insurance	0.0000	—
Iron, coal and steel	0.0082	0.0048
Mines	0.0734	0.0855
Motor traction, etc.	0.0002	—
Nitrate	0.0031	0.0040
Oil	0.0109	0.0052
Rubber	0.0110	0.0020
Shipping	0.0002	—
Tea and coffee	0.0060	0.0079
Telegraphs and telephones	0.0117	0.0217
Trams	0.0209	0.0130
Railways		
Colonial	0.0825	0.0701
Indian	0.0379	0.0457
American	0.1659	0.2227
Foreign	0.1230	0.1064
Total rails	0.4094 ⎫	0.4451 ⎫
Municipal	0.0397 ⎪	0.0218 ⎪
	⎬ Total 0.7073	⎬ Total 0.7261
Governments	⎪	⎪
Colonial	0.1818 ⎪	0.1973 ⎪
Foreign	0.0764 ⎭	0.0619 ⎭
Total	1.0000	1.0000

Source: Table E1.

Table E4. *Investment in the years 1907–1913 (inclusive) by destination*

Area	Amount invested in £s
Canada and Newfoundland	£253,526,387
Australasia	64,795,960
South Africa	55,252,619
West Africa	15,631,427
India and Ceylon	64,712,975
Straits Settlements	23,135,538
Hong Kong	—
Br. N. Borneo	3,069,021
Miscellaneous other colonies	1,406,000
Total colonial	£481,529,927
U.S.	£164,201,850
Cuba	14,563,385
Philippines	2,238,283
Argentina	118,339,585
Brazil	88,227,036
Mexico	33,822,322
Chile	27,563,340
Uruguay	—
Peru	6,989,691
Miscellaneous American	11,128,188
Russia	46,214,906
Egypt	6,427,577
Spain	—
Turkey	4,745,869
Italy	—
Portugal	—
France	—
Germany	—
Miscellaneous European	48,831,730
China	27,805,737
Japan	22,447,240
Miscellaneous foreign	21,359,470
Total foreign	£645,901,202
Grand total	£1,127,431,129

Source: Paish (1914: 81).

Table E5. *Capital public invested by Great Britain in other lands (DEC. 1913)*

Area	(1) End 1913 (£000s)	(2) percentage of total portfolio, 1913	(3) percentage of 1913 total added since Dec. 1906
Canada and Newfoundland	£514,870	13.8	49.2
Australasia	416,446	11.2	15.5
South Africa	370,192	9.9	14.9
West Africa	37,305	1.0	41.9
India and Ceylon	378,776	10.1	17.0
Straits Settlements	27,293	0.7	84.7
Hong Kong	3,104	0.1	—
Br. N. Borneo	5,820	0.2	52.7
Miscellaneous other colonies	26,189	0.7	5.3
Total colonial	£1,779,995	47.9	27.0
U.S.	£754,617	20.3	21.7
Cuba	33,075	0.8	44.0
Philippines	8,217	0.2	27.2
Argentina	319,565	8.6	37.0
Brazil	147,967	3.9	59.6
Mexico	99,019	2.6	34.1
Chile	61,143	1.6	45.0
Uruguay	36,124	0.9	—
Peru	34,173	0.9	20.4
Miscellaneous American	25,538	0.6	43.5
Russia	66,627	1.7	70.8
Egypt	44,912	1.2	14.3
Spain	19,057	0.5	—
Turkey	18,696	0.5	25.3
Italy	12,440	0.3	—
Portugal	8,136	0.2	—
France	8,020	0.2	—
Germany	6,364	0.1	—
Miscellaneous European	54,580	0.4	98.1
Japan	62,816	1.6	35.7
China	43,883	1.1	63.3
Miscellaneous foreign	69,697	1.8	30.6
Total foreign	£1,934,666	52.1	33.3
Grand total	£3,714,661	100.0	30.3

Sources:

Col. (1) – Paish (1914: 84).

Col. (2) – calculated from column (1).

Col. (3) – calculated from Table E4.

Note: Percentage totals may not sum to 100.0 due to rounding error.

Part II. Estimates of Yields on British Domestic Fixed Capital

The purpose of this section is to present an estimate of the average rate of return on domestic fixed capital. (See Table E6.) The results are necessarily approximations because the income that is derived from fixed assets alone is difficult to calculate, especially when combined with income from self-employment, and because capital stock estimates are crude. Nevertheless, even under assumptions which bias downwards the estimate of the return to real domestic capital, that return is still nearly twice the rate Paish calculated was earned on the great majority of British foreign investments. The rate of return is calculated for the years 1910–1914 only, rather than for the entire period. This was done because the estimates of property's share of domestic income are more reliable than for earlier years. However, Feinstein believed that it was considerably more likely that property's share fell between 1865 and 1914 than that it rose.[3] Hence, to extend the proportion of domestic property which was held in 1910–1914 to the rest of the period would be to under-estimate the average rate of return; the conclusions drawn from the years 1910–1914 thus are not reversed but strengthened by examination of the entire period.

Even under assumptions which are clearly under-estimates of the rate of return on real industrial capital, a wide differential of at least three percent existed between the average return on domestic capital as contrasted with foreign. The rate of return on capital in industries with rapidly growing markets, industries in which rather little British domestic captial was ventured, must have been considerably higher.

Table E6. *Estimation of real rate of return on the domestic fixed capital stock*

	(a) Compromise GDP (at factor cost) (£m)	(b)[1] 0.398 × (a) = property's share of GDP (£m)	(c) Domestic gross capital stock at current replacement cost (£m)	(d) (b) ÷ (c) Average rate of return on all property gross of depreciation
1910	1971	784	7310	0.1072
1911	2050	816	7600	0.1071
1912	2131	846	8010	0.1056
1913	2232	886	8500	0.1042
	Source: Feinstein (1972: col. 5, Table 4)		*Source:* Feinstein (1972: col. 5, Table 46)	

	(e) Rent (£m)	(f) (b) − (e) Property's share exclusive of rent on land and buildings (£m)	(g) Value of dwellings (£m)	(h) (c) − (g) Value of gross capital stock exclusive of dwellings (£m)
1910	239	545	1750	5560
1911	243	573	1830	5770
1912	246	600	1910	6100
1913	249	637	1980	6520
	Source: Feinstein (1972: col. 6, Table 1)		*Source:* Feinstein (1972: col. 1, Table 46)	

Table E6. (cont.)

	(i) (f) ÷ (h) Rate of return on real capital exclusive of dwellings gross of depreciation	(j)² Value of public capital stock (£m)	(k)² (h) − (j) Value of gross private capital stock exclusive of dwellings (£m)	(l) (f) ÷ (k) Rate of return on private capital stock (exclusive of dwellings) gross of depreciation
1910	0.0980	772	4788	0.1138
1911	0.0993	789	4981	0.1150
1912	0.0984	806	5294	0.1133
1913	0.0970	826	5694	0.1119

	(m) capital consumption (£m)	(n) (f) − (m) property's share (exclusive of rent) exclusive of capital consumption (£m)	(o) (n) ÷ (h) rate of return on capital stock (exclusive of dwellings) net depreciation
1910	100	445	0.0800
1911	103	470	0.0814
1912	110	490	0.0832
1913	116	521	0.0799

Source: Feinstein (1972: col. 12, Table 1)

[1] Feinstein (1968: column 4, Table 5, p. 126) gives 39.8% as property's share of gross domestic product for the years 1910–1914.

[2] The value of the capital stock exclusive of dwellings includes national and local government capital whose benefits were largely excluded from the national income accounts. Therefore, to determine the rate of return on the capital stock which did generate a yield measured by the national income statistics, the government capital stock should be subtracted. Government capital was assumed to last forty years, hence the stock was estimated summing the previous forty years' capital investment outlay of national and local governments. The annual investments are found in Feinstein (1972: cols. 9 and 10, Table 39). To the extent that government capital did earn a measured return or that government funds were used to build dwellings, col. (l) is an overestimate. This caution is not important for pre-1914 Britain; for example, see W. Ashworth (1960:225–7).

Part III. Exports and domestic consumption of selected commodities produced in Britain in 1907

By using the 1907 Census of Production, it is possible to make an estimate of the value of particular commodities produced in Britain and to determine how much of the output was consumed domestically and how much was exported. Some adjustments must be made to the export figures to make them comparable to those for domestic consumption. Export values are given free on board ship (f.o.b.); hence the cost of transportation and handling must be deducted in order to obtain the cost of the goods at works, which is the point at which domestically consumed goods are valued. This is most simply done for coal, where all values are given at the pithead and the number of tons exported for each category of coal is given. It is then easy to calculate the average value of a ton of coal from each category and multiply that value by the number of tons exported. This gives a value of exported coal at works of £11.4m less than the f.o.b. value. This is not surprising since almost 50% of the total railway receipts for goods traffic in 1907 came from the hauling of minerals, the most important of which by far was coal.[4] For all the other goods examined here 5.86% of their f.o.b. value was deducted for transport and handling in order to make the export value correspond to the value of the goods at works.[5] All the data comes from the Census of Production, 1907 (Cd. 6320) unless otherwise noted; the page numbers given in parentheses beside the data refer to the Census.

Coal (p. 43)	(1) Tons raised (millions)	(2) Value (£m)	(3) Tons Exported (millions)	(4) Imputed value of Exports (£m)
anthracite	3.909	2.297	2.128	1.250
steam	128.204	58.704	46.730	21.397
gas	29.039	12.779	10.445	4.596
household	53.060	25.705	1.510	0.731
other sorts	52.348	20.069	2.788	1.043
	266.560	£119.554	63.601	£29.043

col. (4) = [col. (2) ÷ col. (1)] × [col. (3)]

An additional 18.613 million tons of steam coal was shipped for use by the merchant marine. If some of this coal were sold to a foreign ship, that amount would effectively be exported. It was assumed in order to underestimate the amount exported that the high percentage of 80% of this coal was sold to British ships and only 20% to foreign. The value of the steam coal exported in this manner was calculated as follows:

(18.613m tons) × (0.20) × (£58.704m/128.240m tons)
= £1.705m value exported.

Total value at pithead of coal exported was:

£29.043m.	coal
1.705m.	steam coal

£30.748m

The total value at pithead given to coal raised in Britain was £119.554 millions (p. 42).

The total value at works of cotton textiles made in Britain was given as £132.0m ± £1m free of duplication (p. 291). The value of the exported goods at works was £98.89m (= £105.043m × 0.9414).

The total value at works of woollen and worsted textiles produced in Britain was £65.5m free of duplication (p. 301). The f.o.b. value of exports was £28.2m (Mitchell and Deane, 1962: 305); the value of the exported goods was taken to be £26.56 (= £28.2 × 0.9414) at works.

The total value of jute, hemp and linen textiles manufactured in Britain was £23.0m (p. 308) and the f.o.b. value of exports was £10.751m (p. 308); this was adjusted to give a value of £10.12m at works.

The value of engineering output was given as £116,621,000. This figure, however, was estimated to contain duplications amounting to £11,600,000 (upper estimate, p. 130). The lower estimate of engineering output in Britain (broadly, steam engines, internal combustion engines, prime movers, machinery, structural work and electrical engineering products) was therefore £105,021,000. The value of rolling stock and locomotives made by private railway companies was added to this figure of the value of engineering output:

locomotives	£7,918,000	(includes repair work)	(p. 166)
rolling stock	302,000	(includes repairs)	(p. 866)

£8,220,000

Value (f.o.b.) of engineering output exported:

£7,900,000	steam engines (including locomotives)
22,848,000	non-electrical machinery
3,466,000	electrical goods
273,000	ordnance made by private firms

£34,487,000

The value of engineering exports at works was taken to be £32.47m (£34.487 × 0.9414). Value at works:

goods exported	£361.4m (see footnote 5)
goods made and consumed in the U.K.	£1020m (p. 29)

Commodities produced domestically	Exported	Consumed domestically
Coal	£30.7m	£88.9m
Cotton	98.9m	33.1m
Woollen, worsted	26.6m	38.9m
Jute, hemp, linen	10.1m	12.9m
	£166.3m	£173.8m

The commodities listed comprised 46.0% $\left(= \dfrac{£166.3}{£361.4} \right)$ of the value of exports at works;

the same commodities compromised $17.0\% \left(= \dfrac{£173.8}{£1020.0} \right)$ of home consumption of traded goods produced domestically. The structure of foreign demand for British goods is thus seen to be sharply different from that generated by the domestic economy. Nearly half the export demand fell on only four commodities; there was no similar concentration of domestic demand for domestic output. Since a consequence of foreign investment was to stimulate the export industries at the expense of domestic demand, foreign investment was an important cause of British resources being concentrated in export industries; had less foreign investment been made, and consequently had export demand relative to domestic demand been less, fewer resources would presumably have been committed to those important export industries and greater incentive would have been given to diversification.

Foreign investment did not stimulate demand for the output of the engineering industries in a similar manner. Half of British investment was made abroad in 1907 yet only 28.7% of engineering output was exported.

Commodity	Exported	Consumed domestically
Engineering output	£32.5m	£80.8m

Engineering output was 9% of total exports (value at works) while engineering output was just under 8% of total domestic consumption of domestically produced traded goods.

Notes

1. Introduction

1. A representative sample of the variety of approaches to the puzzle may be found in the following selections from a massive literature: A.L. Levine (1967); S.B. Saul (1969); D.H. Aldcroft (1968); and D.N. McCloskey (1970).

2. For stylistic convenience and in order to reflect the natural historical unity of the period that has been perceived by many writers – for example G.M. Young (1936: vi–vii), an observer especially sensitive to such nuances – Victoria's reign is considered to extend to August, 1914. Certainly the British economy of the five or six decades before the war is most sensibly seen as a smoothly evolving, unified entity.

3. Bairoch's data, in view of the conceptual problems encountered in measuring economic performance and the added difficulties created by the sparseness of historical information, must be considered tentative at best and capable of indicating no more than rough orders of magnitude, although they do possess the virtues of wide coverage and rough accord with contemporary assessments. For an extended discussion of the conceptual problems inherent in measuring economic performance, see Kennedy (1983).

4. Byatt (1968: 273) argues that 'electrification in Britain was probably little delayed by weaknesses among manufacturers'. This claim would appear to be unfounded considering the speed at which development in electrification progressed in the late nineteenth century. Reliance on foreign electrical manufacturers always guaranteed that British firms got electrical equipment after their most advanced foreign competitors. This competitive disadvantage, combined with less skill in the deployment of electrical equipment, a lack of skill that arose for the same reasons that electrical equipment manufacture was backward, may have been decisive in determining the fate of new ventures in their most vulnerable stage. Guido Semenza, an Italian engineer writing in the mid-1890s in the *Journal of the British Institution of Electrical Engineers*, succinctly assessed the state of British technical capabilities in electrical engineering before 1914 when he noted that, in comparison with the Swiss experience, British engineers exhibited 'little novelty, no dash, no tendency which indicates impending progress' (quoted in Brittain, 1974: 113–14). A similar line of argument is advanced by T.P. Hughes (1962; 1983: 77–78). The connection between mass production and electrification is stressed by R.B. DuBoff (1967: 513–16).

5. Rosenberg emphasizes the manner in which the capability to produce one type of complex machined part has encouraged the development of the capacity to produce other types, which have often found their uses in the manufacture of quite unrelated items. The ability of the engineering sector to transfer manufacturing capability from one application to another 'constitutes an external economy of enormous importance to other sectors of the economy' (Rosenberg, 1963:415). Ian Lloyd (1978:3–5) in his history of Rolls–Royce has stressed the advantages and skills F.H. Royce was able to bring to automotive engineering from his experience as an electrical engineer.

   Electrification was particularly important in this process because it allowed much greater flexibility of plant layout since it made it possible for each machine tool or work station to have, where it would be most useful, its own independent electric motor without regard to the positioning of motors elsewhere in the plant. Each independent motor could draw, or not draw, power as required without regard to the power demands in the rest of the plant, so long as total demand was no greater than total supply capacity, a very general constraint in sharp contrast to the previous necessity to run continuously the steam engines supplying power by belts and pulleys to particular work stations.

6. The basis for judging performance here is similar to that used in modern portfolio theory. Assessment of relative performance between 1899–1914 and 1919 (or 1924)–1938 depends upon how the observer's preferences value growth compared with variance. An interesting assessment of the strengths and weaknesses of the most common procedures employed to calculate growth rates may be found in Pesek (1961). The regression analysis used here provides the additional benefit that the standard deviation of the growth rate estimator offers some indication of the reliability of the estimator as well as providing the natural measure of the stability of economic performance.

7. Matthews *et al.* (1982:537–8) also accept the argument that Britain's improved productivity performance in the inter-war period was at least in part due to making good the gap between British technology and that employed in the other advanced countries of the time. However, they also argue that the improvement represented more than mere catching up and that the effort to close the gap also appears to have stimulated British innovation.

8. For yields on electrical engineering see Byatt (1979:157, Table 34, Panel A). The unweighted average rate of profitability for the years 1904–1913 of the seven firms reported there is 3.0%. A weighted average would have yielded a rate closer to 2.6%. Cable makers did rather better – the unweighted average rate of return for cable makers in the years 1903–13 was 5.9% – but represented (see Byatt, 1979: Table 34, Panel B) a much smaller segment of the entire industry, comprising assets accumulated between 1896 and 1914 worth in Byatt's calculations, only £3.7m or 52% of the similarly computed value of assets accumulated by the major electrical machinery manufacturing firms, £7.1m (Byatt, 1979: Tables 31 and 33). Byatt's figures over-estimate the proportion of electrical engineering assets held by all cable makers because among the large machinery manufacturers he does not report Siemens Brothers Dynamo Works at Stafford (with assets accumulated in the period worth approximately £1m) or GEC, while he excludes only Siemens' Woolwich cable-making establishment with assets accumulated in the period apparently worth

approximately £700,000. For more details see Byatt (1968:262–5). British cable makers were not noted for their technological capability especially in the area of high voltage transmission which was to become so crucial later. See Hannah (1979:32). For yields on selected English supply companies – given as 2.1% per year – see Edelstein (1976:292, Table 1) and sources cited there. Edelstein's calculation for yields in investment in electrical equipment manufactures are based on cable makers only. See Edelstein (1970:254–5).

9. For an essay that brings out clearly the possibilities inherent in such a line of argument, see Arrow (1974).

10. For a challenging and influential (and controversial) analysis of the way in which cultural values affect attitudes towards economic endeavour and risk-taking, see Martin J. Wiener (1981:especially Chapter 7).

2 Economic growth and structural change

1. The procedure is explicitly based on the premise that conventional measures of output, despite conceptual defects, nevertheless capture the crucial characteristics and trends of economic development. The defects in the conventional national income accounts are reviewed by Kuznets (1966:220–34), one of the pioneers of national income accounting. A detailed investigation of those defects and of their quantitative significance is contained in the seminal paper by William Nordhaus and James Tobin (1972) who have found a close correlation between the movements in the conventional accounts and the movements in their Measure of Economic Welfare (MEW). Both measures move in the same direction, although the rate of growth of conventional income is consistently greater than the rate of growth of MEW. Nevertheless, this implies that within certain limits, which are most closely associated with the provision of voluntary leisure and the nature of urban amenities and disamenities and which were not violated in the late Victorian period, increases in the growth rate of conventional income will also imply increases in the growth rate of MEW. This finding has been corroborated by King (1974) on the basis of correlations in the movements of indices of social indicators intuitively reflecting welfare changes difficult to quantify (e.g. life expectancy, health levels, etc.) and movements in conventional incomes. For a comprehensive survey of these and related issues in measuring economic activity, together with review of the most promising strategies for accounting improvements and their likely significance for economic analysis, see Kennedy (1983).

2. The example of textiles serves to illustrate the argument that even if a sectoral analysis of total factor productivity were possible, it would only complement but not replace the sectoral analysis treated in this book. In order for aggregate output to expand faster than the weighted sum of factor inputs, technological progress in one form or another must take place. Yet that progress need not occur in the industries that produce the equipment and services which make technological progress possible in the rest of the economy. In view of the data difficulties inherent in estimating productivity – separate output price indices, factor price indices, and knowledge of the elasticities of factor substitution in production are needed – and the numerous sources of error which these difficulties create, it is a more robust procedure to

concentrate on measuring and correctly weighting sectoral output indices. While indices of output are not without error, since they would still be required in any estimations of productivity, productivity estimates necessarily cannot be more accurate than output indices. Of course, knowledge of productivity advance is extremely useful in charting the way in which technological advance occurs. The strategic sectors are important because they promote productivity advance in the rest of the economy, but without precise productivity estimates, knowledge of how the strategic sectors achieve their impact must remain speculative.

3. It should be noted that a number of historians have refused to acknowledge the significance of structural change on the scale considered here. Both J.A. Dowie (1968) and B.W.E. Alford (1972: 20–25) have questioned whether the 'new' industries, many of which have been designated strategic in this book, were, even as late as the inter-war period, large enough to affect substantially aggregate economic performance. Neither writer stresses the intermediate good nature of much of the output of the 'new' industries (most notably electrical engineering and chemicals; more subtly, vehicles also constituted an intermediate good in the distributive trades). Thus neither writer links rapid growth of the 'new' industries to improved productivity performances in the 'old', although Dowie does recognize the possibility. More recently, Neil K. Buxton (1975) has also questioned, on the basis of their relatively small levels of investment and labour uptake, the importance of the 'new' industries in bringing about recovery in Britain from the Great Slump of 1929–32. It should be noted that the strategic industries considered in this paper are a larger group than that Buxton considered and that the contribution of his category 'new industries' to total net output was much greater than that made by either investment or employment in those industries. How this latter discrepancy is reconciled is not at all clear for Buxton is also highly sceptical of the claim that productivity growth in the 'new' industries was unusually great.

While the argument of this paper focuses on the importance of strategic industries in long-term growth and thus can say nothing directly about the role of these industries in cyclical recovery, Buxton's conclusions do not give enough weight to the ability of a group of industries to sustain higher than average growth rates over long periods of time. He offers no way of measuring the importance of an industry other than to look at its relative size whereas the significance of an industry to aggregate growth is a product of *both* its relative size *and* its growth rate. In contrast, the importance of these combined considerations are well illustrated by Matthews *et al.* (1982: 256–258), where the importance of the 'new' industries is discussed. A different line of argument has been taken by G.N. von Tunzelmann (1982). He dismisses the argument that the new industries were a group (or block) of industries with few input–output links to the rest of the economy, particularly the traditional export staples. In his treatment of the new industries von Tunzelmann is in close accord with the arguments of this paper, which stress the importance of the strategic industries as sources of intermediate inputs to the rest of the economy. Unlike Buxton, von Tunzelmann does try to measure the importance of the 'new' industries and when he takes account of the importance of inputs from the 'new' industries to the rest of the economy, the 'new' industries appear significant indeed, although input–output calculations subject to counterfactual constraints, by understating adjustment possibilities, may overstate the loss due to the constrained expansion of strategic sectors.

A complete assessment of the 'new' industries, particularly their contribution indirectly, would require the comparison of two input–output tables, one showing the input–output matrix of an economy with a counterfactually large strategic industry sector and the other the input–output matrix of the actual economy, with a smaller strategic industry sector. Some elements in one matrix would be larger than the corresponding element in the other and these differences can be utilized to indicate the aggregate savings, if any, permitted by the presence of a larger group of strategic industries in meeting any level of final demand. In particular, the column sums of the input–output matrix, that is each $\sum_{i=1}^{n} a_{ij}$, where a_{ij} is the value of the ith input needed to produce one pound's worth of the jth commodity, must equal the total (non-labour) cost of producing the jth good. Therefore $1 - \sum_{i=1}^{n} a_{ij}$ equals the payment to the non-produced good (assumed to be labour). The sum $\sum_{i=1}^{n} a_{ij}$ will on average be smaller for the more efficient economy. After all, if the strategic industries enhance productivity, as has been argued here, then even after allowing for greater use of their output, the economy is able to produce at any given level using fewer resources overall. This overall saving represents the potential increase in real incomes (appearing here as higher real wages) permitted by using a technologically superior set of production techniques. Whether the economic response to technological change – particularly in terms of prices, investment, and employment – will be such as to permit full realization of the potential increase in real income is another matter, one which cannot be lightly dismissed in the context of a discussion of economic performance in the 1930s. Matthews *et al.* (1982: Ch. 9) find that TFP (Total Factor Productivity) appears to move comparatively uniformly across most major sectors and conclude therefore that shifts in resources among sectors are not a major factor in raising TFP and hence real incomes. As the example of machinery and textiles cited above indicates, however, the sectoral incidence of TFP may not reveal the ultimate origins of productivity advance. (For further discussion of this point, and an illustration of how misleading cursory treatments of structural change can be, see below, Appendix D, section III, and related Table D4.) In fact, the marked differences in sectoral output growth rates contrasted with the limited differences in sectoral TFP growth suggest that the consequences of sustained technological change are more likely to be registered on the factors determining sectoral output growth than on the possibilities of sectoral differences in TFP gains.

4. The industrial structure of modern Japan is a clear example of how a country very poor in resources has allocated its resources so as best to compensate for the barrenness of the land. Greatest stress is placed on those activities which exploit most fully the one great asset of the country, the technological and organizational skills of the people, skills whose acquisition and maintenance are the object of much expenditure of time, money and effort (Denison and Chung, 1976: 13). For students of British economic growth, the Japanese growth rates are simply astonishing. Over the period, 1953–71, real output of general machinery, electrical machinery, transport equipment and precision instruments maintained an average annual growth rate of 19%, implying a doubling of output every 3.8 years. Nor can this explosive growth, which was twice the growth rate for the economy as a whole, be attributed to expansion from a small base. The 1937 level of output was reached by 1952–4, making the industrial base in 1953, therefore, among the largest in the world. Furthermore, the

averages conceal an *acceleration* of growth in the late 1960s and early 1970s, by which time the Japanese economy had become the world's third largest.

5. Limitations of the published census do not permit a more detailed breakdown. Experimentation with the consequences of various possible redefinitions of the engineering sector indicates that the present definition with its large 'traditional, low technology' component tends to under-estimate the growth potential of sectoral change. In these circumstances, since counterfactual changes are biased downward, recourse to a more detailed breakdown does not appear to be worth the considerable effort involved. It is hoped that more information on the sector will emerge as a by-product of business history research responding to Clapham's injunction to determine 'how much'.

6. Labour force data are taken from Appendices IIA and IIB (Kennedy, 1975: 152, 171), where the U.K. and U.S. labour forces are allocated across sectors on a comparable basis. The U.K. data is for 1911, the U.S. data for 1909. To obtain an estimate for the approximate number of workers in each sector in 1907, the later observation-year figure was multiplied by the ratio of employed workers in 1907 to employed workers in the later year. Employed workers data in the U.K. are taken from Feinstein (1972: Table 57, column 3); in the U.S. from U.S. Bureau of the Census (1975: series D 127). The U.K. ratio is 0.959; the U.S. ratio is 0.968.

7. It is sometimes thought that the utilization of electricity which occurred much more readily in the U.S. than in the U.K. is explained by comparatively high American wages. This is highly improbable for electrically driven or controlled manufacturing processes dominated alternative techniques over a very wide range of relative capital and labour costs. Indeed, Minami (1977: 946–7, 956) has argued that Japanese manufacturers, in the early twentieth century, embraced electrification with even more enthusiasm than their American counterparts precisely because Japanese levels of productivity (and hence levels of wages) were so low that only a major technological advance could redress the situation. Furthermore, workers in very small Japanese establishments which previously could not afford to provide non-human sources of power gained more proportionately from the advent of cheap electric power than did workers in larger, better equipped plants. Thus, it is considerably more accurate to claim that compared with Britain, American wages were high because of the wide usage of electricity than it is to claim that American electricity usage was widespread because of high American wages.

8. The enormous requirements placed on the engineering industry in executing the task of mass producing automobiles is fairly readily comprehended. What may not be so obvious is that the successful design of automobiles generated advance in the design of machine tools as well. Thus Rosenberg (1963: 426) has written that: 'important features of the automobile itself were actually transferred and embodied into machine tools. Thus the transmission for the drive and feed mechanisms of machine tools was considerably improved when machine tool builders adopted the alloy steel sliding gears and integral keyshafts developed by automobile designers. Moreover, the introduction of antifriction bearings into key points of the machine tool resulted from the demonstration of their usefulness in automobiles. Finally, the whole approach to the lubrication of machine tools was radically revised as a result of the automobile.'

9. Interestingly, there is some evidence that technologically advanced industries were

unusually dependent upon telecommunications. Harold C. Passer (1952: 387) has observed that by 1895 General Electric's offices in New York City generated more telephone traffic than any other two companies in that city combined. This seems to be explained by General Electric's creation of a national marketing capability in the 1890s. It is not surprising that the manufacture and sale of complex, highly heterogeneous equipment to a broad range of users at a time of intense technological ferment would generate exceptional communications demands.

10. R.C. Floud (1976: 101–18) has argued that the performance of the British machine tool industry was creditable and that the surge of American imports into free-trade Britain, at the end of the nineteenth century, was only the result of the American industry's reaching European levels of efficiency after long shelter behind tariff barriers. This argument fails fully to recognize, however, that the machine tool industry as a separate entity was, in any case, only a product of the second third of the nineteenth century and had evolved in all industrial countries very rapidly. The 'mature' phase of the industry anywhere did not occur until after 1880, when demands for transport equipment, first bicycles and then automobiles, led to machine tool developments which had applications in almost all manufacturing activities (see Rosenberg, 1963: 422 and footnote 5, Chapter 1 above). The U.S. led in these transport developments and also in electrification, a process that both contributed to and benefited from the developments in the manufacture of transport equipment. Although imprecise trade data before 1914 make definitive statements difficult, it would appear that the commercial ascendancy of American machine tool producers was the result of a rapid technological advance which produced new types of automatic and semi-automatic equipment necessary for the implementation of mass production methods, rather than the consequence of marketing machine tools which were comparable to British tools in all respects but price. Rosenberg's discussion of the use of more durable metal alloys, of new drive mechanisms, and of new applications for machine tools makes it very unlikely that the U.S. exports of the 1890s were qualitatively similar to British machine tools. Indeed in making his case, Floud carefully states his assumptions, ranking them in descending order of plausibility; his last, least plausible assumption is that machine tools were a 'homogeneous product' (pp. 115–16). No other historian of machine tools, nor even Floud himself in the rest of his book, accepts this assumption. Without this assumption, however, Floud cannot make his case with the available evidence. In this book it is argued that American and British machine tool production and practices were more similar in the first three quarters of the nineteenth century than they were in the last quarter. New metal alloys, electrification and a rapidly changing pattern of final output, in which mass produced goods such as bicycles, automobiles, electric motors, office machines, and telephones quickly became important for the first time, led to a sharp change in the demand for machine tools. Note that a crucial element of simultaneity inevitably arises for without supply side changes, demand for mass produced goods would not have been generated in the first place. This change took place first in the U.S. or at least was complete earlier in the U.S., and was subsequently exported. An important factor determining the import of American machine tools was the shift in patterns of final output in Britain. Only when bicycles became mass produced, did American machine tools become attractive, or indeed, necessary.

11. Byatt (1962: 369–70; 1968: 255–8). It has often been pointed out (see Byatt, 1968: 258–62) that the large foreign investments in Britain were not particularly profitable before 1913. In part, especially in the cases of Westinghouse and Siemens, this was due to market misjudgment and bad management. A much more important reason, however, was the decline in British expenditure on plant and machinery by more than a third from 1903 to 1908 followed by only a weak recovery to 1913, the 1903 level of purchase not being regained until 1914 (Feinstein, 1972: Table 39, column 3). In real terms, 1913 British gross domestic fixed capital formation was only 83% of that of 1903 (Feinstein, 1972: Table 40, column 3). It is this very sharp fall in domestic investment rather than fundamentally mistaken commercial judgment that produced the poor showing. Electrical engineering in this period was almost entirely a producer of intermediate goods and was thus unusually exposed to sudden fluctuations in investment. See Chapter 6 for further discussion.

12. The most consistent case for a systematic relationship between emigration and U.K. home construction has been made by Brinley Thomas (1973). Thomas's argument has been questioned by H.J. Habakkuk (1962) and S.B. Saul (1962). Thomas (1973: 202–22) has replied to these criticisms. While Thomas has shown that most regional business cycles were correlated with demographic trends of which emigration was especially important, the relationships among domestic and foreign investment, emigration and migration are too complex to support unambiguously any causal argument advanced so far.

13. A complete explanation is likely to be complex for if electricity supply costs were the entire answer one would expect electric welding to have predominated in the NESCO supply area (Newcastle). Welding in Britain before 1914 also suffered because of difficulty in making the welded joints sufficiently strong (Pollard and Robertson, 1979: 123). However, if electricity in all British shipbuilding centres had been as cheap and reliable as in the NESCO area a much greater incentive would have existed to encourage the research and experimentation that eventually produced a solution to the problem of weak welds. As it was, the solutions were found more quickly abroad and British shipbuilders later found themselves struggling to keep abreast of foreign techniques in an area of ship construction where they, but a short while before, had led.

14. The advantage to Brunner, Mond of the inferior technology of its far larger competitor was very similar to the advantages factory-based manufactures of yarn and cloth reaped a century earlier from the existence of a large technologically inferior cottage-based industry for the production of the same goods. As long as United Alkali determined prices and wages in the inorganic chemical industry Brunner, Mond would earn super-normal profits *and* be shielded from the full consequences of adverse price fluctuations, the main impact of which would fall on chemical workers and United Alkali profits and production. The anaemic profits of United Alkali were testimony of its usefulness as Brunner, Mond's financial 'shock absorber'. See Joel Mokyr (1976) for a comprehensive discussion of the advantages a technologically superior firm would enjoy in a technologically weak industry.

15. How small is the comparative advantage allowed by size and geography may be inferred from 1970 data. Gross farm product in the U.S. (including farm rents paid to non-farm owners) in that year was 3.65% of GNP; in the U.K. GNP originating in agriculture, forestry and fishing was 3.00%. Both countries subsidize their farmers, the

Americans more so than the British. Therefore, at the very most, it would appear that the richer resource endowment of the U.S. permits an agricultural sector of only 125–50% of that of the U.K. U.S. data is from U.S. Bureau of Economic Analysis (1973: series A2 and A22, adjusted to Kendrick's definition); U.K. data from CSO (1976:19).

16. This factor is important to bear in mind when comparing U.S. and British growth performance. The U.S. by no means whatever represented an ideal example of growth. Faster transfer of resources from agriculture to the rest of the economy is but one obvious way in which more rapid growth could have been achieved in the nineteenth-century American economy.

17. It is important to note that it was foreign demand and not an uncontrolled appetite for energy which explains much of the relatively large size of the U.K. coal mining sector. The relative unimportance of electricity generation in the U.K. also indicates that the most efficient means of obtaining useful energy from coal was comparatively neglected.

18. This claim needs some qualification. It would only be true if the introduction of mechanical aids, primarily cutters and conveyors, on a larger scale than actually occurred would necessarily have been more costly than the methods employed. This has in fact been claimed by Rhodri Walters (1975: 297–8) and A.J. Taylor (1968: 56–60). However, if earlier adoption of mechanical devices had led to improvements in the skill with which they were deployed, to incremental improvements in machine design, and to improvements in overall mine operations as a result of the reorganization required to accommodate the new equipment, the initial cost of the equipment and its medium term maintenance would not have been the relevant costs to use in the decision of whether to mechanize or not for those costs would, in such cases, be properly attributed to future, not current output. Whether technological progress induced by more aggressive mechanization would have lowered or raised mining's share in national income would depend on both the income and the price elasticity of demand for coal. The rent component of mining's share clearly depended on low costs per ton.

19. For an enlightening account of the classical illustration of this process, see Gary Saxonhouse (1974).

20. Sandberg (1974: 139–74) notes that Britain's share of world exports of cotton goods declined after 1882–4. This was due to the rapid growth of markets in French colonies and in Eastern Europe, both markets in which British participation was limited for political and diplomatic reasons and, more importantly, to unavoidable competitive pressure from low-wage industries in the American South, Italy and Japan. Nevertheless, Sandberg (1974: 141) records that in 6 years from 1905 to 1913, Britain exported over 6 billion yards of cloth; never before or since that time has any nation managed to export such a volume of cloth.

21. Tyszynski (1951:277–8). The same broad features also emerge from Maizels' somewhat more comprehensive data. See Maizels (1970: 178).

22. Feinstein (1972: T14–T15, T114–115). Compare the growth of column 10, Table 5, with that of column 10, Table 52.

23. This claim is justified by the following calculations. From Feinstein, (1972) Table 5, column 10, the index number for 1907 GNP is 89.2 (1913 = 100). From Feinstein (1972) Table 52, column 10, the index number of real output in paper and printing is

84.4 (1913 = 100). From the same sources, the index number for 1938 GNP is 120.2 (1913 [1938 market prices] = 100) and for paper and printing is 186.9 (1913 = 100). Obviously over the period 1907–1938, paper and printing grew much faster than did real GNP. To be precise, the ratio of the index of paper and printing to GNP is 0.946 in 1907 and 1.555 in 1938, implying an increase in the relative share of GNP of paper and printing in 1938 GNP of 164.4% compared with the share of GNP in 1907 (1.555/0.946 = 1.644). The 1907 share of GNP was 1.47%. From Table 2.1 above, 1.47 × 1.644 = 2.417. The figure of 2.42% of GNP may be compared with the 1909 U.S. figures 2.35%.

24. John W. Kendrick (1961:471) provides an output measure for the industries of paper manufacture and printing and publishing. Public consumption of books, magazines and newspapers is given in U.S. Bureau of the Census (1975: Series P324 and P370).

25. Du Boff (1967: 516, footnote 4) notes that printing and publication led in the industrial application of electricity in the late nineteenth century and that this application was intimately linked to greater productivity advances there than occurred in any other sector before 1909. So rapid was electrification in U.S. printing that the 1905 Census of Manufactures took special note of the fact.

26. In the U.S. manufacturing census of 1909, the manufacture of cash registers and calculating machines was recorded as an important middle rank industry (ranked in the third of six categories) in terms of value added in production. The category is not mentioned at all in the 1907 U.K. production census. See U.S. Bureau of the Census (1914b: 41). The absence of office equipment in British firms before 1914 is vividly illustrated by Payne (1967: 534–5).

27. Such a claim has been advanced for example, by Charles Wilson, (1965: 185–6), who quoted approvingly Robert Giffen's 1887 speech to the British Association. Giffen argued: 'industry by a natural law is becoming more miscellaneous and as populations develop, the disproportionate growth of the numbers employed in such miscellaneous industries, and in what may be called incorporeal functions, that is, as teachers, artists and the like, prevents the increase of staple products continuing at the former rate.'

28. Chandler (1962: 12–16). Contrast this situation with that set out by Payne (1967: 527–36) for Great Britain.

29. Table 2.10 shows the proportion of GDP of value added in the professional sector in the U.S. to be 83.8% of the similar proportion in the U.K. When the occupational census data is used, the proportion of the U.S. labour force counted as legal, scientific or engineering professional is 89.2% of the relative size of its U.K. counterpart. (The U.S. proportion is 0.66%; the U.K. proportion 0.74%.) Accountants and cashiers (the two groups cannot be distinguished) were much more important in the U.S. In all, then, there would appear to be no significant differences in the functional importance of professional workers, including accountants, as a group in the two countries.

30. Note that this argument does *not* imply that total payments to factors in transport would fall. What is implied is that new capital goods were so effective relative to their cost that they earned very high yields. Capital losses were likely to accrue to owners of older vintage transport equipment (i.e. railroads) and it is these losses which acted to hold down overall returns on capital. Exactly the same kind of argument would apply to labour earnings: wages paid to workers would rise, but wages per efficiency unit of labour could nevertheless fall. Thus the earnings accruing to factors of production

rose less rapidly than output of transport services. This argument does assume that demand for transport is not highly price elastic. If it were, then a clear tendency for transport's relative share of GNP to increase would exist. It is also likely that the national income accounts as they are presently defined tend to under-estimate value added in transportation since the labour cost of individuals driving themselves in their own vehicles is generally not recorded. Thus the rise of automobile ownership to the extent that it diverted passengers from public transport, where factor costs are recorded, would cause value added arising in transport to appear less than it actually was if proper 'welfare' accounting were employed. For a more complete discussion of this point see W.D. Nordhaus and J. Tobin (1972: 38–47).

31. Evidence for this claim comes from three sources. First, data for value added in distribution (gross of capital depreciation) for census years in the period 1869–1948 are found in Harold Barger (1955: 70, Table 20 and 77, Table 23). Barger's series with minor adjustments is then compared with GNP. The results of this comparison are set out below. Barger's series, which includes the net sales of eating and drinking establishments is not directly comparable to the wholesale–retail trade entry in Table 2.2, which counts the value added in such establishments in personal services. Other adjustments to the data are described in Data Appendix B.

Value added in wholesale-retail trade as a percentage of U.S. GNP

1869	20.9%	1919	19.2%
1879	20.1%	1929	17.3
1889	19.1	1939	17.8
1899	18.2	1948	19.4
1909	18.2		

Source: Value added in distribution: Barger (1955: Tables 20 and 23). GNP: U.S. Bureau of Economic Analysis (1973: series A7). GNP data for 1939 and 1948 are from U.S. Bureau of Economic Analysis (1973: series A8).

The trend is not monotonic, clearly being sensitive to fluctuations in business activity which affect wholesale–retail trade less than overall economic activity, a tendency which increases trade's relative importance during recessions. Nevertheless, at the very least it is clear from these data that there is no tendency for trade's relative importance to increase over time.

This conclusion is supported by comparing net value added at factor cost in retail–wholesale trade (U.S. Bureau of the Census, 1975: series T1 plus T2) with net national income (U.S. Bureau of the Census, 1975: series F7). The same downward trend reversed by recession is again evident. It also emerges when gross value added in distribution (series F138) is compared with GNP (series F130) over the years 1947–70, a period when better data are available. It is interesting to note that the relative importance of gross value added in distribution to GNP is uniformly greater than the relative importance of net value added in distribution to NNI. This finding suggests that distribution gives rise to more substantial capital depreciation than American economic activity in general. The substantial use of capital in the sector can most early be interpreted as the result of a systematic attempt to boost labour productivity.

32. From 1870 to 1913, output of distribution services grew slightly more rapidly than did GNP (compare Feinstein, 1972: Table 53, column 1 with Table 7, column 7). After

1918, this process was sharply reversed; by 1938, distribution services were, in relative terms compared with GNP, only 96.4% of the 1913 level and by 1965 this figure had fallen to 78.9%. Since 1965, the same trend continued to be observed until 1971; between 1972 and 1975 distribution increased its relative share but this reflects the same cyclical pattern as was noted in the U.S. where distribution increases its relative share during recession. See CSO (1976: 18–19).

33. For evidence of the labour-intensive nature of distribution, see Barger (1955: 3–18) and Margaret Hall, John Knapp and Christopher Winsten (1961: 46).

34. The Anglo-American Productivity Council Report *Retailing* placed great emphasis on consumer transport as the explanation for the enormously greater sales productivity recorded in American distribution when contrasted with that of Britain: 'It is the regular and consistent use of the private car which has caused the most recent changes and developments in American retailing. It has affected the development of both large department stores and the chain food stores to a particular degree and has fostered the creation of new shopping centres comprising groups of shops and stores which are sited in the new suburbs or in open country, in some cases several miles from a city, large town or main shopping centre of the older type ... Practically all the trade of such centres is based on the private motor car' (quoted in Hall *et al.* 1961:82). Although the use of automobiles was much more widespread in the early 1950s than had been true before 1914, the rapid growth of automobile ownership early in the century had even then begun to change shopping habits.

35. This passage was quoted in E.H. Hunt (1973: 140, Footnote 2). Hunt systematically uses the growth of employment in domestic services as a gauge of under-employment. In those regions where workers in all industries were paid relatively low wages, domestic employment as a fraction of total employment was higher than the national average. Even if service employment were falling in a low-wage region, it fell less rapidly than the national average, and if agriculture's share were rapidly declining, a portion of that decline would be offset by rising employment in domestic services. Conversely in high wage areas domestic workers were far fewer. The inference may be easily drawn that if any alternative to domestic service could be found, it would be preferred by most workers. Since the demand for domestic servants may be reasonably supposed to be income elastic, since at any point in time cross section data reveal the wealthly consistently to hire more servants, the increase rising more rapidly than estimated wealth, supply-side factors must account for the bulk of the sector's persistent contraction.

36. There is, of course, no reason *in principle* why domestic capital formation should suffer so long as markets were *equally* good at projecting *all* the relevant information needed to make rational decisions. There is very good reason to believe that this informational neutrality was not observed. See Chapter 4 for a more complete discussion.

3 The consequences of structural change in the Victorian economy

1. Concentration on sector growth invites, but does not directly answer, the question of how such growth comes about. The mechanics of sectoral growth (assuming no changes in the degree of vertical integration in the sector) may be summarized under

two broad headings. First, productivity advance in industries facing price elastic demand allows an outward shift in supply curves, thereby increasing industry revenue. If demand is income elastic as well, the capacity for expansion can be very great. The automobile industry may serve as an illustration of this first mechanism. Secondly, productivity in an industry may not be great but demand shifts in its favour, thereby raising industry revenues relative to the rest of the economy. An illustration of this process may be found in the machinery industry in the twentieth century where the price of final output may rise sharply due to secular increases in demand. However, product innovation in this sector is often rapid, creating severe index number problems. Prices when measured in 'efficiency' terms, in terms of what a given machine is capable of doing, may, in fact, reveal a decline even when the nominal cost of the machine itself rises. For a discussion of this problem in connection with machine tools, see Roderick Floud (1971: 321–23). The discussion following Floud's paper is also useful. Obviously, if an industry were to achieve relative expansion, one of these mechanisms, or a combination of both, would have to operate.

2. While iron and steel products were becoming increasingly important in international trade, Britain's share of world markets was declining and British imports were rising, even though British exports were also increasing rapidly (Tyszynski, 1951: 277–8).

3. Construction is an activity in which international trade is relatively unimportant and for which, therefore, those measures of performance which rely on international trade flows are largely irrelevant.

4. The cold statistics of this decline are in Feinstein (1972: T60). Between 1870 and 1913 agricultural rents in current prices declined by 18.9%; the wages of agricultural workers rose by only 5.3%; farmers' incomes declined by 15.2%. All this occurred while the price index of GDP at factor cost rose by 3.4%. Nor did the decline halt in 1914. By 1938, agriculture accounted for only 3.28% of U.K. GNP (at factor cost). This figure is artificially low due to the partition of Ireland which caused an almost entirely agricultural region to be removed from the U.K. economy. Feinstein's data for 1920 show that in that year Southern Ireland accounted for 29% of the agricultural output of the unpartitioned U.K. Hence the comparable 1938 proportion would most likely have been 4.23% (= 3.28 × 1.2906), assuming that the relative share of Southern Ireland's agricultural output in unpartitioned U.K. output would have been unchanged in 1938 from 1920. If Southern Ireland would have industrialized in any event 4.23% is obviously an over-estimate to agriculture's share in 1938 on a basis comparable to that used in 1913. Some drama (and a few qualifications concerning structural adjustments in agriculture) associated with British agriculture's long decline can be found in T.W. Fletcher (1960–1: 420–22) and in F.M.L. Thompson (1963: 308–20).

5. It should be noted that the difference is not statistically significant although it is certainly more likely that U.S. distribution output grew more slowly than did national income. With observations restricted to Census years, the OLS estimate of U.S. distribution growth is characterized by an unusually large standard error. Nevertheless, except for a negligible reversal in 1909, the sector continually declined in relative importance in the U.S. from 1869 to the First World War. See also footnote 31, Chapter 2.

6. It should be noted that the selection of a rapidly growing sector for counterfactual contraction tends to reduce the impact of the proposed structural changes.

7. Feinstein (1972: Table 46, columns 2, 3, 4; and Table 50). The reader is warned that all capital stock estimates are difficult to compile, and that while Feinstein's estimates have been prepared with exemplary care and are by far the best available they must nevertheless be considered only provisional.

8. Cairncross (1953: 3–4) estimates that British foreign investment 1870–1914 occurred at a rate comparable, when adjusted for the relative sizes of the economies, to an American Marshall plan every *six months* during the post 1945 period.

9. The only exception to this general rule was the U.S. construction sector. Kendrick's data show the real output of U.S. contract construction rising by only a third between 1909 and 1929, while GNP rose by 89% in the same period. However, the slow rate of growth of real output in construction may be statistical artifact rather than an historical reality. Kendrick's data (1961: Table A.IX and A.XI) show employed man hours worked in the sector increased as a proportion of both total employment and hours worked in the economy over the period 1909–1929. Although productivity gains in the sector were almost surely less than those of the economy as a whole, there is no reason to believe that relative incomes earned in the sector fell (Kendrick, 1961: 497). Thus the sector's relative share of total output after 1909 is greater than the measure of real output growth would suggest, since the real output measure does not reflect a greater preponderance of national income originating in the sector, but only reflects physical production. If the relative shift of expenditure was heavily in construction's favour, a measure of physical output will under-estimate the relative significance of the increases in the industry's output.

10. The calculation which supports this claim was made in the following manner. Feinstein (1972: Table 17, column 4) sets out per capita gross domestic product at constant factor cost (1913 prices). To make this comparable with the GNP estimates at (slightly modified) market prices, the values in column 4 were multiplied first by 1.079 (the ratio of GNP to GDP in 1913) and the resulting value multiplied then by 1.075 (the ratio of GDP at market prices to GDP at factor cost). The result was to produce a series of per capita GNP (rather than GDP) at 1913 market prices (rather than 1913 factor costs). Net property income from abroad declined markedly after 1914 and indirect taxes of all sorts became much larger. To maintain the 1913 ratios of GNP to GDP and GDP at market prices to GDP at factor cost is to over-estimate substantially (by about 10% by 1965) real per capita GNP at market prices as derived from Feinstein's series for GDP at constant factor cost. Making this conscious over-estimate of comparable GNP after 1913, if the 1913 value of £49 per capita per year is multiplied by 1.268, the result of £62.1 was not matched in peacetime until 1946. The value was, however, surpassed for every year from 1940 to 1945 (inclusive). This was the result of unusual wartime conditions which stimulated high-value engineering output relative to the rest of the economy. Therefore, the date of 1946 for the overtaking by the actual economy of the counterfactual 1913 economy can be seen as quite conservative; a later date could easily be justified by making any reasonable adjustment for the decline of foreign property income or the increase in indirect taxes over 1913 levels.

11. This level, 25% larger than the relative size of the U.S. textiles industry in contrast to a

situation where the relative sizes of the textiles industries in the two countries were equal, was selected to reflect the powerful position in international markets which Britain had established by 1880.

12. This value was chosen as follows: from Feinstein (1972: Table 23, column 1) total factor income in 1938 in agriculture was £170m. This was 3.28% of 1938 GNP at factor cost, obtained by adding column 6 to column 9 of Table 3 and dividing £170m by the result. But this percentage is not comparable to pre-1914 data because the partition of Ireland in 1922 removed a heavily agricultural sector from the U.K. economy, making what remained proportionately less agricultural. The extent of this reduction is calculated from Feinstein's estimate of agricultural factor income in the unpartitioned U.K. in 1920 (£385m) divided by agricultural factor income in the partitioned U.K. in the same year (£306m). The resulting ratio is 1.2906. Consequently the 1938 agricultural sector size comparable to the 1907 size was 4.23% (3.28 × 1.2906). The difference between the 1907 size of 6.66% and the adjusted 1938 size of 4.23% was 2.43%. Half of this share was assumed to come from pre-1914 British agriculture and the other half from net property income from abroad.

13. This sector was too highly aggregated in Blue Book (CSO, 1976) Table 2.2 to permit approximation of its true size in 1970. Since the purpose of the calculations based on 1970 sector sizes is for illustration only, more precise definition is not necessary.

14. Data are taken from OECD (1973). The value was that of value added by distribution in the American economy in 1969.

4 Limits to British growth? The balance of payments and supply of labour

1. Due allowance must be made for the effect of accumulated experience in generating and then applying new technology. British adoption of electricity in the late nineteenth century may have been as rapid as, or perhaps even more rapid than, the adoption of new textile machinery in the mid eighteenth, but it is only reasonable to believe that the degree of transformation remarkable and progressive in a pre-industrial society would appear less remarkable and less progressive in an advanced economy a century later. The crucial distinction is that in the eighteenth century, Britain was a pioneer; by the late nineteenth century not only was Britain no longer an industrial leader but was showing increasing strain in maintaining even a semblance of competence in assimilating the advances made elsewhere.

2. All calculations have been made in terms of 1907 prices. Given the magnitude of the suggested changes, 1907 prices would almost surely have been altered had faster growth occurred. Exactly how they would have altered is a complex question which cannot be resolved here, although the factors involved can be identified. Supplies of engineering output would have been much larger, as would the level of construction acitivity. But these enhanced supply capabilities would have occurred in an environment of rising incomes (indeed they are the real counterpart of rising money incomes) and, therefore, demand would also have been higher. Future research may resolve this question by examining what, if any, equilibrium price vectors would support the counterfactually higher level of output. Nevertheless, even assuming relative prices would have changed, the calculations here still leave the historian with a measure of the volume of real consumption implied by the counterfactual variants even if the interpretation of the value of this new volume is not straightforward.

3. J.R. Meyer (1955: 12–34). C.K. Harley (1974: 411) has reported serious errors in Meyer's input–output table which make it unusable as a cross-check on the structural changes proposed here. In any case there are intrinsic difficulties in using input–output tables for counterfactual calculations. The input–output coefficients observed at any point in time are generated by a capital stock and labour force of many different vintages; in circumstances of rapid technical change the coefficients may change rapidly with relatively few retirements of some vintages and additions of others.

4. L.H. Jenks (1927: 332–6). In particular, Jenks notes that: 'She (Britain) could scarcely balance her requirements of food and raw materials with the manufactures she could export and the freights her merchant marine could collect. The export of surplus capital was over. Her further investments were to come for a generation from the accruing profits of those which had already been made. They were to consist in what a German writer has termed "the secondary export of capital".'

5. A higher figure for the counterfactual level of consumption could have been obtained by increasing manufactured imports while holding the aggregate domestic investment total fixed at £769.4m and aggregate exports of goods and net services fixed at £631.6m, thus causing net foreign investment to fall. The increased consumption would be provided by foreigners who would receive fewer investment resources but would still provide the U.K. with more imports. This would be one obvious benefit of the enormously strong balance of payments position Britain built during the first half of the nineteenth century.

6. Non-durable consumption is over-stated by the procedures used in Table 4.5 because investment in human capital (accounted for primarily as part of the increased value of government and professional services) is treated as consumption rather than invest-ment. For a persuasive argument that human capital formation, particularly by means of formal technological and managerial education, was a necessary adjunct of economic advance from the late nineteenth century onwards, see Robert R. Locke (1984). There can be little doubt that improved Victorian economic performance would have entailed greater rates of both human and physical capital formation.

The distortion caused by counting investment in human capital in the category of consumption should not, however, be exaggerated because the same training that enhanced work skills and capability was (and still is) often valued for its own sake. Many in positions of authority and responsibility thoroughly enjoyed their work and would have been at a loss without it. For such people, investment in human capital formation and consumption were inextricably intertwined. In addition, the sums involved, at least for technical education, were comparatively small, although, as Locke shows, the impact of these expenditures was disproportionately great. Locke (1984: 34, Table II.1) reports that Germany had only 16,568 students in attendance at Technical Institutes in 1910. To support a similar number of students in Britain at a total cost of £200 per student per year – at a level nearly 25% greater than 1907 counterfactual average per capita income, a purposefully generous estimate – would have cost only £3.3m. Even if this figure were doubled to include technical education at secondary level and elsewhere outside the universities, the sum of £6.6m is still only 1.48% of the total value of increased output available for current (non-durable) consumption (£475.3m, from line 15, Table 4.5).

7. This is a somewhat artificial result arising from the mechanical procedure of allocating labour according to relative shifts in sector size. An equally plausible procedure would

have been to allocate relatively less labour to the expanding sectors in order to reflect greater capital intensity there. Such a procedure would have removed any appearance of unrealistically high productivity levels in contracting sectors which, in such a procedure, would have kept a larger share of their labour force.

5 Institutional obstacles to structural change: British capital markets to 1913

1. The discussion that follows is based on the emerging theory which relates choice under uncertainty to financial market operations. The theory began to take its present shape with a series of publications by Markowitz (1959), Sharpe (1964), Lintner (1965) and Mossin (1966). This work, which is primarily concerned with the equilibrium conditions of demand for securities given a fixed supply, has been extended to encompass some considerations of production and investment. A sample of this literature is found in Diamond (1967), Stiglitz (1972), Leland (1974) and Ekern and Wilson (1974). Surveys of this rapidly growing literature have begun to appear. Five of the more accessible are Sharpe (1970, 1981), Mossin (1973), Copeland and Weston (1983), and Elton and Gruber (1984). Mossin's survey in particular clearly describes the importance of investment and production decisions and indicates how these activities may be related to the more extensively analyzed problem of demand for risky assets. The literature is still in a state of flux in which few of the major theoretical problems can be considered satisfactorily resolved. However, the theory that does exist now offers the opportunity of approaching the history of capital market development and operation with the prospect of asking questions of fundamental importance. Although the theory is still incomplete, at least the areas of significance are now reasonably well defined and the theory can act as a useful guide to the historian seeking to understand a complex but fundamental process. Without such a guide, historical studies can only too easily become lost in a mass of uninterpretable data. On the other hand, the historian must exercise care for the theory is, after all, incomplete and is operational, as opposed to inspirational, in only a most limited fashion.

2. This assumption of zero variance is adopted only for convenience of exposition. As long as the risk characteristics of the new opportunity were substantially different from the risk characteristics of the firm's pre-existing aggregate portfolio of investments, the argument would obtain.

3. If the firm in the example has issued non-recallable bonds and was unable to reduce the interest rate it was paying, it would be unable to undertake the investment unless it could create an independent subsidiary whose borrowing terms would be determined by the marginal risk (in this case zero) of the new project alone. Since such financial separations are likely to be expensive and time-consuming to arrange, firms often attempt to keep a balanced portfolio of debt obligations in order to take advantage of new opportunities without exposing themselves unduly to adverse developments. Moreover, within Mossin's example it is possible to find riskless projects with a yield greater than 3% but less than 4% which should be undertaken but which will not be *unless* explicit recognition is made of the impact of the new project's yield on the existing firm. Any attempt at financial separation in these circumstances would lead to

incorrect rejection of the new project. In such a case, restructuring of the firm's existing debt is a necessary condition of the firm's acceptance of the new project.

4. Capital and capital goods should be interpreted widely to include investments in research and knowledge.

5. As long as the institution were effectively constrained to invest all savings efficiently, charging only the 'market' price for management services, the absence of competition would not be a cause for worry. However, the possibility that the institution would act as a monopolist in the securities market and a monopsonist in the deposit market suggests that some of the technical efficiency of centralization might usefully be sacrificed to maintain a desired level of competition in both markets.

6. The continuous revaluation of firms' worth, as investors adjust their portfolios in a perfect capital market in response to new information, yields an interesting but not obvious implication concerning portfolio equilibrium. Because all investors are assumed to share identical information which is interpreted by all in the same way, each investor holds the same percentage of stock of every homogeneous risk class. The actual percentage varies according to the wealth and risk aversion of the investor, but if 0.001% of the total market value of the stock of one distinct firm is held by an investor, he also must hold, in efficient equilibrium, 0.001% of the stock of every other distinct firm. (Different firms whose earnings are highly correlated are treated as effectively comprising a single firm.) This result stems directly from the way in which assets are evaluated in the same manner by all investors; if there were anything to be gained by one person in holding a different combination of risky assets all would want to hold the same different portfolio and the subsequent bidding up and down of various securities would cause, finally, all investors to hold balanced portfolios of risky assets. Investors differ only in the percentage of their wealth which they hold in the risky portfolio, not in the composition of risky assets in their portfolios. Mossin (1973: 82–3) provides evidence for this claim by showing that an investment firm, Eaton and Howard, held 'balanced' portfolios in two of the mutual funds it managed. For each of five distinct classes of risky securities, the aggressive fund's holdings were 2.2 times those of the conservative fund. That is, the two funds differed only in the percentage of the homogeneous, risky portfolio that each held, with the aggressive fund having a smaller proportion of its assets in the least risky assets.

7. Wilson's paper considers in some detail various market conventions by which prices might be formed, an issue slighted here. Nonetheless whatever the convention (e.g. buyers or sellers set the price at which trading begins) and whatever the distribution of quality, owners of low quality assets benefit most from unequal information.

8. It is a reasonable assumption that the financial instruments Davis is concerned with were homogeneous in their risk characteristics even though it is possible that regional fluctuations in economic activity would justify some interest differential.

9. Commenting on the portfolio policies of the London clearing banks, which had absorbed most of the local banks through amalgamation, Goodhart (1972: 135) notes that: 'The major gap in portfolios was, as is well known, the absence of industrial, especially domestic industrial, stocks from their holdings.'

10. Goodhart (1972: 162–65) makes clear that the oversight of local bank managers was a 'delicate problem'. It was not conspicuously solved with imagination. A more efficient use of available information would surely have involved, as Arrow has

suggested in another context, greater joint risk sharing (co-insurance) rather than such a marked avoidance of risk by intermediaries and a consequent concentration of risk on borrowers.

11. I am indebted to Christopher J. Napier of the Department of Accounting and Finance at the London School of Economics for this reference.

12. One factor which King stresses is the difficulty shareholders may very plausibly have in reaching agreement on what the firm's objectives should be. King (1977: 132–44) demonstrates that it may be unreasonable to expect shareholders to ignore their own interests as consumers or as suppliers of inputs.

13. Readers who are persuaded of the arbitrage capabilities of modern financial markets are invited to ponder footnotes 22 and 23 of Grossman and Hart's paper.

14. Byatt (1962: 350). It should be noted that Viscount Emlyn, the Chairman of the company who was quoted on the management reorganization, was at least partially justified in his desire for control over technological extravagance. Crompton in 1896 had started an electric cooking and heating section which did not have good prospects (Byatt, 1962: 351). However, complete suspension of experimentation when technological change was as rapid as it was in the 1890s, when British firms were falling far behind foreign developments, was not a satisfactory response to the problem.

15. In 1900 prices, total investment fell from £222m in 1903 to £142m in 1908, a fall of 36% from the 1903 peak. Total investment recovered briefly in the next two years, then fell to £138m (1900 prices) in 1912. The 1912 (constant price) figure was 62.2% of 1903s; in 1913, 70.7%. By sector, ships between 1903 and 1908 fell only 29.4% and by 1913 had reached 141.2% of the 1903 level. In constant 1900 prices, land-based transport equipment was very steady, rising to only £8m and falling (only once) to £6m. The 1913 level (£9m) was 128.6% of the 1903 level (£7m). Plant and machinery in constant 1900 prices slumped 35.9% between 1903 and 1908. In 1912 the level was 62.5% of 1903; in 1913, 82.8%. Investment in dwellings fell steadily from 1903; the level in 1908 was 70.7% of 1903; in 1913, 39.0%. Other new buildings and works reached a pre-war nadir in 1909, when the level was 49.5% of 1903; the 1913 level was 59.1%, slightly above the 1908 level. (All data from Feinstein, 1972: Table 40.) The pattern of gross domestic fixed capital formation in current prices was very similar. See Feinstein (1972: Table 39) and Chapter 6 below.

16. Between 1908 and 1913, U.S. output rose from 63,500 cars with a value of $135m to 461,500 cars with a value of $400m. The crisis in the U.S. did not faze this explosive growth. In 1913, only 40% of the cars were Ford's. See Chandler (1964: 3–4).

17. The following treatment of the financial histories of the major chemical firms has relied heavily on W.J. Reader (1970: 24–27, 48–56, 103–23).

18. A further difficulty is that the pricing model is assumed to apply to circumstances in which portfolios are efficiently diversified although there is much evidence that efficient diversification across all securities did not take place. Hence, first class securities are even more firmly established as deriving their value largely in isolation from the rest of the economy.

6 The economics of British foreign investment in the late nineteenth century

1. The quality of British foreign investments was sometimes amazing. In 1891 Argentina repudiated its public debt; yet the railroads and export facilities whose construction

incurred the debt were built and by the turn of the century the debts were made good. See Ford (1962: 141–65).

2. The information on new purchases is much better than that on sales, which is almost nonexistent. Hence it is not possible to know precisely how aggregate portfolio holdings compared with the annual flow of assets into the portfolio. There is no reason, however, to assume that bonds were more likely to be sold than equities. In fact the reverse was probably true; those who bought shares probably took a more aggressive, and perhaps more professional attitude towards the management of their portfolios and were hence more likely to prune their portfolio more frequently, meaning that the gross inflow of shares relative to fixed interest securities very likely over-represented their importance in the aggregate British portfolio of foreign securities.

3. C.K. Hobson (1914: 159) noted in his book that: 'There is however, a new characteristic visible in the course of foreign investment during the past few years, namely a tendency to invest in manufacturing and industrial concerns... A considerable amount of United States Steel Corporation is held here.' The explicit mention of U.S. Steel is revealing. (George Paish, in a discussion of his 1911 paper before the Royal Statistical Society, also mentioned the U.S. Steel Corp. See George Paish, 1911: 197.) Such mention evokes a strong image of what the consequences of a different pattern of foreign investment might have been. In 1889 Andrew Carnegie had offered to sell out to a group of English capitalists (Hughes, 1966: 261). If they had taken him up and had bought the most dynamic steel company in the U.S. rather than U.S. railway bonds, their returns would have been much larger. Such a direct stake in the active management of real capital abroad, if it had occurred, would have put British foreign investment before 1914 in a rather different perspective than that which followed from the more limited stake owned by bond holders. As it was, it was not until Morgan created U.S. Steel twelve years later that the entrepreneurial profits from the formation of a giant, quasi-monopolistic firm were reaped. There were other examples: Hughes (1966: 287–8) cites the spectacle of James Couzens, Henry Ford's finance manager, sitting on a Detroit curb, crying from frustration at not being able to raise money for Ford's operations. The Ford in the world's future could have been quite different had the agents of English investors been as quick to spot promising American industrial issues as they were to spot railway bonds and tea and rubber plantations. Ford eventually raised the money, mainly from individuals; would it have been possible had Detroiters been accustomed to investing heavily in foreign railways?

4. The method of calculating these yields was to equate the income from the relevant gross domestic capital stock, valued at current replacement prices, with property's share of GDP. See Appendix E, Part II. Inadequacies of data make calculations for earlier years more speculative. The period 1910–13, however, is interesting, for it was a time of heavy foreign investment. Furthermore, the average rate of return on domestic capital does not seem to be unusually high during those years. See Phelps–Brown and Weber (1953: Figs. 3 and 5.) Matthews *et al.* (1982: 184–191) also find the yield on domestic capital just before the war to be noticeably below that achieved earlier. The yield rates reported here are below those found by Matthews *et al.*

5. The converse would appear to be true. First, over this period, the domestic net capital stock valued at current replacement costs increased by almost 10% more than the sum

of the gross investment, suggesting substantial capital gains in money terms on real assets. Secondly, although the average rate of return on all property valued at current replacement costs fell over the years 1910–13, the drop was consistent with a marginal rate of return of nearly 9%, assuming that all of the change in yields was brought about by the most recent investment. Of course, if the structure of yields had changed so as to inflict heavy capital losses on previous investments, it would still be possible that the most recent investments, perhaps concentrated in new sectors, would offer very high marginal returns.

Little more can be gleaned from further study of these aggregates. Data are still needed on marginal rates of return at the firm level. Such micro-studies will be complicated, however, by the fact that rates of return will depend in part on the values of macro-variables beyond the control of individual firms, as well as on the type of investment made.

6. Kuznets (1966: 257–8) has noted the tendency in modern economies for producers' equipment to become a relatively more important component of GDFCF.

7. Data for the value of exports of plant and machinery are taken from Mitchell and Deane (1962: 303–5, columns for 'machinery' and 'electrical goods'). Data for the value of domestic installation of plant and machinery are taken from Feinstein (1972: Table 39, column 3).

8. Note that exports of machinery as a proportion of total exports of goods and services rose steadily from 1.6% in 1870 to over 5.0% in 1913 with no clear tendency for the intensity of foreign investment to alter the trend.

9. The smaller importance earlier in the century of machinery in total exports may perhaps be explained by the greater relative importance of railroad construction, which was labour and material intensive rather than equipment intensive.

10. This effect is also discussed by Matthews *et al.* (1982: 455–6).

11. It may be noted however that J.M. Keynes, in his discussion of Paish's 1911 paper, expressed reservations about Paish's estimate, suspecting that it may have been too high. See Paish (1911: 195–6).

12. A recent study of the evolution of Hobson's thought is found in P.J. Cain (1978). There is a strong similarity between the impact on the domestic economy argued here for nineteenth-century foreign lending and the impact upon the contemporary British economy attributed to North Sea Oil by P.J. Forsyth and J.A. Kay (1980). In both cases the domestic economy had to accommodate large resource inflows from abroad which tended, *ceteris paribus*, to reduce the size of the traded goods sector of the economy.

13. Successful foreign efforts to meet debt repayment deadlines would have the same impact as a systematic tendency for the propensity to import to rise over time.

14. One important consequence of a reduction in labour's share of national income would have been to constrict the domestic British market for mass produced consumer goods, the manufacture of which were characterized by the high wages paid to workers. Thus the squeeze on labour income is seen to have come from several directions and to have constituted a pervasive influence.

Appendix E. Characteristics of British foreign investment

1. C.H. Feinstein (1972: 155–156). Feinstein, (1972: 204–205) presents with caution two estimates of Britain's stock of overseas assets in 1913. Even making a generous

allowance for foreign income and using the lower asset value, the average rate of return on all foreign assets was no more than 5.5%, which is virtually Paish's estimate.

2. There is no complete check on Paish's figures, but the 'Report of the Dollar Securities Committee', *Sessional Papers of the House of Commons*, 1919, paper number 212, Vol. xiii, from page 523, contains a list of dollar securities requisitioned during the First World War. Since the securities were valued at their market price at the time the government took control of them and since the pound fluctuated against the dollar during the war, it is not possible to state the value of the securities in 1913 without much further research. However, the *Report's* data lends some support to Keynes' claim, made during the Statistical Society's discussion of Paish's paper, that Paish over-estimated the holdings of American securities in 1913. The *Report* recorded only approximately £300,000,000 of U.S. securities sold or held on loan by the Committee. This is incomplete in many ways, particularly due to the failure to record sales made before July 1915 and to evasion, but, if correct, would imply a capital loss on realization of approximately 50% of the securities' value at the end of 1913.

3. C.H. Feinstein (1968: 129) has written: 'The outside limits would appear to be a fall of one percentage point (from 1865–1869 to 1910–1914) in labour's share of the domestic product or a rise of four percentage points.'

4. Rail revenue totalled £29,400,000 from the carriage of minerals in 1907; see Cd. 6320 (1912: 22). See B.R. Mitchell and P. Deane (1962) for the f.o.b. value of coal, given as £42.1.

5. Census data indicates that, after allowing for the cost of transportation and handling of coal, £22.5m to £42.5m should be allowed for the cost of transporting and handling of all other exports. The value of exports (f.o.b.), excluding coal, gold, silver and diamonds, was £383.9m. The value at works of this amount was taken to be £361.4m, which was reached by the following calculation:

$$(1 - [£22.5m/£383.9m])[£383.9m] = £361.4m$$

$$1 - [£22.5m/£383.9m] = 0.9414$$

See Cd. 6320 (1912: 28) for estimates of transport and handling between works and ports.

Bibliography

Abramovitz, M. and David, P.A. (1973). Reinterpreting economic growth: parable and realities. *American Economic Review (Papers and Proceedings)*, **63**, 428–439.

Adler, J.H. (ed.) (1967). *Capital Movements and Economic Development.* London: Macmillan.

Akerlof, G.A. (1970). The market for 'lemons': quality uncertainty and the market mechanism. *Quarterly Journal of Economics*, **84**, 488–500.

—(1976). The economics of caste and the rat race and other woeful tales. *Quarterly Journal of Economics*, **90**, 599–617.

Aldcroft, D.H. (1964). The entrepreneur and the British economy, 1870–1914. *Economic History Review*, **17**, 113–134.

—(ed.) (1968). *Development of British Industry and Foreign Competition, 1875–1914.* London: Allen & Unwin.

Aldcroft, D.H. and Richardson, H.W. (eds.) (1969). *The British Economy, 1870–1939.* London: Macmillan.

Alford, B.W.E. (1972). *Depression and Recovery? British Economic Growth, 1918–1939.* London: Macmillan.

Allen, R.C. (1977). The peculiar productivity history of American blast furnaces, 1840–1913. *Journal of Economic History*, **37**, 605–633.

—(1979). International competition in iron and steel, 1850–1913. *Journal of Economic History*, **39**, 911–938.

Ames, E. and Rosenberg, N. (1963). Changing technological leadership and industrial growth. Reprinted in *Purdue Faculty Papers in Economic History 1956–1966* (1967), 363–382.

Anderson, B.L. (1978). Institutional investment before the First World War: the Union Insurance Company, 1897–1915. In Marriner (ed.) (1978), 37–79.

Arrow, K.J. (1974). Limited knowledge and economic analysis. *American Economic Review*, **64**, 1–10.

Ashworth, W. (1960). *An Economic History of England: 1870–1939.* London: Methuen.

—(1965). Changes in the industrial structure, 1870–1914. *Yorkshire Bulletin of Economic and Social Research*, **17**, 62–74.

Ayers, G.L. (1934). *Fluctuations in New Capital Issues on the London Capital Market.* University of London: Unpublished MSc. Thesis.

Bairoch, P. (1976). Europe's Gross National Product, 1800–1975. *Journal of European Economic History*, **5**, 273–340.

Barger, H. (1955). *Distribution's Place in the American Economy Since 1869*. Princeton: Princeton University Press (for National Bureau of Economic Research).

Baumol, W.J. (1967). Macroeconomics of unbalanced growth: the anatomy of urban crisis. *American Economic Review*, **57**, 415–426.

Bowley, A.L. (1921). *The Division of the Product of Industry: An Analysis of National Income Before the War*. Oxford: Oxford University Press.

—(1937). *Wages and Income in the United Kingdom Since 1880*. Cambridge: Cambridge University Press.

Bowley, M.E.A. (1966). *The British Building Industry: Four Studies in Response and Resistance to Change*. Cambridge: Cambridge University Press.

Brainard, W.C. and Tobin, J. (1968). Pitfalls in financial model building. *American Economic Review (Papers and Proceedings)*, **58**, 99–122.

Brainard, W.C., Shoven, J.B. and Weiss, L. (1980). The financial valuation of the return to capital. *Brookings Papers on Economic Activity – 2, 1980*, 453–511.

British Parliamentary Papers (1908). *Annual Statement of Trade – 1907 (Cd. 4100)*. London: HMSO.

—(1911). *Census of Ireland: Census, Province of Leinster (Cd. 6049)*. London: HMSO.

—(1911). *Census of Ireland: Census, Province of Munster (Cd. 6050)*. London: HMSO.

—(1912). *Census of Ireland: Census, Province of Connaught (Cd. 6052)*. London: HMSO.

—(1912). *Census of Ireland: Census, Province of Ulster (Cd. 6051)*. London: HMSO.

—(1912). *Census of Production: Final Report, 1907 (Board of Trade) (Cd. 6320)*. London: HMSO.

—(1913). *Census of Scotland, 1911, Vol. 1 (Cd. 6097)*. London: HMSO.

—(1914). *Annual Statement of Trade 1913 (Cd. 6970)*. London: HMSO.

—(1914). *Census of England and Wales, 1911: Vol. X. Occupations and Industries (Cd. 7018)*. London: HMSO.

—(1915). *Census of England and Wales, Summary Tables (Cd. 7929)*. London: HMSO.

—(1919). Report of the Dollar Securities Committee. *Sessional Papers of the House of Commons*, Vol. XIII, No. 212.

—(1930). *Census of Scotland, 1911, Vol. II (Cd. 6896)*. London: HMSO.

Brittain, J.E. (1974). The international diffusion of electrical power technology, 1870–1920. *Journal of Economic History*, **34**, 108–121.

Burton, H. and Corner, D.C. (1968). *Investment and Unit Trusts in Britain and America*. London: Elek.

Buxton, N.K. (1975). The role of 'new' industries in Britain during the 1930s: a reinterpretation. *Business History Review*, **49**, 205–222.

Byatt, I.C.R. (1962). *The British Electrical Industry, 1875–1914*. Oxford University: Unpublished PhD. Thesis.

—(1968). Electrical products. In Aldcroft (ed.) (1968), 238–278.

—(1979). *The British Electrical Industry, 1875–1914*. Oxford: Clarendon Press.

Cain, P.J. (1978). J.A. Hobson, Cobdenism and the radical theory of economic imperialism, 1898–1914. *Economic History Review*, **31**, 565–584.

Cairncross, A.K. (1953). *Home and Foreign Investment, 1870–1913: Studies in Capital Accumulation*. Cambridge: Cambridge University Press.

Cameron, R.E. (ed.) (1967). *Banking in the Early Stages of Industrialization*. London: Oxford University Press.

Central Statistical Office (CSO). (1976). *National Income and Expenditure, 1965–1975*. London: HMSO.

Chandler, A.D. (1962). *Strategy and Structure: Chapters in the History of Industrial Enterprise*. Cambridge, Massachusetts: MIT Press.

—(1977). *The Visible Hand: The Managerial Revolution in American Business*. Cambridge, Massachusetts: Belknap Press, Harvard University Press.

Chandler, A.D. (ed.) (1964). *Giant Enterprise: Ford, General Motors and the Automobile Industry – Sources and Readings*. New York: Harcourt, Brace & World.

Checkland, S.G. (1975). *Scottish Banking: A History, 1695–1976*. Glasgow: Collins.

—(1977). *The Upas Tree: Glasgow, 1875–1975*. Glasgow: University of Glasgow Press.

Chiang, A.C. (1967). *Fundamental Methods of Mathematical Economics*. New York: McGraw-Hill/Tokyo: Kogakusha (International Student Edition).

Cipolla, C.M. (ed.) (1973). *The Fontana Economic History of Europe: The Emergence of Industrial Societies – 2*. Glasgow: Collins.

Clapham, J.H. (1936, fourth edition). *The Economic Development of France and Germany, 1815–1914*. Cambridge: Cambridge University Press.

Copeland, T.E. and Weston, J.F. (1983, second edition). *Financial Theory and Corporate Policy*. Reading, Massachusetts: Addison-Wesley.

Cottrell, P.L. (1980). *Industrial Finance, 1830–1914: The Finance and Organization of English Manufacturing Industry*. London: Methuen.

Crafts, N.F.R. (1979). Victorian Britain did fail. *Economic History Review*, **32**, 533–537.

Crouzet, F. (1972). Editor's introduction. In Crouzet (ed.) (1972), 1–69.

Crouzet, F. (ed.) (1972). *Capital Formation in the Industrial Revolution*. London: Methuen.

David, P.A. (1973). Labor scarcity and the problem of technological practice and progress in the nineteenth century. *Discussion Paper 297, Harvard Institute of Economic Research*. Cambridge, Massachusetts.

Davis, L.E. (1965). The investment market, 1870–1914: the evolution of a national market. Reprinted in *Purdue Faculty Papers in Economic History, 1956–1966* (1967), 119–160.

—(1966). The capital markets and industrial concentration: the U.S. and U.K., a comparative study. Reprinted in *Purdue Faculty Papers in Economic History, 1956–1966* (1967), 663–682.

Deane, P. and Cole, W.A. (1962). *British Economic Growth, 1688–1959*. Cambridge: Cambridge University Press.

Denison, E.F. (1967). *Why Growth Rates Differ*. Washington: Brookings Institution.

Denison, E.F. and Chung, W.K. (1976). *How Japans Economy Grew & Fast: the Sources of Postwar Expansion*. Washington: Brookings Institute.

Diamond, P. (1967). The role of a stock market in a general equilibrium model with technological uncertainty. *American Economic Review*, **57**, 759–776.

Dickson, P.G.M. (1960). *The Sun Insurance Office, 1710–1960*. London: Oxford University Press.

Dixit, A.K. (1976). *Optimization in Economic Theory*. London: Oxford University Press.

Dowie, J.A. (1968). Growth in the inter-war period: some more arithmetic. *Economic History Review*, **21**, 93–112.

DuBoff, R.H. (1967). The introduction of electric power in American manufacturing. *Economic History Review*, **20**, 509–518.

Dunning, J.H. (1956). The growth of U.S. investment in U.K. manufacturing industry,

1856–1940. *The Manchester School*, **24**, 245–269.

Easterlin, R.A. (1961). Influences in European overseas emigration before World War I. *Economic Development and Cultural Change*, **9**, 331–351.

Ebery, M.G. and Preston, B.T. (1976). *Domestic Service in Late Victorian and Edwardian England, 1871–1914*. Reading: Reading Geographical Papers, No. 42.

Edelstein, M. (1970). *The Rate of Return on U.K. Home and Foreign Investment, 1870–1913*. University of Pennsylvania: Unpublished PhD. dissertation.

—(1971). Rigidity and bias in the British capital market, 1870–1913. In McCloskey (ed.) (1971c), 83–105.

—(1974). The determinants of U.K. investment abroad, 1870–1913: the U.S. case. *Journal of Economic History*, **34**, 980–1007.

—(1976). Realized rates of return on U.K. home and overseas portfolio investment in the age of high imperialism. *Explorations in Economic History*, **13**, 283–329.

—(1977). U.K. savings in the age of high imperialism and after. *American Economic Review (Papers and Proceedings)*, **67**, 288–294.

—(1982). *Overseas Investment in the Age of High Imperialism: The United Kingdom, 1850–1914*. London: Methuen.

Edwards, J.R. (1981). *Company Legislation and Changing Patterns of Disclosure in British Company Accounts, 1900–1940*. London: The Institute of Chartered Accountants.

Eichengreen, B.J. (1982). The proximate determinants of domestic investment in Victorian Britain. *Journal of Economic History*, **42**, 87–95.

Ekern, S. and Wilson, R. (1974). On the theory of the firm in an economy with incomplete markets. *Bell Journal of Economics and Management Science*, 5 (Spring), 171–180.

Elton, E.J. and Gruber, M.J. (1984, second edition). *Modern Portfolio Theory and Investment Analysis*. New York: John Wiley.

Feinstein, C.H. (1968). Changes in the distribution of the national income in the United Kingdom since 1860. In Marchal and Ducros (eds.) (1968), 115–148.

—(1972). *National Income, Expenditure and Output in the United Kingdom, 1855–1965*. Cambridge: Cambridge University Press.

—(1978). Capital accumulation and economic growth in Great Britain, 1760–1860. In Mathias and Postan (eds.) (1978), 28–96.

Feis, H. (1930). *Europe: The World's Banker, 1870–1914*. New Haven: Yale University Press.

Fletcher, T.W. (1960–1961). The great depression of English agriculture, 1873–1896. *Economic History Review*, **13**, 417–432.

Floud, R.C. (1971). Changes in the productivity of labour in the British machine tool industry, 1856–1900. In McCloskey (ed.) (1971c), 313–344.

—(1974). The adolescence of American engineering competition. *Economic History Review*, **27**, 57–71.

—(1976). *The British Machine Tool Industry, 1850–1914*. Cambridge: Cambridge University Press.

Fogel, R.W. and Engerman, S.L. (eds.) (1971). *The Reinterpretation of American Economic History*. New York: Harper and Row.

Ford, A.G. (1962). *The Gold Standard 1880–1914: Britain and Argentina*. London: Oxford University Press.

—(1965). Overseas lending and internal fluctuations, 1870–1914. *Yorkshire Bulletin of Economic and Social Research*, **17**, 19–30.

Forsyth, P.J. and Kay, J.A. (1980). The economic implications of North Sea oil revenues. *IFS Working Paper No. 10*. London: Institute for Fiscal Studies.

Frank, R.H. and Freeman, R.T. (1978). *Distributional Consequences of Direct Foreign Investment*. London: Academic Press.

Freeman, C. (1974). *The Economics of Industrial Innovation*. Harmondsworth, Middlesex: Penguin Books.

Fremdling, R. (1977). Railroads and German economic growth: a leading sector analysis with a comparison to the United States and Great Britain. *Journal of Economic History*, 37, 583–604.

Fremdling, R. and O'Brien, P.K. (eds.) (1983). *Productivity in the Economies of Europe*. Stuttgart: Klett – Cotta.

Gallman, R.E. (1960). Commodity Output of the United States, 1839–1899. Conference on Research in Income and Wealth, *Studies in Income and Wealth, Vol. 24*. New York: National Bureau of Economic Research.

Gallman, R.E. and Howle, E.S. (1971). Trends in the structure of the American economy since 1840. In Fogel and Engerman (eds.) (1971), 25–37.

Goodhart, C.A.E. (1972). *The Business of Banking, 1891–1914*. London: London School of Economics and Political Science and Weidenfeld and Nicolson.

Green, A. and Urquhart, M.C. (1976). Factor and commodity flows in the international economy of 1870–1914: a multi-country view. *Journal of Economic History*, 36, 217–252.

Grossman, S.J. and Hart, O.D. (1980). Takeover bids, the free-rider problem, and the theory of the corporation. *Bell Journal of Economics*, 11, 44–64.

Habakkuk, H.J. (1962). Fluctuations in housebuilding in Britain and the United States in the nineteenth century. *Journal of Economic History*, 22, 198–230.

Hahn, F.H. (1973). *On the Notion of Equilibrium in Economics: An Inaugural Lecture*. Cambridge: Cambridge University Press.

Hall, A.R. (1963). *The London Capital Market and Australia, 1870–1914*. Canberra: The Australian National University.

—(1968a). Editor's introduction. In Hall (ed.) (1968b), 1–19.

Hall, A.R. (ed.) (1968b). *The Export of Capital from Britain, 1870–1914*. London: Methuen.

Hall, M. Knapp, J. and Winsten, C. (1961). *Distribution in Great Britain and North America: A Study in Structure and Productivity*. Oxford: Oxford University Press.

Hannah, L. (1974a). Managerial innovation and the rise of the large-scale company in interwar Britain. *Economic History Review*, 27, 252–270.

—(1974b). Takeover bids in Britain before 1950: an exercise in business 'pre-history'. *Business History*, 16, 65–77.

—(1976b). *The Rise of the Corporate Economy: The British Experience*. London: Methuen.

—(1979). *Electricity Before Nationalisation: A Study of the Development of the Electricity Supply Industry in Britain to 1948*. London: Macmillan.

Hannah, L. (ed.) (1976a). *Management Strategy and Business Development*. London: Macmillan.

Harbury, C.D. and Hitchins, D.M.W.M. (1979). *Inheritance and Wealth Inequality in Britain*. London: Allen & Unwin.

Harley, C.K. (1974). Skilled labour and the choice of technique in Edwardian industry. *Explorations in Economic History*, 11, 391–414.

Harrison, A.E. (1969). The competitiveness of the British cycle industry, 1890–1914. *Economic History Review*, **22**, 287–303.

Hart, O.D. (1975). On the optimality of equilibrium when the market structure is incomplete. *Journal of Economic Theory*, **11**, 418–443.

Higgs, R. (1971). *The Transformation of the American Economy*. New York: John Wiley.

Hill, T.P. (1971). *The Measurement of Real Product: A Theoretical and Empirical Analysis of the Growth Rates for Different Industries and Countries*. Paris: OECD.

Hobson, C.K. (1914). *The Export of Capital*. New York: Macmillan.

Hughes, J.R.T. (1960). *Fluctuations in Trade, Industry and Finance: A Study of British Economic Development*. Oxford: Clarendon Press.

—(1966). *The Vital Few: American Economic Progress and Its Protagonists*. Boston: Houghton Mifflin.

—(1968). Wicksell on the facts: prices and interest rates, 1844 to 1914. In Wolfe (ed.) (1968), 215–255.

Hughes, J.R.T. and Reiter, S. (1958). The first 1945 British steamships. Reprinted in *Purdue Faculty Papers in Economic History, 1955–1966* (1967), 453–483.

Hughes, T.P. (1962). British electrical industry lag, 1882–1888. *Technology and Culture*, **3**, 27–44.

—(1983). *Networks of Power: Electrification in Western Society, 1880–1930*. Baltimore: Johns Hopkins University Press.

Hunt, E.H. (1973). *Regional Wage Variations in Britain, 1850–1914*. London: Oxford University Press.

Imlah, A.H. (1958). *Economic Elements of the Pax Britannica*, Cambridge, Massachusetts: Harvard University Press.

Irving, R.J. (1975). New industries for old? Some investment decisions of Sir W.G. Armstrong, Whitworth & Co. Ltd., 1900–1914. *Business History*, **17**, 150–175.

James, J.A. (1978). The welfare effects of the antebellum tariff: a general equilibrium analysis. *Exploration in Economic History*, **15**, 231–256.

Jefferys, J.B. (1938). *Trends in Business Organization in Great Britain since 1856*. University of London: Unpublished PhD. dissertation.

Jenks, L.H. (1927). *Migration of British Capital to 1875*. New York: Knopf.

Jones, R. and Marriott, O. (1970). *Anatomy of a Merger: A History of G.E.C., A.E.I. and English Electric*. London: Cape.

Jörberg, L. (1973). The Nordic countries, 1850–1914. In Cipolla (ed.) (1973), 375–485.

Kaldor, N. (1966). *Causes of the Slow Rate of Economic Growth of the United Kingdom: Inaugural Address Delivered at Cambridge University*. Cambridge: Cambridge University Press.

Kendrick, J.W. (1961). *Productivity Trends in the United States*. Princeton: Princeton University Press.

Kennedy, W.P. (1974). Foreign investment, trade, and growth in the United Kingdom, 1870–1913. *Explorations in Economic History*, **11**, 415–444.

—(1975). *The Economics of Maturity: Aspects of British Economic Development, 1870–1914*. Northwestern University: Unpublished PhD. dissertation.

—(1976). Institutional response to economic growth: capital markets in Britain to 1914. In Hannah (ed.) (1976a), 151–183.

—(1982). Economic growth and structural change in the U.K., 1870–1914. *Journal of Economic History*, **42**, 105–114.

—(1983). Problems of accountancy and interpretation in assessing long-term economic performance. In Fremdling and O'Brien, (eds.)(1983), 57–77.

—(1984). Notes on economic efficiency in historical perspective: the case of Britain, 1870–1914. In Uselding (ed.) (1984), 109–141.

Keynes, J.M. (1936). *The General Theory of Employment, Interest, and Money.* London: Macmillan.

Kindleberger, C.P. (1964). *Economic Growth in France and Britain, 1851–1950.* Cambridge, Massachusetts: Harvard University Press.

Kindleberger, C.P. and Di Tella, G. (eds.) (1982). *Economics in the Long View: Essays in Honour of W. W. Rostow – Volume 3, Applications and Cases, Part II.* London: Macmillan.

King, M.A. (1974). Economic growth and social development: a statistical investigation. *The Review of Income and Wealth,* **20**, 251–272.

—(1977). *Public Policy and the Corporation.* London: Chapman and Hall (John Wiley).

King, W.T.C. (1936). *History of the London Discount Market.* London: G. Routledge & Sons Ltd.

Klein, B.H. (1977). *Dynamic Economics.* Cambridge, Massachusetts: Harvard University Press.

Kocka, J. (1978). Entrepreneurs and managers in German industrialization. In Mathias and Postan (eds.) (1978), 492–589.

Kuznets, S.S. (1961). Quantitative aspects of the economic growth of nations: VI. Long-term trends in capital formation proportions. *Economic Development and Cultural Change,* Vol. 9 (No. 4), Part II (July), 1–124.

—(1966). *Modern Economic Growth: Rate, Structure, and Spread.* New Haven: Yale University Press.

Landes, D.S. (1969). *The Unbound Prometheus.* Cambridge: Cambridge University Press.

Lavington, F.E. (1921). *The English Capital Market.* London: Methuen.

Lazonick, W. (1981a). Competition, specialization and industrial decline. *Journal of Economic History,* **41**, 31–38.

—(1981b). Factor costs and the diffusion of ring spinning in Britain prior to World War I. *Quarterly Journal of Economics,* **95**, 89–109.

Lehfeldt, R.A. (1913a). The rate of interest on British and foreign investments. *Journal of the Royal Statistical Society,* **76**, 196–207.

—(1913b). The rate of interest on investments in 1912. *Journal of the Royal Statistical Society,* **76**, 415–416.

—(1914). The rate of interest on British and foreign investments. *Journal of the Royal Statistical Society,* **77**, 432–435.

Leland, H.E. (1974). Production theory and the stock market. *Bell Journal of Economics and Management Science,* 5 (Spring), 125–144.

Levine, A.L. (1967). *Industrial Retardation.* London: Weidenfeld and Nicholson.

Lindert, P.H. and Trace, K. (1971). Yardsticks for Victorian entrepreneurs. In McCloskey (ed.) (1971c), 239–274.

Lintner, J. (1965). The valuation of risk assets and the selection of risky investments in stock portfolios and capital budgets. *Review of Economics and Statistics,* **47**, 13–37.

Lloyd, I. (1978). *Rolls-Royce: The Growth of a Firm*. London: Macmillan.

Locke, R.R. (1984). *The End of Practical Man: Entrepreneurship and Higher Education in Germany, France and Great Britain, 1880–1940*. London: JAI Press, Inc.

McCloskey, D.N. (1968). Productivity change in British pig iron, 1870–1938. *Quarterly Journal of Economics*, **82**, 281–96.

—(1970). Did Victorian Britain fail? *Economic History Review*, **23**, 446–459.

—(1971a). Editor's introduction. In McCloskey (ed.) (1971c), 1–10.

—(1971b). International differences in productivity? Coal and steel in America and Britain before World War I. In McCloskey (ed.) (1971c), 285–309.

—(1973). *Economic Maturity and Entrepreneurial Decline: British Iron and Steel, 1870–1913*. Cambridge, Massachusetts: Harvard University Press.

—(1979). No it did not: a reply to Crafts. *Economic History Review*, **32**, 538–41.

McCloskey, D.N. (ed.) (1971c). *Essays on a Mature Economy: Britain after 1840*. London: Methuen.

McCloskey, D.N. and Sandberg, L.G. (1971). From damnation to redemption: judgements on the late Victorian entrepreneur. *Explorations in Economic History*, **9**, 89–108.

Maddison, A. (1964). *Economic Growth in the West: Comparative Experience in Europe and North America*. London: Allen & Unwin.

Maizels, A. (1970). *Growth and Trade*. Cambridge: Cambridge University Press.

Marchal, J. and Ducros, B. (eds.) (1968). *The Distribution of National Income*. London: Macmillan.

Markowitz, H.M. (1959). *Portfolio Selection: Efficient Diversification of Investments*. New Haven: Yale University Press.

Marriner, S. (ed.) (1978). *Business and Businessmen: Studies in Business, Economic and Accounting History*. Liverpool: Liverpool University Press.

Martin, R.F. (1939). *National Income in the United States, 1799–1938*. New York: National Industrial Conference Board.

Mathias, P. (1969). *The First Industrial Nation*. London: Methuen.

—(1973). Capital, credit, and enterprise in the Industrial Revolution. *Journal of European Economic History*, **2**, 121–143.

Mathais, P. and Postan, M.M. (eds.) (1978). *Cambridge Economic History of Europe, Vol. VII, Part I – The Industrial Economies: Capital, Labour, and Enterprise*. Cambridge: Cambridge University Press.

Matthews, R.C.O., Feinstein, C.H. and Odling-Smee, J.C. (1982). *British Economic Growth, 1856–1973*. Oxford: Clarendon Press.

Melman, S. (1956). *Dynamic Factors in Industrial Productivity*. Oxford: Oxford University Press.

Meyer, J.R. (1955). An input–output approach to evaluating the influence of exports on British industrial production in the late nineteenth century. *Explorations in Entrepreneurial History*, **8**, 12–34.

Milward, A. and Saul, S.B. (1977). *The Development of the Economies of Continental Europe, 1850–1914*. London: Allen & Unwin.

Minami, R. (1977). Mechanical power in the industrialization of Japan. *Journal of Economic History*, **37**, 935–958.

Mitchell, B.R. and Deane, P. (1962). *Abstract of British Historical Statistics*. Cambridge: Cambridge University Press.

Mitchell, B.R. and Jones, H.G. (1971). *Second Abstract of British Historical Statistics.* Cambridge: Cambridge University Press.

Mokyr, J. (1976). Growing-up and the industrial revolution in Europe. *Explorations in Economic History,* **13,** 371–396.

Morgan, E.V. and Thomas, W.A. (1962). *The Stock Exchange: Its History and Functions.* London: Elek.

Mossin, J. (1966). Equilibrium in a capital asset market. *Econometrica,* **34,** 768–783.

—(1973). *Theory of Financial Markets.* Englewood Cliffs, New Jersey: Prentice-Hall.

Navin, T.R. and Sears, M.V. (1955). The rise of a market for industrial securities, 1887–1902. *Business History Review,* **29,** 105–138.

Neal, L. and Uselding, P. (1972). Immigration: a neglected source of American economic growth, 1790–1912. *Oxford Economic Papers,* **24,** 68–88.

Nerlove, M. (1968). Factors affecting differences among rates of return on investment in individual common stocks. *Review of Economics and Statistics,* **50,** 312–331.

Neuberger, H. and Stokes, H.H. (1974). German banks and German growth, 1883–1913: an empirical view. *Journal of Economic History,* **34,** 710–731.

Nordhaus, W.D. (1972). The recent productivity slowdown. *Brookings Papers on Economic Activity,* **3,** 493–545.

Nordhaus, W.D. and J. Tobin (1972). Is growth obsolete? In *National Bureau of Economic Research, Economic Research: Retrospect and Prospect – Fiftieth Anniversary Colloquium,* V, *Economic Growth.* New York: Columbia University Press.

Olson, M. (1974). The United Kingdom and the world market in wheat and other primary products, 1870–1914. *Explorations in Economic History,* **11,** 325–355.

Organization for Economic Cooperation and Development (OECD). (1973). *The Distribution Sector: Evolution and Government Policies – A Report by the Industry Committee.* Paris: OECD.

Paish, G. (1909). Great Britain's capital investments in other lands. *Journal of the Royal Statistical Society,* **72,** 465–495.

—(1911). Great Britain's capital investments in individual colonial and foreign countries. *Journal of the Royal Statistical Society,* **74,** 167–200.

—(1914). The export of capital and the cost of living. *Transactions of the Manchester Statistical Society, 1913–14.* 63–92.

Passer, H.C. (1952). Electrical manufacturing around 1900. *Journal of Economic History,* **12,** 378–395.

—(1953). *The Electrical Manufacturers, 1875–1900: A Study in Competition, Entrepreneurship, Technical Change and Economic Growth.* Cambridge, Massachusetts: Harvard University Press.

Patrick, H.T. (1967). Japan, 1868–1914. In Cameron (ed.) (1967), 239–289.

Patterson, D.G. (1976). *British Direct Investment in Canada, 1890–1914: Estimates and Determinants.* Toronto: University of Toronto Press.

Payne, P.L. (1967). The emergence of the large-scale company in Great Britain. *Economic History Review,* **20,** 519–542.

—(1978). Industrial entrepreneurship and management in Great Britain. In Mathias and Postan (eds.) (1978), 180–230.

Pesek, B.P. (1961). Economic growth and its measurement. *Economic Development and Cultural Change,* **9,** 295–315.

Phelps-Brown, E.H. and Weber, B. (1953). Accumulation, productivity and distribution in the British economy 1870–1939. *The Economic Journal*, **63**, 263–288.

Pollard, S. (1957). British and world shipbuilding, 1890–1914: a study of comparative costs. *Journal of Economic History*, **17**, 426–444.

Pollard, S. and Robertson, P. (1979). *The British Shipbuilding Industry, 1870–1914*. Cambridge, Massachusetts: Harvard University Press.

Postan, M.M. (1935). Recent trends in the accumulation of capital. *Economic History Review*, **6**, 1–12.

Pressnell, L.S. (ed.; S. Nishimura, translator) (1973). *Money and Banking in Japan*. London: Macmillan.

Prest, A.R. and Adams, A. (1954). *Consumer Expenditure in the United Kingdom 1900–1919*. Cambridge: Cambridge University Press.

Purdue Faculty Papers in Economic History, 1956–1966 (1967). Homewood, Illinois: Irwin.

Reader, W.J. (1970). *Imperial Chemical Industries: A History – Vol. I, The Forerunners, 1870–1926*. London: Oxford University Press.

Reisser, J. (1911). *The German Great Banks and their Concentration in connection with the Economic Development of Germany*. Senate Document No. 593 (National Monetary Commission), 61st Congress, 2d Session. Washington: Government Printing Office. Reprinted 1977 by Arno Press, New York.

Reiter, S. (1977). Information and performance in the (new)^2 welfare economics. *American Economic Review (Papers and Proceedings)*, **67**, 226–234.

Richardson, H.W. (1965a). Over-commitment in Britain before 1930. Reprinted in Aldcroft and Richardson (eds.) (1969), 190–218.

—(1965b). Retardation in Britain's industrial growth, 1870–1913. *Scottish Journal of Political Economy*, **12**, 125–149.

—(1968). Chemicals. In Aldcroft (ed.) (1968), 274–307.

Rosenberg, N. (1963). Technological change in the machine tool industry, 1840–1910. Reprinted in *Purdue Faculty Papers in Economic History, 1956–1966* (1967), 405–430.

Rotella, E.J. (1977). *Women's Labor Force Participation and the Growth of Clerical Employment in the United States, 1870–1930*. University of Pennsylvania: Unpublished PhD. dissertation.

—(1981). The transformation of the American office: changes in employment and technology. *Journal of Economic History*, **41**, 51–57.

Rubinstein, W.D. (1977). Victorian middle classes: wealth, occupation and geography. *Economic History Review*, **30**, 602–623.

Samuelson, P.A. (1965). *Foundations of Economic Analysis*. New York: Atheneum.

Sandberg, L.G. (1974). *Lancashire in Decline: A Study in Entrepreneurship, Technology and International Trade*. Columbus: Ohio State University Press.

—(1978). Banking and economic growth in Sweden before World War I. *Journal of Economic History*, **38**, 650–681.

—(1979). The case of the impoverished sophisticate: human capital and Swedish economic growth before World War I. *Journal of Economic History*, **39**, 225–242.

Saul, S.B. (1960). The American impact on British industry, 1895–1914. *Business History*, **3**, 19–38.

—(1962a). House building in England, 1890–1914. *Economic History Review*, **15**, 119–137.

—(1962b). The motor industry in Britain to 1914. *Business History*, **5**, 22–44.

—(1965). The export economy, 1870–1914. *The Yorkshire Bulletin of Economic and Social Research*, **17**, 5–18.

—(1968a). The engineering industry. In Aldcroft (ed.) (1968), 186–237.

—(1968b). The machine tool industry in Britain to 1914. *Business History*, **10**, 22–43.

—(1969). *The Myth of the Great Depression, 1873–1896*. London: Macmillan.

—(1972a). The market and the development of the mechanical engineering industries in Britain, 1860–1914, In Saul (ed.) (1972b), 141–170.

Saul, S.B. (ed.) (1972b). *Technical Change: The United States and Britain in the Nineteenth Century*. London: Methuen.

Saxonhouse, G. (1974). A tale of Japanese technological diffusion in the Meiji period. *Journal of Economic History*, **34**, 149–165.

Sayers, R.S. (1936). *Bank of England Operations, 1890–1914*. London: P.S. King.

Scarf, H. (1973). *The Computation of Economic Equilibria*. New Haven: Yale University Press.

Scherer, F.M. (1970). *Industrial Market Structure and Economic Performance*. Chicago: Rand-McNally.

Schumpeter, J.A. (1939). *Business Cycles: A Theoretical, Historical and Statistical Analysis of the Capitalist Process*. New York: McGraw-Hill.

—(1962, third edition). *Capitalism, Socialism, and Democracy*. New York: Harper and Row (Harper Torch-books).

Seltzer, L.H. (1928). *A Financial History of the American Automobile Industry*. Boston: Houghton Mifflin.

Sharpe, W.F. (1964). Capital asset prices: a theory of market equilibrium under conditions of risk. *Journal of Finance*, **19**, 425–442.

—(1970). *Portfolio Theory and Capital Markets*. New York: McGraw-Hill.

—(1981, second edition). *Investments*. Englewood Cliffs, New Jersey: Prentice-Hall.

Sheppard, D.K. (1971). *The Growth and Role of U.K. Financial Institutions, 1880–1962*. London: Methuen.

Shergold, P.R. (1976). *The Standard of Living of Manual Workers in the First Decade of the Twentieth Century: A Comparative Study of Birmingham, U.K., and Pittsburgh, U.S.A.* London School of Economics: Unpublished PhD. dissertation.

Shoven, J.B. and Whalley, J. (1972). A general equilibrium calculation of the effects of differential taxation of income from capital in the U.S. *Journal of Public Economics*, **1**, 291–321.

Siemens, G. (1957). A.F. Rodger, translator. *History of the House of Siemens – Vol. I: The Era of Free Enterprise*. Freiberg/Munich: Karl Alber.

Simon, M. (1967). The pattern of new British portfolio foreign investment, 1865–1914. In Adler (ed.) (1967), 30–60.

Solow, R.M. (1963). *Capital Theory and the Rate of Return*. Amsterdam: North Holland.

—(1970). *Growth Theory: An Exposition*. Oxford: Clarendon Press.

Stiglitz, J.E. (1972). On the optimality of the stock market allocation of investment. *Quarterly Journal of Economics*, **86**, 25–60.

Supple, B. (1970). *The Royal Exchange Assurance: A History of British Insurance, 1720–1970*. Cambridge: Cambridge University Press.

Svennilson, I. (1954). *Growth and Stagnation in the European Economy.* Geneva: United Nations.

Taylor, A.J. (1961). Labour productivity and technological innovation in the British coal industry, 1850–1914. *Economic History Review,* **14,** 48–70.

—(1968). The coal industry. In Aldcroft (ed.) (1968), 37–70.

Thomas, B. (1971). Demographic determinants of British and American building cycles. In McCloskey, (ed.) (1971c), 39–74.

—(1973, second edition). *Migration and Economic Growth: A Study of Great Britain and the Atlantic Economy.* Cambridge: Cambridge University Press.

Thomas, W.A. (1973). *The Provincial Stock Exchange.* London: Frank Cass.

Thompson, F.M.L. (1963). *English Landed Society in the Nineteenth Century.* London: Routledge & Kegan Paul.

Tunzelmann, G.N. von. (1982). Structural change and leading sectors in British manufacturing, 1907–68. In Kindleberger and Di Tella (eds.) (1982), 1–49.

Tyszynski, H. (1951). World trade in manufactured commodities, 1899–1950. *The Manchester School,* **19,** 272–304.

United Nations, Economic Commission for Europe. (1970). *Economic Survey of Europe in 1969, Part I: Structural Trends and Prospects in the European Economy.* New York: United Nations.

United States Bureau of the Census. (1914a). *Thirteenth Census of the United States, Vol. IV: Occupational Statistics.* Washington: U.S. Government Printing Office.

—(1914b). *Thirteenth Census of the United States, Vol. VIII: General Report and Analysis, Census of Manufactures.* Washington: U.S. Government Printing Office.

—(1975). *Historical Statistics of the United States, Colonial Times to 1970.* Washington: U.S. Government Printing Office.

US Bureau of Economic Analysis. (1973). *Long Term Economic Growth, 1860–1970.* Washington: US Government Printing Office.

Uselding, P. (ed.) (1984). *Research in Economic History: A Research Annual, Volume 9.* London: JAI Press, Inc.

Veverka, J. (1963). The growth of government expenditures in the United Kingdom since 1790. *Scottish Journal of Political Economy,* **10,** 111–127.

Walters, R. (1975). Labour productivity in the South Wales steam-coal industry, 1870–1914. *Economic History Review,* **28,** 280–303.

Webb, S.B. (1980). Tariffs, cartels, technology and growth in the German steel industry, 1879–1914. *Journal of Economic History,* **40,** 309–330.

Wiener, M.J. (1981). *English Culture and the Decline of the Industrial Spirit, 1850–1980.* Cambridge: Cambridge University Press.

Wilson, C. (1965). Economy and society in late Victorian Britain. *Economic History Review,* **18,** 183–198.

Wilson, C. (1980). The nature of equilibrium in markets with adverse selection. *Bell Journal of Economics,* **11,** 108–130.

Wolfe, J.N. (ed.) (1968). *Value, Capital and Growth: Papers in Honor of Sir John Hicks.* Chicago: Aldine.

Young, G.M. (1936). *Victorian England: Portrait of an Age.* London: Oxford University Press.

Index